Ethnologia Europaea

Journal of European Ethnology

Volume 43:1
2013

MUSEUM TUSCULANUM PRESS · UNIVERSITY OF COPENHAGEN

Printed in Sweden by Exakta, Malmö 2013
Cover and layout Pernille Sys Hansen
Cover illustration Morten Krogh Petersen
ISBN 978 87 635 4115 2
ISSN 0425 4597

This journal is published with the support of the Nordic board for periodicals in the humanities and social sciences.

Museum Tusculanum Press
University of Copenhagen
Birketinget 6
DK-2300 Copenhagen S
Denmark
www.mtp.dk

In memoriam
Bjarne Stoklund
1928-2013

Editor of Ethnologia Europaea
1984–2004

CONTENTS

WHAT IT FEELS LIKE TO BE A TOURIST
Explorations into the Meaningful Experiences of Ordinary Mass Tourists

David Picard

Based on ethnographic data gathered through observations made as a tour guide in the Indian Ocean island of La Réunion, I explore "what it feels like to be a tourist". My aim is to articulate observations of subjective tourist experience with theory about the structural frames of tourism culture and the touristic realms these have brought about. I argue that the individual experience of sites evolves within broadly shared aesthetic cultures, but that the emotions generated by the encounter of such sites are negotiated through highly personalised stories. Tourism attractions in this tropical island indicate the presence of shared aesthetic dispositions and feelings of national belonging among the German tourists observed there, while tourists struggle for words to affirm the individuality, authenticity and magic of their experiences.

Keywords: tourism, experience, transformation, La Réunion, German national romanticism

Tourists have learnt to behave like tourists. They know how to follow signs, read maps, take planes, visit sites, interact with hotel staff, order food in restaurants and respond to specific attractions. Tourists are often dressed similarly, ask similar questions, move their bodies in similar ways, and stay in similar places. Because travel practices and touristic norms of behaviour appear to show relatively little variation among specific tourist groups, tourism is often considered a highly standardised mass phenomenon emanating from, and somehow mirroring the structure of, industrialised modern society. However, while being subjected to collectively held norms and values, tourism – like most practices in social life – is experienced in a highly personal way. While the experience of travel may be framed by powerful narratives and representations about the destinations visited, tourists encounter the realms of their travels and holiday destinations through their own bodies and senses. The aim of this research is to explore the articulation between this individual experience and the structural framework of tourism as a wider social institution. The article builds on Graburn's (1989) theoretical framework of the "sacred journey", considering tourism in terms of a ritual transgression of the everyday which leads tourists outside their usual life contexts and circumstances, with the potential to induce a personal transformation at the individual level. It points out the social and societal relevance of individual cases and stories of tourists evolving within the structural framework of tourism – thus articulating Graburn's initially structuralist approach alongside work on the more fluid aspects of learning how to be a tourist (Löfgren 2002), forms of performance and experience in tourism (Edensor 1998; Larsen 2001; Coleman & Crang 2002; Franklin 2004) and related processes of transformation (Crossley 2012). The article contributes to different, earlier attempts to study tourists from a phenomenological perspective, to understand how tourism realms are perceived – and thus brought into being – from the subjective perspective of tourists and travellers while on tour or after the tour (Adler 1989; Frey 1999; Cohen 2004b; Bruner 2004; Harrison 2003; Hom-Cary 2004).

Besides this theoretical aspiration, the research also has a polemic goal, which lies in its attempt to re-emancipate the meaningful experience of the ordinary mass tourist, frequently looked down upon by academics and other eclectic folks. Mass tourism, it is often claimed by these cultural elites, is a form of superficial consumption symptomatic of a society emptied of real values. In any case, it does not constitute a meaningful activity, so it is not worth being studied as an ethnographic object. Over the past forty years, the sentimental colonialism of such institutionalised anti-tourism discourses by academics, and the common-sense elevation of peripheral Others as noble savages threatened by the contagions and pollutions of modernity, have become objects of study themselves (Fabian 1983; Clifford 1989). In his still influential book *The Tourist*, MacCannell (1976) suggests that tourism in particular evolves within symbolic structures akin to those of religious pilgrimages observed in other social contexts. He proposes studying tourism in terms of a social institution that allows modern subjects to bring to life and renew the big mythical figures and moral principles of the modern world. Also, the historic analysis of Western tourism practice demonstrates the relative stability of the particular culture from which it emanates, and from which it periodically reinvents itself by adopting new names, categories and sites of attraction (Löfgren 2002; Spode 2011). Tourism thus appears to be a "serious" and important academic topic with the potential to reveal a deeper understanding of the normative processes underlying modern life.

Observing Tourists during the Tour and back Home

To achieve my aim, I use an ethnographic research design based upon the observation of actual tourist practice as it unfolds normally in a quotidian tourist context. As Graburn (2002) stresses, in order to study tourism ethnographically, it makes little sense for the researcher to approach tourists only at one particular moment of the journey, without being able to articulate the observations made during this moment within the wider context of the journey and the tourists' everyday lives. An ethnographic approach towards tourists hence ideally follows tourists from long before their departure until long after their return home. How to achieve such an objective? Tourism evolves within a transnational ethnoscape, making it actually rather difficult to follow the subject of investigation throughout tourists' journeys (Clifford 1997; Appadurai 2003). Also, tourism is usually profoundly personal and intimate; tourists, even if they often appear to be part of a large "crowd", habitually travel alone or in small groups, as couples or with friends. While ethnographers can get themselves accepted as fellow tourists/participant observers, such an approach remains ethically and socially ambivalent – for example a honeymoon with an ethnographer as a constant companion may no longer be a honeymoon. Finally, tourism generally is a rather expensive type of leisure activity, and it appears difficult to convince any research council to fund a vast number of holiday trips to the Seychelles, Samoa or Bahamas for the sake of ethnographic observations of what tourists do before, during and after being on holiday.

A pragmatic way to respond to these logistic, ethical and financial challenges is to do participant observation by taking on the role of the tour guide. Building on the experience of other researchers who have adopted such an approach (Amirou 1995; Cohen 1985; Bruner 2004), I gained employment as a guide for a tourism agency in La Réunion. Between 1998 and 2000, I guided twenty four-day round trips on the island. These always followed the same itinerary, stopped in the same hotels, passed the same sites and included the same food. Because of the invariance of its spatial and temporal structure, this research achieved an almost experimental outlook. The groups were composed mainly of Germans who had booked their trip via a German tour operator. Their numbers varied between three and eight. I stayed with these tourists all day long, sharing meals and drinks, driving the minibus, performing a guide discourse and engaging in informal, often long conversations. I also spent the night at the same hotels, though in a separate room. At the end of the round trip, I left the groups at the airport. However, I stayed in contact through correspondence, and later revisited many of them in their homes in Germany. I also asked them to print and send me the "ten most significant photos" of their holiday in La Réunion, together with comments and text (I offered to cover the cost of the prints and postage). By consciously and voluntarily putting myself within the frame of observation (Tedlock 1991), I became part of the realms of the tourists' journeys and the memories these generated. At the same time, by performing similar sets of discourses, including humour and ways of connecting to the tourists, I remained, to a large degree, an invariable element of the research setting. This particular research approach allowed me to observe in great detail what actually happens when tourists "do" tourism and what happens when they return back home. The major limitation of this approach lies in the difficulty to study the processes of "coming home" – the journey home and the reintegration into the home environment – which seems to be a moment of crucial importance for the anthropological understanding of tourism.

Experience, Sense-Making and Magical Memory

During the journey the tourists experienced a large number of visual, sensual and mental encounters. I took them to viewpoints, led them into museums and interpretation sites, entered forests and directed them to beaches and riversides. The experience of these sites usually engaged all the senses. The tourists felt the heat of the sun and the coolness of the rain; they watched the land, objects and people that appeared in front of their eyes, they smelled the odour of the streets, mountains and forest; they tasted food and drink; they immersed themselves in small lakes, rivers and lagoons. While sensually engaging with their exotic surroundings, they listened – more or less attentively – to my explanations about the island and its populations and about myself. In the evenings and during breaks, I recorded and wrote up the sequences of dialogues and conversations that unfolded during the daily journeys and during the stopovers in the hotels. I noticed that these dialogues and conversations seemed to unfold in very personal, individualistic ways, taking into account personal concerns, tastes and preoccupations.

At the same time, I also noticed that the ways they unfolded were very similar, as if the participants were following the same cognitive processes. This involved (usually) several sequential phases. During the first phase, the "Wow-Phase" of the first contact with a specific site or story, the tourists were usually speechless. Arriving at a spectacular viewpoint or facing a large waterfall, the sole visible or audible articulations I could record were "ah" and "oh", sometimes also "oh my God" (*oh mein Gott*) or "oh shit" (*oh Scheisse*). Often, their eyes were wide open, and sometimes their mouths as well. On rare occasions, tourists became short of breath, sweated, trembled, felt dizzy or said they "needed to sit down" – visibly displaying symptoms of shock or extreme awe (I have elsewhere discussed these extreme cases in terms of a commonly observed travel syndrome [Picard 2012]). In the second phase, the "Amazement-Phase", the tourists usually verbally articulated the emotions induced by the encounter in absolute terms. They used words like "beautiful" or "amazing!". Often they shook their heads, looked at their friends, smiled; couples exchanged kisses and held hands. In the third phase, the "It's Like-Phase", the tourists typically searched for known analogies, namely by saying, "it's like..." ("it's like in Bali"; "it's like on the moon"; "it's like Chinese food"; "it's like nothing I have seen before" etc.). In the fourth, somehow antithetic "But-Phase", the tourists normally dialecticised the encounter and the analogy they had used, sometimes also introducing a moral judgement ("but in Bali, the site was much bigger"; "but this is so much nicer than the moon"; "but it tastes much better"; "this space is just incredible" etc.). In the fifth phase, the "Me-Phase", the antithetic images generated associations with personal memories or preoccupations, which in turn often triggered conversations disconnected from the actual encounter ("We were in Bali with our children last year..."; "I feel like a small grain in the universe, though I am not religious like my parents..."; "there are lots of Chinese restaurants now in Germany..."; "we used to travel a lot when we were young..."). In most cases, the encounters with the exotic Other thus induced emotions and cognitive processes that would eventually let the tourists talk about themselves. People, sites and stories thus worked as triggers to work out personal preoccupations and embed them in narratives, and eventually reconstitute forms of Self. The exotic Other thus worked as a tool to transgress, transform and eventually maintain Self.

While these phases of touristic cognition followed a similar sequence, the speed of this sequence and the means by which it was articulated varied largely from one to the other. Some tourists – especially those with a lot of travel experience – often appeared much less impressed by certain sites or stories than others with less experience. For the first category, the whole process was frequently articulated through the uttering of a single phrase. Fabian,[1] for instance, a tourist who had substantial travel experience, reacted very quickly when facing a large Hindu temple. "Ah!" he said, "a Hindu temple. With all the colours. Looks a bit kitschy." He took a photo, then explained: "I have seen similar ones in Bali, but there they are even bigger. They have the most beautiful ones I have seen so far." After less than a minute, Fabian was ready to go back to the bus. He articulated his astonishment ("Ah"), then succinctly defined the encounter and gave it a valuation ("a Hindu temple"; "a bit kitschy"). After taking a photo, he found an analogy from a previous journey ("like in Bali") and linked the encounter to his personal life ("the most beautiful ones I have seen so far").

In other cases, this process took much longer: sometimes hours, weeks or even months. In one case, representing the other extreme, a woman, Donata, with whom I continued to exchange letters after the journey, seemed to work out the experience of a volcanic caldera over several weeks. At the actual site, she reacted, typically, with an "ah", and then said, after a short while: "This is so beautiful." Later, in the bus, she explained: "This had something artistic; perfect lines and forms. Like on the moon. I had the impression of seeing something prehistoric." Several weeks after the trip, I received a letter from her in which she described a photo she had taken at the same site. "This allows me to imagine how evolution has taken place. While I am not part of any religious community, when facing this landscape I had the impression to be a small grain in the universe," she wrote. The outer journey was accompanied by an inner one which was far from over when this tourist returned home. It took months for her to translate and stabilise the experience into a form of memory, possibly leaving her deeply transformed.

What this last case also points to is that the observation of tourism during the tour needs to be extended beyond the actual journey and be articulated with an observation of home contexts. I therefore suggest two further phases as part of the touristic cognition process here observed, which extend into the home environment. Within the frame of this study, I could not observe these phases directly, but had to rely on descriptions by the tourists made during interviews when I visited them in their homes in Germany several months later. In this sense, a sixth phase, the "Coming Home-Phase", describes the event when tourists come home, integrate their souvenirs into their home environment (by means of incorporating material objects into existing collections, using ingredients in welcome-home dinners or giving them away as gifts), and talk about their journey among themselves and with friends or relatives. This phase also includes home re-appropriation rites, like walking through all the rooms, having a pee, cleaning the house, having a drink and/or going to the supermarket to fill the fridge.

This Coming Home-Phase seemed distinguishable from a later phase, the "Souvenir-Phase", when, several weeks or months later, the encounters of the journey appear transformed into more or less rigid souvenirs that have become part of the tourists' everyday normality. When I met the tourists later, most of what had happened during the journey was reduced to a set of key memories and stories. Paradoxically, while the tourists' conversations during the trip were mainly focused on their home concerns (their children, jobs, partnerships, memories etc.), in this post-tourist context, the memories where about the actual trip and sites encountered. I, as the guide, had become part of these objectivisations, and was often confronted with funny anecdotes of the trip that I had long forgotten. In this Souvenir-Phase, material souvenir objects acquired during the trip had frequently become part of existing collections. These included often very anodyne-seeming bits and pieces – stones, shells and small art-and-craft objects – whose value seemed to lie less in their specific form or artistry, but in a metonymic quality perpetuating the material realm of the journey in the home context.

Asked about meanings and usages of such souvenir objects, most of the tourists actually gave explanations that made me think about practices related to religious relics. The objects were usually exhibited in cupboards, on shelves or in set boxes, all of which in many ways seemed to constitute contemporary forms of living-room shrines. Photos were framed and put on walls or in photo albums, as if their visual invocation of the island and their actual physicality perpetuated an "authentic link" (Stewart 1984) between the island and the fragment of the island taken home. The tourists and their cameras had actually been on the island where they had captured the sites – thus creating a sympathetic relation[2] between the spaces of the journey and the images and objects taken home and incorporated into their mundane home environments. What had been captured by the tourist cameras during the journey was a reflection of the realms encountered, as if this process were able to transfer the quality of the visited island onto the photographic memory – similar to Renaissance practices of capturing the sacred aura of a religious shrine via hand mirrors that pilgrims would take to a sacred site, and subsequently back to their homes (Robinson & Picard 2009). Similarly, many tourists/informants explained to me how they had felt their bodies "recharged", full of energy and sunshine, when they had returned from the journey. Because most tourists considered home and away as evolving in ontologically differentiated realms, once they had returned home these material remnants of the island gained a symbolically and materially heightened quality. In a way, their metonymic qualities only became visible once tourists had returned home. In this context, these souvenirs were subjected to different ceremonial usages, once again reminiscent of different forms of religious practice. They were shown to those selected visitors who were granted access to the living room or shown the holiday photo albums, accompanied with stories about the trip. Moreover, they were "activated" at a very personal level in specific moments – for example when the tourists felt down or stressed because of bad weather, difficult work relations, relationship problems etc. – as a means to invoke the good memories of the journey. Many tourists told me that this evocation had happened to them by actually touching small souvenir objects and even photos, as if such acts were able to bring back memories and the marvellous realm of the journey. Others used consumable objects like spices or soap bought while on the trip to prepare a meal or take a bath, which would make them feel better.

Transgressions of Home, Transformations of Travel

The emotions induced by the experience of the journey led to highly differentiated and personalised reflections about the realms of the journey and on those back home, which brings to the surface different layers of the transformational process induced by travel. Facing a mountainous landscape, for instance, one tourist, Valerio, started to talk about a previous trip to Colorado where the landscape had been equally beautiful, "but with less extension". He associated "all these tropical landscapes" with a book, *Treasure Island*, which he had read as a child. He remembered being a child, and thus reiterated a fragment of his life story, connecting his present with a past. At the same site, another tourist, Alessia, started to talk about her own daughter and her daughter's travels abroad, and also about the economic difficulties facing young people due to the high unemployment rate. She thus construed quite a different narrative than Valerio, reiterating a story articulating her relationship with her daughter. Another tourist, Sepp, found the water pools and cascades "better than those of the aqua-parks in Germany", and then told us stories about previous experiences. Here again, the site induced a different type of story. I suggest that these stories and the way they mediate the engagement with specific sites can be related to different travel motives and related layers of experience – "recreational", "existential" and "social" – which appear in all forms of tourism, yet which are unequally considered. For some tourists, the break from home represented an opportunity to spend time with friends and relatives, for others to get away from a stressful work environment or to bring some movement into a boring, everyday life. These travel motifs and related layers of experience during the journey thus appear to respond to specific circumstances marking the tourists' home contexts. In most cases, the tourists were seeking a ritual reversal of these circumstances and their temporal or definite transformation. The transgression of home became a premise of the journey, with the aspiration that it would provide what was lacking at home – social proximity, existential order, social flow – and thus reunite Self with otherwise separate provinces of life and meaning. In the following, I will further explore each of these travel aspirations and the transformational processes they are associated with.

Recreating Social Life

Some of the tourists among the sample appeared to have had a stressful working life in their home contexts, which did not allow them to spend a lot of time together. This was the case for Nicolas and Francesca, but also for Valerio and Hisako. The latter were both insurance brokers, and explained to me that they often worked for ten hours a day and therefore did not have much time to maintain their couple's life and the love that had once brought them together. Nicolas owned a company, and told me he spent most of his time apart from his wife, who would stay at home. Travelling thus seemed a means of escaping these contexts of alienation and spending time together, to "generate shared experiences", as Nicolas explained to me one day.

The desire to transform a deficient social life by means of the journey was usually fulfilled through the way in which these tourists experienced sites and then talked about their experiences. In most situations, they related their encounters to the spaces that marked their everyday life – allowing them to reflect upon, and recreate, the symbolic fabric of their social relations. These couples frequently projected themselves, as couples, into the social spaces of La Réunion and wondered about how it would be to live "here". They then eventually usually talked about their common lives back in Germany, for instance that they actually liked their lives there. Nicolas, for instance, tasting a passion fruit found in a forest inside the island, said, "Wow! This is delicious! It tastes like a multi-vitamin juice, almost artificially. At home, we had these once in a dessert." Francesca, his wife, responded, "Yes, and since recently, you can buy these in the supermarket as well." In a different context, facing my explanations about local religious practices related to a particular saint, Nicolas defended the "real God" who "had said not to admire other symbols". Francesca responded, with an ironic, but sympathetic smile, that "all these saints are part of the Catholic mysticism". She explained that she was a Protestant and wouldn't be "scared by this". In another situation, facing an isolated hamlet in the mountains, she said, "This is so isolated. How can people live here? Is there a school, or a supermarket, or a doctor?" He said, "It looks okay for a holiday house. You can come up here from the coast in less than two hours." She responded, "Never in my life I would want to live here. To go shopping, you will spend an entire day on these mountain roads." I explained to them that with the poverty and competition over land during the colonial time, people tended to go further and further away from the coast to have their own land. He responded, "Okay, if you grow up here, if you are used to the solitude, you will surely feel fine here. You wouldn't want to live in the city. If these people here arrived in our town in Germany, they would probably not like it very much either." The observations of these three situations show how Nicolas and Francesca almost always systematically negotiated their encounters in terms of their context back home. The passion fruit is associated with previous experiences of passion fruits in this home context and related gender roles (he talked about a dessert, she about the supermarket). The encounter of a local saint challenged them to reflect upon their own beliefs and to reaffirm their distinguished visions of religion, but also an amicable tension between their own religious difference (he is a Catholic, she a Protestant). Facing the isolation of a small hamlet, both imagined living in such a place and finally seemed to agree that "you feel fine where you grow up", the people here in their hamlet, and the two in their town in Germany.

Similar to this case, Valerio and Hisako almost systematically put what they encountered during the journey in parallel with realities that marked their life back in Germany. On top of a mountain, gazing inside one of the island's valleys, Valerio said, "Oh this is magnificent. This depth and these colours. When we were in Colorado, we have been at similar viewpoints, but the land didn't have the same extension. It must be a very different life when you live in a valley like this." Hisako later commented, "Yes, but we are fine where we live. There are all our friends, our parents and the job. Maybe it is sometimes difficult, the bad weather, the stress, but it is our home." Facing this and other landscapes, both frequently talked about "back home" ("we are happy at home", "at home, it is different...") and thus brought this "back home" back into being. The journey seemed to work as a means to transform meaning and relations that marked their everyday life, both that of the couples and that of their broader life worlds. When I revisited Valerio and Hisako, and also Nicolas and Francesca in their respective homes, I found neatly organised households in which the souvenirs of the journey had been integrated in similar ways. Nicolas had hung prints of the volcano in the corridor, and some smaller material objects had been arranged in a cabinet above the television, together with objects taken home from other journeys. The photos had been put into an album arranged in a living-room cupboard, together with other photo albums. Valerio and Hisako had their photo prints still in the envelope, in a drawer with other envelopes that were awaiting to be put into albums – "maybe during the autumn, when we have time", Hisako told me. The movement away from home, the related transgression of quotidian rhythm and practice, and the socially concentrated and emotionally heightened space of the journey in these cases become means to reassemble fragments of social life, recreate affective links among friends and couples, and embed these in personal narratives. Attractions here primarily work as means to evoke and renew memories of past experiences and, from there, to re-invoke memories through which to think and articulate social life at this small intimate scale.

Recreating Existential Order

Another motif of travel seemed to lie in the hope that the experiences of the touristic journey would allow the tourists to transform their lives at a more existential level. In these cases, life back home frequently seemed to be marked by different degrees of boredom or existential feelings of senselessness. This was, for instance, the case for Lula-Maria who, after divorcing her husband, went through what she called a "psychologically difficult phase" and thus joined the trip, with her best friend, Donata, to "see something else", "without husbands". For Donata, herself in a transitional period of her life, the journey made her engage with ideas of the supernatural and to rethink her relations to a wider cosmos and the religion of her parents. Facing different religious sites, she seemed to engage in a long process of reflection (as mentioned earlier) that went beyond the relationships of her immediate social environment. In her later conversations with me, she questioned a deeper meaning of the world: of evolution, nature and truth in human life.

At a different level, this existential search for meaning also seemed to underpin Arianna and Sepp's travels: an elderly couple, both retired, who, in their own words, were "bored of life" and "didn't know what to do all day long in their home". They told me they saw life like "a film that would soon be over". During the journey, they hardly engaged at all with what I told them or what they saw, but persistently talked about themselves, their "sad life", their youth during the Hitler Regime in Germany, their difficult relationships with their children, the problems their daughter had at work and the "black people you see more and more in Germany now". They explained to me that they had hoped that travelling would allow them to "leave this sad environment" (*die traurige Umgebung verlassen*) for a while, to "see some colours" and "rediscover their optimism" (*ihren Optimismus wiederfinden*). I am not sure the journey allowed them to find this form of transformation.

At a different level, this existential search also marked the journey of tourists who, by travelling, fulfilled what they called "a childhood dream" (*Kindheitstraum*) – a project they had been cherishing over many years. Alessia and Ben, for instance, told me they had always dreamt about travelling together to exotic places. Yet, when they eventually had the means to do so, their parents fell ill, and they had to look after them for many years. Only when their parents had passed away could they "finally" travel, they said. Likewise, Carmen, an elderly woman, explained to me that she had a souvenir photo of her father standing in front of the Victoria Falls in East Africa, and that she had always dreamt about going there, "as a means to find my father". She told me that she had realised this project the year before, and "a circle had been closed" (*ein Kreis hat sich geschlossen*).

For many of the tourists who had lived in the former German Democratic Republic (GDR) (where travel had been strictly regulated), the fact of being on a tropical island was very frequently put into perspective alongside memories of the suppressive regime of the former Socialist country. Many encounters within the island were here directly related to the lack of freedom to travel before the fall of the Berlin Wall, and the wider circumstances that had led to German reunification in 1991. A particular case – that of Sepp[3] and Arianna – was symptomatic. Both related their encounters – be it of graffiti on a wall, poor neighbourhoods or a dinner beside a hotel swimming pool – to memories of social life in the former GDR and the changes brought about by unification. Entering a poor neighbourhood in one of the coastal towns, Sepp said: "Oh, so these are the slums then, aren't they?" (*Dies sind dann die Slums, oder nicht?*). I explained that many people live in sheet-metal houses, and that I was not sure that he could talk about "slums". I further explained that life on the island had quickly changed since the 1960s, and that many people had difficulties integrating into the new society on the island. He responded with a long reflection about his own life world, saying: "Me as well, I had big problems to integrate myself in the society that had come from the West. Everything went quite fast after the fall of the wall. Before there was a certain conviviality in our quarters and villages, even at work. But now, everyone fears to lose their jobs." In other contexts, confronting various sites induced violent emotional reactions. For instance, when we arrived at the volcano, he spontaneously started to cry, cursing the former political leaders of East Germany (the GDR). He murmured: "That I can still see this, all this beauty..." He later added:

> I had thought I would never see a volcano in my life. If you live in East Germany you cannot imagine that such beauty exists. While there are lots of difficulties following the opening of the wall, this liberty to travel, to see other countries, compensates them all. No one can take these moments away from us any longer, we should live while being alive. An accident can easily happen or you lose your job. But these souvenirs will remain.[4]

Common to these very different cases was that the encounters and experiences of the journey challenged the tourists' life worlds in a deeper, existential way. It made them rethink their wider being in the world as humans and as social actors in a specific historical context. Travel made them reflect upon, and recreate, personal life histories by articulating public events that had marked their personal lives, thus relating their personal belonging to more generic narratives, for example of nation, family and humankind. It eventually allowed them to become new persons, where memories of a violent past, or of a life that no longer existed, were transformed and objectified into stories. The distance from home allowed these tourists to encompass these existential dimensions of social life and rearticulate them with their present context. It allowed them to move on in life.

Recreating Social Flow

Another travel motif for most tourists seemed to lie in a search for immediate sociability. The act of travelling and creating social flow became in itself the motif for the journey. Especially for those tourists living in relative solitude back home, the space of the journey became a means to generate human contact. For instance, Carmen, an 82-year-old woman living alone in a major German city, had been going on two "big" journeys, in her words, each year throughout the ten years preceding the trip to La Réunion. She joined group tours, often with a travel companion, another elderly lady from another city whom she had met on one of these trips. According to Carmen, the sociability of these journeys was formed around a shared interest in "different cultures and people". Fabian, who lived alone and, in his words, had no real friends or friendship network in his hometown, was a similar case. Travelling had become his *raison d'être*, he told me, as it allowed him to meet fellow travellers and talk about his shared interest in foreign places and tourist destinations. During the trip, both Carmen and Fabian revealed themselves to be highly knowledgeable about a wide range of tourist destinations around the world. Encounters with sites in La Réunion were systematically related to previous experiences, and triggered stories of "similar" – or "dissimilar" – hotels, places, guides and anecdotes experienced during previous journeys. Both were excellent dinner-table raconteurs, sharing stories about other places, often focusing on tourism infrastructures – certain hotels, travel guides, sites etc. – and consequences of tourism development. A typical dialogue emerged, for example, when we arrived at the volcano and Fabian said:

> Oh, this is magnificent, the cleanliness, the intensity of the landscape, the forms, the width of the land. There is no comparison with Mauritius. Such landscapes, one cannot find in Mauritius. What a pity that such sites lose their beauty with tourism development, like it has happened in Spain and even in Bali.

One night over dinner he explained that the hotel we were staying in was "very, very beautiful", and then told a story about a hotel in which he had previously been staying in Morocco, with showers in the corridors and dogs hanging out in the kitchen. This led him to talk about another hotel, somewhere in Africa, where he had to pump water from a well every morning. "Compared to these hotels," he said, "this one here is pure luxury." He then went on to wonder why it only had two stars. In front of a large Hindu temple, I explained that a revalorisation of Hinduism had been happening in La Réunion in recent years, and that many people had started constructing new temples. I told them about the cultural transformations that Hinduism had undergone on the island, and about the use of animal sacrifices. Fabian interrupted me and started to tell a story about a previous travel experience in Bali, when he had taken part in religious ceremonies. He concluded his explanations by saying that this ceremony had been "real", "not staged for tourists". Almost any story he told situated him as an expert within a wider tourism world; he rarely or never talked about himself in other terms.

When I later revisited Fabian and Carmen, in their respective homes, I found surprising similarities in the ways they used tourist souvenirs to decorate their home spaces. In principle, this did not differ from most of the other tourists, yet it seemed to take on a different dimension. The ground floor of Fabian's house was almost entirely filled up with touristic objects from various places he had visited. There was hardly any way to get through the living room, which looked like a touristic curiosity cabinet with souvenirs on the floor, in cupboards and glass cabinets, and hanging on the walls. As he had no friends, he would enjoy these on his own. Similarly, the living room in Carmen's apartment was decorated with travel objects wherever I looked, though they were smaller and organised in themed collections. She told me that she took home similar sets of objects from each destination – a small art-and-craft sculpture or doll, a stone and a shell – which were integrated into separate collections. Additionally, she had images and image-like craft art hanging on the walls, and a neatly organised collection of photo albums, all in the same format, allowing her to recollect images and stories from each of her journeys. Both told me, in their respective ways, that the act of travelling induced a form of social flow with fellow travellers that was rare in their home environment.

German National Romanticism and the "Power of Nature"

The tourists all arrived in La Réunion by plane following an 11-hour flight. I first met them either at the airport or at their hotel the morning after their arrival. At this early stage of the journey, comments made about La Réunion frequently defined the island as a "place out of this world" (*ein Platz ausserhalb der Welt*), or a "place far from everything" (*ein Ort weit von allem*) that constituted a "world on its own" (*eine Welt in sich selbst*). They talked about the island as an "enclosed space" (*ein abgeschlossener Raum*) and a "continent in a microformat" (*ein Kontinent im Mikroformat*). In the eyes of the tourists, La Réunion thus emerged as a form of enclosed space encompassing a wider world in a miniaturised format: a large garden concentrating and making visible the symbolic elements of time and being (Picard 2011). Among the infinite possibilities of forms that could have been recognised in the space of this journey, the tourists consistently responded to a similar set of sights and, equally, remained consistently unperceptive of other possible encounters. Despite their social differences, they shared very similar feelings of seduction and awe induced by specific sites, in particular those bringing about what they usually referred to as the "power of tropical nature" (*die Gewalt der tropischen Natur*), which materialised in various forms, for example the "play of colours" (*das Farbenspiel*), the "contrasts in light" (*die Lichtkontraste*), the "intensity of the sunshine" (*die Intensität der Sonne*), the "abundance of water" (*das viele Wasser überall*) or the "uncanny atmosphere of fog" (*die unheimliche Atmosphäre des Nebels*). Specific areas of the island were thus transformed into meaningful landscapes conceived of in terms of a powerful, often uncanny and sometimes bizarrely magnified nature. Nature appeared as a realm imbued with divine grace and power, a transfiguration of transcendental forces into the materiality of the land, transforming land into enchanted natural landscapes.

In the weeks following the trip, I asked the tourists to send me what they considered to be the "ten most significant photos" of their journey, and to comment on each of them briefly. Seven tourists responded to this request, and sent me between eight and twelve photos respectively. By far the largest proportion of photos (more than eight on average)[5] represented panoramic shots of landscapes. One quarter of all photos were snapshots of the volcano, and one third of the island's mountains. Surveying the comments and captions the tourists attached to each photo, I then explored common themes, which I regrouped into three semantic fields: "power of nature", "lush nature" and "local life". The semantic field of the "power of nature" regrouped, once again, more than eight photographs on average, which variously depicted clouds and fog moving in and out, light and shadow games, water crashing on rocky sea shores and in waterfalls, and small villages inside huge landscapes. Photos regrouped in the field of "lush nature" mainly included close-up pictures of flowers, plants and fruits; "local life" pictures included shots of the town centre, markets, museums and religious sites. The last step of the image analysis was to explore the density of experience articulated through photos taken. To do so, I compared the distribution of photographed sites with the actual time spent at these sites during the journey. The entire journey included approximately 52 hours of "conscious time", if a sleeping period from 22:00 p.m. to 7:00 a.m. was deducted. Approximately 30 hours (58%) of this total time was spent in hotel and service spaces (hotel rooms and lobbies, restaurants and airport lounges), whereas only 3% of the images represent such spaces. On the other hand, while only 3 hours (6%) were spent on the volcano, 25% of all photos were taken there. In this sense, the volcano generated almost 60 times more photos than the hotel and service environment.

What these observations seem to indicate is that the individual tourist experiences were framed by "aesthetic dispositions" (Roger 1997) largely shared by the tourists. Irrespective of their individuality, the subjects of the study seem to have learnt to experience the Other in more or less the same conventional way. This observation is paradoxical in that these tourists came from different social contexts and geographical origins with apparently no other link to each other than "being German". "Being German" thus seems to relate here to more than a merely subjective feeling of belonging to an "imagined community" of nation (Anderson 1991), but makes manifest elements of a historically formed, shared mindset and culturally specific cognitive processes. This observation induces an epistemic dilemma, as it seems to imply that nationality – that is "being German" – could be considered a pertinent analytical category to study individual mentality and behaviour. As many anthropologists do, I struggle here with a historical explanation for the processes that may have led to the hegemony of specific aesthetic forms of the sublime embedded within a national romanticism among people growing up in Germany. While I do not want to – and cannot – within the context of this article explore the historic formation of a hypothetically common "German" – or else "Western", "European" or perhaps class-related – romantic tourist culture, it would be interesting to follow up on this observation, for example by repeating the study with other national tourist populations.

The "miracle of consensus" (MacCannell 1976), observed here among German subjects, may usefully be explained by a historic approach (Jackson 1998). Following MacCannell, it can be understood in terms of a twofold process of sight sacralisation, met with a corresponding ritual attitude on the part of the tourists. In this sense, a "sacralisation" of specific sights embodying the idea of "power of nature" may have taken place in Germany. Spode (2011) claims that romantic ideas and images of nature were here systematically institutionalised through the humanistic bourgeois education within the realms of the emerging German nationalisms of the eighteenth and nineteenth centuries, and resurface in modern tourism culture. Similarly, Löfgren (2002) observes that the specific cultural forms of nature observed here had already been developed in the eighteenth and nineteenth centuries, following institutionalisation processes of the idea of "terrible beauty" and the quest for the sublime, found, for example, in the form of waterfalls. What seems to have shifted from this faraway historical context is that the sublime art of the seventeenth and eighteenth centuries were transformed into popular media, such as literature. And so we have *Treasure Island* to which one tourist referred to make sense of a specific locale.

It may also be interesting to further explore these and other means by which the tourists of this study have been socialised to this romantic aesthetic. It seems fruitful to focus on one specific form of landscape (e.g. on the volcano, or on the mountains etc.) and deconstruct the processes by means of which each landscape has been historically formed and mediated as an attraction. In another research, which follows the one described in this article, I have focused on the aesthetic constitution of coral reefs, and started to show how a specific idea of nature cultivated in modernist thinking was projected onto the specific geographical realms of coastal environments (Picard 2011). The defining element of this idea resided in an aesthetic of "perfection in nature", with perfection being defined by theological principles of divine symmetry and wholeness. From this point of view, "nature" appeared to be inhabited by a divine force generating such symmetries, while their adoration and study allowed modern subjects to approach, capture or eventually subdue this divine (Lanfant 2009). This observation confirms the analysis of comments made by tourists in this study, associating the perceived "power of nature" with an underlying divine force.

Beyond the prism of a cultural anthropology of German or otherwise national romantic tourist aesthetics, it is important to point out the strong sense of belonging to a German national narrative among the subjects, which seems to have evolved at a different, more fluid level of subjectivity. For instance, I usually told the tourists a popular legend of a slave who escaped from the plantations and found freedom in the mountains, thus evoking a common plot of romantic hero stories. I used this story to talk about wider issues emerging from debates in La Réunion on how to deal with the heritage of slavery. While the heritage of slavery was in most cases not a story of particular interest to the tourists, many spontaneously made an analogy with debates then dominating the German public media sphere on how to deal with the heritage of the Holocaust. Similar to a fable that uses animal characters as metaphors to talk about politics and human relations, the story of dealing with slavery worked as a metaphor to evoke events that for the tourists seemed in their structure similar. I observed on a different occasion that French tourists would react in different ways, often using stories of slavery as metaphors to talk about the perceived confines brought about by modernity and globalisation; topics that were then dominating the French public media sphere.

Conclusion

Many theories of tourism have focused on the structural frames of tourist experiences, and the political dimension of disciplining individuals to submit to specific concepts of time and nature encountered through the journey. Over the past fifty years, touristic travel has variably been theorised as a form of ritualised escape (Enzensberger 1958; Dumezedier 1967; Nash 1989), a quest for an authentic realm whose form itself was said to be embedded in the ideology of modernity (MacCannell 1976), a form of modern pilgrimage in its structure analogous to historical forms of religious pilgrimage (Turner & Turner 1978; Graburn 1989; Cohen 2004a) and as a form of modern festivity allowing the modern subject to recreate the social and moral fabric of modern social life (Graburn 1989; Hennig 1997). Through its focus on the social and societal relevance of individual stories, this study shows how these broader frames and cultures of tourism are articulated at the level of personal tourist experience.

So what does it feel like to be a tourist? While we can never "fully" access the inner worlds of tourists (or anyone else for that matter), the study demonstrates that the journey makes tourists feel perplexed, even speechless when experiencing certain sites – always searching for the right words. Tourism is emotionally intense and mentally challenging. Tourists, while on the tour, are challenged to make the unfamiliar familiar, to impose aesthetic forms upon the realities encountered. They are often emotionally moved without being able to explain why. They are confronted with the moral boundaries of social life, gender, the body and death, and are challenged to engage with these boundaries and what they hold to be normal and natural. Many encounters have a highly metaphorical value, representing analogies with issues that preoccupy the tourists in their home contexts. For example, encounters with children or stories of crisis lead them to reflect on their own children or crises back in Germany. The encounter with the Other thus becomes a tool to engage and transform these issues from home. This works equally at the scale of the national public sphere – for instance, where events in La Réunion are used to reflect on events preoccupying the public media sphere in Germany, such as how to deal with the memory of the past: slavery in La Réunion and the Holocaust in Germany. Confronting and engaging with the story about debates on how to deal with slavery thus eventually reaffirms a strong sense of belonging to a German national narrative. The encounter with the Other thus enables individuals, couples and friends to rethink and reaffirm, but also to readjust, the emotional and affective foundations of what makes them individuals, couples and friends and, at a more existential level, human beings participating in the wider history and nature of the world. The journey away, which constitutes a transgression of the continuity of the home context, thus enables tourists to transform the circumstances of home – either temporarily, where tourists feel that they can "recharge their batteries" and recreate social links and flow, or permanently, where they return as transformed persons, able to "move on in their lives".

At the same time, regardless of their individual experience, the tourists observed all learnt to experience the Other in highly similar, conventional ways. The study shows the presence of widely shared aesthetic dispositions, articulated in particular through the dominant trope of the "power of nature", variably perceived in dramatic landscapes, sea shores, waterfalls, light contrasts and fast-moving clouds. The collective nature of these individual aesthetic dispositions seems related to historical institutionalisation processes through which the art of the sublime of the seventeenth and early eighteenth centuries flowed into the foundations of national romanticism in Germany – and elsewhere in Europe – and in its settler colonies. These appear to be resurfacing today in popular art forms such as literature, television, museums and mass-reproduced visual art, mediating ideal forms of approaching and experiencing the exotic in a given social context. Yet, in whatever collective ways aesthetic cultures and norms articulate experience, this experience is always made by an individual person. Tourism is, in a way, always frustrating because the best words that tourists find to articulate their experiences are often those used in public representations of sites, including those used in tourism marketing; tourists usually fail to convince others about the authenticity of their experiences when all they say is all that has always been said about a specific site in a tourism advertisement: "It was truly magical!"

Notes

1 All the names of the tourists are pseudonyms.

2 Originally developed by anthropologist James Frazer, the notion of sympathetic relations relates to the power objects or entities that had once been in contact with each other and are believed to continue to exert influence upon each other (e.g. a relic of a saint perpetuating the realm of the saint), or the ability of a metaphor or a copy with similar traits to an original to affect the original (e.g. an image of the divine) (Greenwood 2009).

3 Sepp appears under the pseudonym of Eberhard in two other texts of mine (Picard 2011, 2012).

4 For a more elaborate treatment of travel syndromes using Sepp's (also known as Eberhard's) case, see Picard (2012).

5 The visual content of these photos could broadly be grouped into four content-related, thematic categories: panoramic shots of landscapes; hotel and service spaces; local populations and cultural sites. The statistic analysis of the photos in terms of these categories revealed a standard variation (a measure of how spread out data values are around the mean, defined as the square root of the variance) lower than 15%. This means that, among this very small sample, the different tourists sent me sets of photos that were more or less similar in content; the different samples varied only by one photo on average. This significant homogeneity allowed me to analyse this sample based on the average distribution of visual contents.

References

Adler, J. 1989: Travel as Performed Art. *American Journal of Sociology* 94:6, 1366–1391.

Amirou, R. 1995: *Imaginaire touristique et sociabilité du voyage*. Paris: Presses Universitaires de France.

Anderson, B. 1991: *Imagined Communities: Reflections on the Origin and Spread of Nationalism*. London: Verso.

Appadurai, A. 2003: Global Ethnoscapes: Notes and Queries for a Transnational Anthropology. In: A. Appadurai (ed.), *Modernity at Large: Cultural Dimensions of Globalization*. Minneapolis: University of Minnesota Press, pp. 48–65.

Bruner, E.M. 2004: The Balinese Borderzone. In: E.M. Bruner (ed.), *Culture on Tour: Ethnographies of Travel*. Chicago: The University of Chicago Press, pp. 191–210.

Clifford, J. 1989: The Others: Beyond the 'Salvage' Paradigm. *Third Text: Third World Perspectives on Contemporary Art and Culture* 6, 73–77.

Clifford, J. 1997: *Routes: Travel and Translation in the 20th Century*. Cambridge, MA: Harvard University Press.

Cohen, E. 1985: Tourist Guides: Pathfinders, Mediators and Animators. *Annals of Tourism Research* 12:1, 1–49.

Cohen, E. 2004a: Tourism and Religion: A Comparative Perspective. In: E. Cohen (ed.), *Contemporary Tourism: Diversity and Change*. Oxford: Elsevier, pp. 145–158.

Cohen, E. 2004b: A Phenomenology of Tourist Experiences. In: E. Cohen (ed.), *Contemporary Tourism: Diversity and Change*. Oxford: Elsevier, pp. 65–86.

Coleman, S. & M. Crang (eds.) 2002: *Tourism: Between Place and Performance*. Oxford: Berghahn.

Crossley, É. 2012: Affect and Moral Transformations in Young Volunteer Tourists. In: D. Picard & M. Robinson (eds.), *Emotion in Motion: The Passions of Tourism and Travel*. London: Ashgate.

Dumazedier, J. 1967: *Toward a Society of Leisure*. New York: Free Press.

Edensor, T. 1998: *Tourists at the Taj: Performance and Meaning at a Symbolic Site*. London: Routledge.

Enzensberger, H.M. 1958: Vergebliche Brandung der Ferne: Eine Theorie des Tourismus. *Merkur* 12, 701–720.

Fabian, J. 1983: *Time and the Other: How Anthropology Makes its Object*. New York: Columbia University Press.

Franklin, A. 2004: Towards a New Ontology of Tourism: Tourism as an Ordering. *Tourist Studies* 4:3, 277–301.

Frey, N.L. 1999: *Pilgrim Stories: On and off the Road to Santiago – Modern Journeys along an Ancient Way in Spain*. California: University of California Press.

Graburn, N. 1989: Tourism: The Sacred Journey. In: V. Smith (ed.), *Hosts and Guests: The Anthropology of Tourism*. 2nd ed. Philadelphia: University of Pennsylvania Press, pp. 21–36.

Graburn, N. 2002: The Ethnographic Tourist. In: G.M.S. Dann (ed.), *The Tourist as a Metaphor of the Social World*. Wallingford: CAB International, pp. 19–40.

Greenwood, S. 2009: *The Anthropology of Magic*. Oxford: Berg.

Harrison, J.D. 2003: *Being a Tourist: Finding Meaning in Pleasure Travel*. Vancouver: UBC Press.

Hennig, C. 1997: *Reiselust: Touristen, Tourismus und Urlaubskultur*. Frankfurt: Insel.

Hom-Cary, S. 2004: The Tourist Moment. *Annals of Tourism Research* 31:1, 61–77.

Jackson, M. 1998: *Minima Ethnographica: Intersubjectivity and the Anthropological Project*. Chicago: The University of Chicago Press.

Lanfant, M.-F. 2009: The Purloined Eye: Revisiting the Tourist Gaze from a Phenomenological Perspective. In: M. Robinson & D. Picard (eds.), *The Framed World: Tourism, Tourists and Photography*. Farnham: Ashgate, pp. 239–256.

Larsen, J. 2001: Tourism Mobilities and the Travel Glance: Experiences of Being on the Move. *Scandinavian Journal of Hospitality and Tourism* 1:2, 80–98.

Löfgren, O. 2002: *On Holiday: A History of Vacationing*. Berkeley: University of California Press.

MacCannell, D. 1976: *The Tourist: A New Theory of the Leisure Class*. New York: Schocken.

Nash, D. 1989: Tourism as a Form of Imperialism. In: V. Smith (ed.), *Hosts and Guests: The Anthropology of Tourism*. 2nd ed. Philadelphia: University of Pennsylvania Press, pp. 37–54.

Picard, D. 2011: *Tourism, Magic and Modernity: Cultivating the Human Garden*. Oxford: Berghahn.

Picard, D. 2012: Tourism, Awe and Inner Journeys. In: D. Picard & M. Robinson (eds.), *Emotion in Motion: Tourism, Affect and Transformation*. London: Ashgate.

Robinson, M. & D. Picard 2009: *The Framed World: Tourism, Tourists and Photography*. Farnham, England: Ashgate.

Roger, A. 1997: *Court traité du paysage*. Paris: Gallimard.

Spode, H. 2011: *Wie die Deutschen "Reiseweltmeister" wurden: Einführung in die Tourismusgeschichte*. Wiesbaden: VS Verlag für Sozialwissenschaften.

Stewart, S. 1984: *On Longing: Narratives of the Miniature, the Gigantic, the Souvenir, the Collection*. Baltimore, MD: Johns Hopkins University Press.

Tedlock, B. 1991: From Participant Observation to the Observation of Participation: The Emergence of Narrative Ethnography. *Journal of Anthropological Research* 47:1, 69–94.

Turner, V. & E. Turner 1978: *Image and Pilgrimage in Christian Culture: Anthropological Perspectives*. New York: Columbia University Press.

David Picard holds a Ph.D. in anthropology (2001) from the University of La Réunion, Indian Ocean, and is currently working at the Centre for Research in Anthropology (CRIA) at the New University of Lisbon, Portugal. He is the author of *Tourism, Magic and Modernity: Cultivating the Human Garden* (Berghahn 2011).
(piccccc@gmail.com)

"TO EACH THEIR OWN PLACE"

Ethnicized Memories and Inter-Ethnic Practices in the Sub-Carpathian Hungarian Social World

Anne Marie Losonczy

The socio-cultural network and strategies of Hungarian villages and towns in the sub-Carpathian region are characterized by an increasing tension between the political reinforcement of cultural boundaries with other regional groups and the growing economic importance of informal inter-ethnic relations. The articulation of contrastive political ethnicity with the local social sphere lies in the local memory of collective deportation of Hungarian speakers in 1945 by the Soviet regime that is ritualized by commemorative monuments and events. Yet the diverse forms of inter-ethnic solidarity and co-operation are interwoven with and simultaneously effective in the fields of trade, exchange, smuggling, and temporary migrations across the border. Thus the ethnography of multi-ethnic regions on the margins of diverse national spaces susceptible to international dispute calls attention to the paradoxical inter-dependence between the durability of political ethnicities relying on the permanence of inter-ethnic solidarities and co-operation.

Keywords: inter-ethnic relations, ethnicities, memorial ritualization, sub-Carpathian Ukraine, transborder activities

This research builds on the following working hypothesis regarding ethnicity in complex inter-ethnic settings: On the one hand, there is an inter-dependence between the institutionalization of an isolationist and contrastive ethnicity – particularly prominent in the ritualization of emblematic *lieux de mémoire*; on the other hand, there remains a local practice of downplaying ethnic frontiers through informal trade, smuggling, and the management of tourism. This is an indispensable condition for a politicized ethnicity which maintains its legitimacy by safeguarding a specific culture, territory, and communitarian sociability in order to avoid destroying what it is meant to save. Thus, the relationship between political ethnicity and the informal economy (Sárkány 2010), the problem of the group boundaries and the ideological representations of these boundaries are at the core of the argument.

The re-emergence of informal trade and smuggling across borders was concomitant with the weakening of the Soviet system as early as 1985, and intensified with the independence of the Ukraine in 1992 which led to a complete breakdown of the economic and monetary system of this country. At this juncture, bartering locally and across borders of agricultural and manufactured goods secured the survival of rural and urban populations – regardless of ethnic or national affiliations – as well as the reproduction of social structures and village solidarities distinguishing the different ethnic groups. At the same time, large-scale smuggling, access to institutional financing and privatization co-occurred alongside the reinforcement of the status of former *apparatchiks*[1]. Their rapid recycling in the new Ukrainian political institutions gave them power in a new setting. Those who most successfully rose in the new hierarchy enjoyed both an extended network of kin and multi-ethnic contacts, locally and across borders, and a constant diversification of their activities and resources.

The Hungarian intellectual elite elaborated a politicized ethnicity and depended on the institutional resources of the new political sphere of the Hungarian State that demanded ritualized discourses and practices, constructing an isolationist and contrastive ethnicity (Comaroff & Comaroff 2009) based on an historical and cultural singularity in this regional context. Building up or re-building *lieux de mémoire* and organizing commemorative rituals around them came to figure as the main axis of a regional touristic offer. This touristic programme, however, requires local acceptance and infrastructures for which all ethnic components must collaborate. The heritage tourism appears thus as the economic spin-off of the ethnic mobilization, its production and its legitimizing device. Managing and maintaining this tourism demands at one and the same time the mobility of ethnic elites for setting it up between Hungarian and Ukrainian institutional resources and a permanent inter-ethnic collaboration locally for the implementation of its activities.

The multiplicity of positions occupied by the elites in social, economic and political domaines is typical of the formation of new post-socialist elites and has been amply documented (e.g., Verdery 2003; Eiyal, Szelenyi & Townsley 1998). In the Transcarpathian context, this multi-positionality permeates all social milieus and integrates the ethnic dimension. Fluency in multi-lingualism as well as activation of diverse familial, ethnic and national networks ensure the permanency and the success of operations, which are both economically profitable and sources of regional and ethnic prestige.

After a brief historical survey of the region, I will illustrate the paradoxical inter-dependence between the practice of inter-ethnic relations and the political and touristic patrimonialization around an isolationist ethnicity. To do so, I discuss three different contexts of Transcarpathian daily life: smuggling, informal trade and its markets, and the dynamics of touristic activities. Smuggling and informal trade sustain investments in accomodation and publicity for tourism; they influence the inter-ethnic division of labor of rural and heritage tourism. The latter is based on visiting various *lieux de mémoire*, considered as emblematic of history, and on staging shows of folklorized rural activities.

The ethnografic research focused on the recomposition of frontiers – multi-ethnic, economic and religious – in the region of Transcarpathia, on both sides of the Hungarian-Ukrainian border. It was mostly conducted among the Hungarian-speaking minority in Hungarian, my native language, and later extended to Ruthenian, Ukrainian and Russian components of this region, with my basic knowledge of Russian, which is a vehicular idiom there. Fieldwork began with stays of several weeks in April and September 2008, and continued in the summer of 2010 and in the autumn of 2011, in the cities of Nyiregháza (Hungary), Munkasevo and Beregovo, in several neighboring villages, including two border villages (Chap Hungarian and Tiszapéterfalva), and briefly in Ruthen-speaking villages close to the Verecke Pass. I worked alone, as a paying guest of families that I accompanied and interviewed amidst their daily routines. In 2011, I collected and registered semi-directive interviews of Hungarian survivors of the Gulag (see Losonczy 2010, 2012).

The Heritage of Periphery

As a consequence of the 1920 Trianon Treaty, Transcarpathia was severed from Hungary and absorbed by the newly created Czechoslovakia. Under Czechoslovakian rule, the region was turned into a territorial unit with a distinctive name, *Podkarpatská Rus* (Carpathian Ruthenia), and many Hungarian families migrated to Hungary and were replaced by Czechs.

In 1938, when Czechoslovakia was dismembered, the fringe inhabited by a majority of Hungarians was incorporated into Hungary, which annexed the rest of the region a few months later. In the autumn of 1944, the Soviet Union forced Czechoslovakia to give up the region, and annexed and integrated it into the Socialist Republic of Ukraine. Once it was incorporated into the USSR in 1945, the name was modified again, this time to *Zakarpatska* or *Zakarpattia*, which means "the region beyond the Carpathian mountains". Thereafter, Moscow compelled Hungary to refer to this region as *Karpat-Ukraina* (Carpatho-Ukraine) in all publications, but the local common language and the standard Hungarian still used the term *Kárpátalja*, which had first appeared at the turn of the twentieth century in scientific publications. After the Soviet breakdown, the term *Kárpátalja* re-appeared in all written communications for the Transcarpathian Hungarians as well as for the Hungarian authorities, while the official name in Ukrainian remained *Zakarpatska* (Fedinec & Vehes 2010).

The majority of Hungarian speakers either live in the agricultural zones along the Hungarian border or in the three important towns of this region: Beregovo (Hungarian Beregszász), Munkasevo (Munkács), and Uzhgorod (Ungvár). There are approximately 600 towns and villages inhabited by Hungarian speakers but more often settlements are a mix of ethnic groups; ever since the 1950s, there has been a network of Hungarian-speaking schools, after the Soviet authorities recognized Hungarians as a "nationality". The mix of ethnic groups includes Ukrainians (a majority), Roma, who are often Hungarian speakers, Ruthenians, dominant in the mountain zones, Slovaks, Rumanians, and Russians, with each group numbering some ten thousand. According to the 2001 census, some 80% of the population are Ukrainian, including Ruthens (roughly one million) and 12,5% Hungarian.

After the demise of the USSR, there was a re-awakening and extension of religious activities from the different denominations that had historically been pillars of the multi-religious character of the region. They quickly recovered and restored their religious buildings and schools which were often in poor repair because they had been destroyed or converted for industrial use.

If religious affiliation plays the role of an ethnic marker to a large extent, being very conspicuous in the local idiom and practice, it can also constitute a privileged inter-ethnic field. Thus, since the sixteenth century, many Hungarian speakers have converted to Protestantism. Nonetheless, some tens of thousands, mainly in the cities, share the Roman Catholic faith of the Slovaks, while others, along with most Ruthenians and Rumanians, say they belong to the most brutally repressed religion in the area and in the whole Ukraine, the Uniate faith (or Greek-Catholic Church). The Soviet regime persecuted them after accusing them of "Ukrainian nationalism" and "collaboration with the Nazi Germans". Among the *pravoslavis* (Russian Orthodox Church), one can still find Ruthenians and Ukrainians, often forcibly converted, but this religion does not concern the Hungarian population (Hann 1993: 201–213).

In the period between the two World Wars, the Jews in this region were culturally and economically active, and numbered approximately 86,000. Most considered themselves Hungarian. After World War II, the survivors of the Holocaust, about 25%, rapidly emigrated to the United States, Palestine, and later to Israel. Today, a few hundred elderly Jews are free to practise their religion in small, informal, recently established urban synagogues. The former synagogues were either destroyed or appropriated for other use during the German occupation or the Soviet regime.

The ethnic identification of persons or families by their religion or their principal language is the dominant usage of everyday ethnicity (Brubaker et al. 2006) in rural milieus, where it is considered the most "polite" form of description. The term "Hungarian", however, is still often reserved for ritual, commemorative occasions, or politically oriented speeches: its use indicates the degree of permeability of the local or personal language to the erudite or political expressions of the Hungarians' memory of their internment in the Gulag, thereby communicating their ethnic claims. Moreover, the idiom of religious affiliation still appears as the only one capable of categorizing the mixed population: namely those born from inter-ethnic marriages as well as their children. This inter-ethnic dimension of local social organizations, already ancient, today performs a fundamental function in economic activities, serving as the only guarantee of survival, such as through informal trade, smuggling, and tourism. It also constitutes one of the more important premises implicit in the political and memorial discourses associated with the Hungarian identity of this region.

The post-communist context has restructured the ethnic environment of Hungarians, revealing new actors and ideological discourses. Ukrainian nation-building, re-initiated in 1992 and still ongoing, revived the historical rift between Western Ukrainians, the *Zapadency* according to the present-day Ukrainian idiom, who lived under the Austro-Hungarian, Czechoslovak or Polish rule, and are mostly Uniates (or Greek Catholics), opposed to the *Skhidnyaki*, the "Easterners" according to the same idiom, Orthodox and very Russified (Fedinec & Vehes 2010). Between them, sharp memorial conflicts cristallize around the genocidal nature of the great famine of 1932–33, the *holodomor*, and the representations of armed anti-Soviet resistance in Ukraine. Moreover, the introduction of the Ukrainian language in the educational system at all levels tends to reduce the importance of Russian as a language of communication and culture. From their scanty demographic numbers, Romanian, Roma and Hungarian minorities of Transcarpathia are but a secondary issue, but suffer nonetheless from the fallout of the Ukrainization of the territory. Some nationalistic movements, such as *Svoboda* ("freedom"), will dispute their rights, through symbolic manifestations, and by repeatedly damaging or destroying Hungarian or Ruthenian commemorative monuments.

In Hungarian daily life in Transcarpathia, mostly in villages and multi-ethnic neighborhoods, the Ukrainian presence assumes two forms: that of the power wielded by administrative officials and the economic and political elites, and that of their neighbors, often partners in the informal trade and smuggling, teachers of their children and service-mates in the compulsory military conscription; few mixed marriages exist, but they are difficult to evaluate.

The Ruthens (today called "Rusyn" in publications) form an ethno-linguistic group belonging to the oriental branch of the Slavic language family, sharing part of their vocabulary with Ukrainian. Their territorial core lies in the peripheral, mountainous zones of the northeastern Carpathian range. Their presence there is confirmed since the ninth century and has been completed by gradual migrations over the centuries, originating out of Volhynia, Galicia, and Bukovina. Woodcutters, small farmers, and shepherds used to transhumance, the Ruthens migrated, periodically or permanently, to Slovakia, Romania, Hungary, Poland and even to Serbian Vojvodina. They dispersed among these countries, with a sizeable diaspora in the USA. The traditionally fuzzy character of the frontiers with their ethnic neighbors has permitted continuous and intense trade and economic relations: there is the century-old tradition of Ruthenian day laborers harvesting in the Great Hungarian Plain, and the exchange of their agricultural products up to the end of the Second World War.

Living on the fringes, the existence of Ruthens oscillates between relative isolation and multiple cultural influences; they appear as an inevitable crossing point for an inter-ethnic economic network across borders. Numbering at present between 900,000 and one million (75% in the Ukraine), the Ruthens write their language either in Cyrillic or Latin script. Their dominant religious affiliation is the Uniate Church, which showed a spectacular revival after the end of persecutions by the Soviet regime. This scattered community never constituted a state of its own, neither did Ruthens have cities. Their first intellectuals were Uniate priests; they appear in older publications, sometimes as Russian, sometimes as Ukrainian or Hungarian, according to the policies of assimilation of majority political external forces which were accepted by a large part of the Ruthens (Magocsi 1997). The multiplicity of ethnonyms designating them is a clear illustration of this identitary fuzziness.

The Soviet Union, repressing all manifestations of ethnic particularism, assimilated the Ruthens with the Ukrainian majority. The demise of communism accentuated internal divisions between assimilationnists (Ukrainians, Slovaks, Hungarians or Poles) and a nascent "political Ruthenism" whose Ukrainian leaders are often supported by Russian anti-Ukrainian interests. Since 1989, the Rusyn ethnic organizations have multiplied in Poland, Slovakia, Romania, the Czech Republic, Vojvodina, and then in Hungary. An emergent intellectual elite manning these organizations generates a form of ethnicity based on the notion that the Rusyn are a people (*narod*) constituting the genuine autochtonous population of the Carpathian Mountains. Hence there is the need to codify and teach the written language (Rucinko 2009) so as to claim and obtain all rights that the regional states grant to their respective ethnic minorities.

However, in Ukraine the Ruthenian ethnic claims so far do not appear to gather a majority. They formulate their identity in terms not of "minority" but of "autochtony". A status of "autonomy", recognized by Czechoslovakia in Transcarpathia before the war was "illegally" suppressed by the Soviet regime. Therefore, they deem it necessary to create a "Republic of Subcarpathian Rus", autonomous within the Ukrainian State. The latter, paradoxically follows Soviet heritage and still considers this population as Ukrainian and does not seem ready to grant them cultural and political rights.

Along with the post-communist opening of borders and the use of new technologies of communication, traditional Ruthenian mobility lends to this emerging ethnicity a new, inter-regional dimension with a characteristic network pattern (Magocsi 1997). Paradoxically, these same factors sustain and reinforce Ruthenian inter-ethnic circulation in commercial and touristic activities, as well as the relative frequency of inter-ethnic marriages. If industrialization, education and compulsory military service did contribute to urbanize a fair amount of the Ruthenians in market towns with a large Hungarian population, the opening of borders let them re-discover their ethnic kindred across the borders in Hungary, Slovakia, Poland and Romania. Along with Romanians, they are, at the present time, the privileged trade and marriage partners of Hungarians.

The explicit meaning of both Hungarian and Russo-Ukrainian denominations for the region – namely "the piedmont of the Carpathians" and "beyond the Carpathians" – implicitly refers to two rival centers of power, one in the West (Hungary), the other in the East (Ukraine). The names still share the same logic of the opposition between center and periphery.

This divided dependence between competing centers characterizes not only spatial representations, but also notions of social time. Though place names have been officially written and taught in Russian, and later in Ukrainian, for the last sixty years, Hungarian speakers and most Ruthenians only express places and itineraries with Hungarian names in their daily speech, yet remain quite at ease with the official (Russian or Ukrainian) denominations in their contacts with authorities. Similarly, although the Ukrainian territory is officially in a time zone one hour in advance of Hungarian (and Western European) time, Hungarian speakers and most Ruthenians and Roma tend to set their watches and clocks, make their appointments, open and close their shops and businesses, listen to radio, and watch television according to "Hungarian time", which is designated in the local inter-ethnic speech as *po misnamu* (local time) and derived from the Russo-Ukrainian lexicon. In sharp contrast, all official institutions, state enterprises, public transports, and street clocks operate on "Kiev time", which also sets the pace of daily life for Russians and Ukrainians who have been established there since 1946. If both temporal codes are known and punctually used by all, this duality certainly draws an identity borderline, figuring two forms of supra-local allegiance.

From National Minority to Peripheral Ethnicity

If the policies of the Soviet Union, as brutal as they were incoherent, never succeeded in suppressing the cultural core of supra-local Hungarian identity, it is, paradoxically, the geo-political re-composition after 1989 that now seems to jeopardize cultural links and identification with Hungary, a primary foundation for the profile of a national minority. A bilateral treaty was signed in 1991 to facilitate cordial relations between Budapest and Kiev, whereby Hungary pledged to abandon all territorial claims and entrusted the fate of the Hungarians of Transcarpathia to the good will of the Ukrainian State. This treaty was felt and experienced as a betrayal by the local Hungarian elites. For the Hungarians of Transcarpathia it presents a new and conflicting image of Hungary as a foreign country.

Finally, the integration of Hungary into the EU and the Schengen Area, which imposes heavy administrative conditions on Ukrainian citizens – including ethnic Hungarians – wishing to travel, settle, or study in Hungary, seems to have spread disappointment amongst the entire population. This has progressively transformed into a widespread mistrust of the Hungarian State. In 2004, under the pressure of the nationalistic right, a referendum was organized in Hungary on the question of granting Hungarian nationality to "ethnic" Hungarians in the adjacent countries. The socialist party, then in power, campaigned for the "no", arguing with economic and political reasons of "good neighborhood". The massive abstention of voters and the victory of the "no" reinforced this representation of political aloofness and of the separation between cultural identity and national affiliation.

On the other hand, since the collapse of the Soviet Union, intense informal trade and smuggling – fundamental economic resources for the survival of this region – have increased and diversified inter-ethnic interactions between Ruthenians, Ukrainians and local Hungarians, while activating and widening family and affinal networks on both sides of the Hungarian-Ukrainian border. These practices have expanded and extended the multi-ethnic social space of Transcarpathia toward the border departments of northeastern Hungary. This is typically accomplished through the installation of families and various trans-border trading activities, thus transforming the urban and social landscape of regional towns and villages. No legal intervention or police regulation can stop these practices, thus they delineate the figure of a regional trans-border identity where the prestige-scale shifts toward social competence for the negotiation and mobilization of multiple cultural, identity and interactional resources.

At the same time, the discourses and practices of younger Transcarpathian generations – such as festivals, touristic performances, or the creation and use of virtual space on the web – display a progressive identification with the Transcarpathian territory itself, thereby giving evidence of an emerging Hungarian identity of Transcarpathia (Karas 2008). In this process, instead of being perceived as a territory artificially separated from a common Hungarian country before 1918, Transcarpathia is turning into the main referent in the passage from a national minority to that of a new local ethnicity, thereby making new identity moorings available. From below, the Transcarpathian territory is the basis of Hungarian ethnicity; from above, the figure of the "Hungarian Nation" appears in local comments as a meta-territorial community of the *ethnos*, disseminated amongst several nation states, but with the Hungarian language demarcating its virtual territory. If the 2010 adoption by the right-wing majority of the Hungarian Parliament of a law giving *de jure* Hungarian citizenship to all descendants of Hungarians in the world brings about practical questions of opportunity and feasability, it does not seem to affect this orientation, since Ukrainian law will sanction naturalization by the forfeiture of Ukrainian citizenship.

Surviving Together: Figures of Inter-Ethnic Mobility across Borders

The revival of the informal economy can also be interpreted as the circulation of economic commodities between regions that, until the beginning of the twentieth century, all belonged to historical Hungary. Before 1920, the Carpathian basin constituted an economically and ecologically autonomous unit in Hungary. Cultural and commercial relations as well as the division of labor between the different regions of Hungary share a multi-ethnic history. After 1920, with the new borders imposed by the Trianon Treaty, these relations have been gradually suppressed. It was only after the internal collapse of the socialist regime in the mid-1980s that the structures of popular commerce and the circulation of goods began to re-emerge. Horváth and Kovatch (1999) argue that the informal circulation of commodities and the smuggling activities (of gasoline and other goods) are nothing more than the slow re-institutionalization of the traditional, ethnic, and regional division of labor adjusting to the new realities at the end of the twentieth century. In other words, one can interpret them as a return to the trade relations which were historically and spontaneously organized between the peoples of the Carpathian basin before 1920, but new ethnic actors have appeared on the scene.

Trade and Smuggling across the Hungarian-Ukrainian Border

Immediately following the Soviet regime change, northeastern Hungary experienced a severe economic recession which included a rising rate of unemployment. Consequently, the illegal transport of petrol and fuel-oil across the border became the main resource of economic survival for hundreds of Hungarian families in this region. The quantities smuggled were relatively small – Horváth and Kovatch (1999: 121) estimated between 100,000 and 200,000 liters per month in the mid-1990s. They calculated that this was sufficient to fuel about half of the agricultural machinery of the Hungarian northeast.

The war in Bosnia brought about yet another new development. Ukrainian petrol and gas-oil were still being smuggled, but were trafficked towards the Hungarian-Rumanian border. From there, groups of Serbs and Hungarians then transported the goods across the Hungarian-Serbian border during the blockade imposed by Western powers. Petrol and gas-oil were bought in the Ukraine at less than two-thirds of the Hungarian price, and were then deposited and sold within the Hungarian border fringe, but fuel was also traded in more distant regions of Hungary. In the late 1990s, several villages on the Ukrainian side of the border specialized in storing petrol and fuel-oil for subsequent sale. These deposits stood – and still stand – in the backyards of houses. The largest houses are equipped with tanks and petrol pumps, and can stock up to ten thousand liters; others keep the fuel in containers and use hand pumps. In 1996, the Ukrainian Parliament passed a law that made the production and labeling of vodka a national monopoly. As a result, smugglers who had specialized in the illegal trade of vodka switched to petrol and gas-oil.

When the illegal transport and passage of fuels became more difficult, or the demand for them slackened, the same routes and vehicles began transporting thousands of cigarette cartons bought from Transcarpathian Rumanians or vodka from the black market of Uzhgorod. The people transporting these goods rarely venture beyond the areas of purchase and resale, where they have acquaintances and local knowledge. They are available twenty-four hours a day and can cross the border at any time, based on precise information gathered through a very efficient network of informants. They use Western cars or minibuses with especially large tanks, also illegally imported from Germany.[2] Most of these petrol-smugglers were former employees of the Hungarian National Railways whose jobs had been cut after the fall of communism. Among the younger generation who do not typically own their own vehicles, there are the so-called "day workers" of petrol; those who drive someone else's car laden with petrol across the border.

Crossing the Hungarian-Ukrainian border usually takes a long time, mainly due to the number of vehicles, but smugglers have a tendency to help each other, often ceding places to one another in the queue for customs. In the late 1990s, about 60% of all vehicles crossing the border were petrol transporters (Horváth & Kovach 1999).

Beyond its initial capital investment, smuggling petrol implies a large amount of moral capital. Trust between buyers and sellers is essential for reproducing this trade, equal in importance to the reliability and quality of the smuggled product. In general, transporters of petrol, cigarettes, clothes and textiles, and occasionally agricultural products, each have their own regular customers; the networks thus established between sellers and buyers have been stable from the late 90s to the present day. Two groups constitute the transporters: Transcarpathian migrants and Hungarian-born citizens. Both of them enjoy a privileged relationship with custom officials and border guards, including the exchange of information, and, in turn, financial compensation for such exchanges. Smugglers are mostly men aged between 30 and 40; the first generation that started to organize this trade in the 90s have already been replaced by a younger, more aggressive one. By and large, it has remained an individual and/or family affair without the presence of the mafia on the Hungarian side.

The mafia controls the supply of backyard pumps and tanks in Transcarpathia, but does not intervene in the transport and commercialization of petrol across the border. There is a hierarchy amongst the smugglers, mainly based on the number of vehicles owned. This allows those who are better off to transport cigarettes, alcohol, and other products in addition to the petrol. The losers in this smuggling business are those who lack sufficient initial capital, those without a network of family and friends across the border, and those who cannot stabilize a pool of regular buyers. As one informant put it, "one who has not been honest enough in the selling, and not aggressive enough in the buying". Yet losers and winners do not exhibit a radically different economic prosperity, and success in the form of stable business and clients are locally attributed more to good luck than to special abilities. Social capital accrues from large families with members on both sides of the border and a wide network of acquaintances.

In the cross-border circulation of goods, services, money and people, transport has become an autonomous activity with a tightly knit network of small mobile drivers in constant communication, either amongst themselves and/or with their clients on their mobile phones. This activity also relies on family ties, those nearby and those on the other side of the border: husbands and wives, parents and children, cousins, and in-laws on either side exploit the family vehicles night and day for all-purpose transport, including a convenient alternative for travellers weary of the slow trains and endless delays due to the change of rail gauge between Hungary and Ukraine.

Today, there is both a re-composition and a fragmentation of this informal circulation of goods and services across the border. The admission of Hungary into the Schengen Area on January 1, 2008, has notably reinforced border control, especially on the Hungarian side, chiefly as a result of new military and technological equipment, particularly the increased use of computers. The intensified challenge of crossing the border checkpoints with cars and smuggled goods has resulted in the re-assessment of crossing points along the "green border", and has consequently capitalized on the local, masculine cultural knowledge of the territory. This knowledge is turning into a prized commodity for new, non-local actors, who are increasingly professional, and are often situated within the pyramidal hierarchy of the Ukrainian mafia. The latter have permanent residency and money-laundering investments in the market towns on the Hungarian side, notably in Nyiregyháza, and sometimes contribute to a certain style of urban modernization in these towns. They have also introduced weapons and "human merchandise" in the trans-border scene, through the transfer of clandestine migrants and/or prostitutes on their way to Western Europe. These actors use extortion, intimidation, and open violence in their relations with their local partners, including border police and customs officials, particularly on the Ukrainian side. In order to smuggle cigarettes, alcohol, and weapons, they use the Uzhgorod-Csap-Zahony railway line as well as trucks; many railway employees also take part in this network.

The professionalization and toughening of smuggling activities following the crystallization of the EU–Ukraine border signals the emergence of new goods and actors in an economic field ruled by trans-border logic and tradition. Thus, local areas communicate and thereby constitute the supra-local aspect in the globalization of a violent economy. The growing danger associated with these activities has fragmented the formerly more inclusive field of the informal circulation of goods and services across the border. Ethnographically, this is remarkably clear: The passing, exchanging, and bartering across the border of both standard and prestigious objects of consumption and based on differential prices and taxes and relative scarcity in either country (such as electric appliances, clothes, shoes, and cosmetics, which are less expensive in Ukraine) formerly involved the same networks of villages and roads, of known and accessible markets, and was part of everyday conversation and commentaries. Now, the field of organized smuggling is dominated by extra-regional actors who are mobile and violent, along with their local partners; they conduct their business under a cloak of silence.[3] The sight of new houses, considered extravagant by the locals, and of brand-new powerful cars, which elicit a few involuntary words from drunken masculine voices or encourage oblique rumours whispered among some women, constitute the sole evidence of this organization. Some local actors, mostly men, may occasionally act as a small actor for one or both systems of smuggling. Neither the local small smugglers nor the customs and border officers are able to make individual, strategic choices. They appear as liminal sidekicks at the intersection and on the frontline of several worlds of norms and constraints.

Informal trade is sometimes the only resource left after the loss of opportunities due to the change of economic and political regimes. It activates and widens the local economic and cultural abilities, contributing to the accumulation of individual and family prestige, both locally and in the border zone. At the core of these abilities – convertible into capital when other sources are absent – is the ability to react to unforeseen events: the capacity to maintain, stabilize and expand (within realistically controlled limits) relational networks between all the ethnic groups present in this region and in the bordering countries of Hungary, Slovakia, and Rumania. Beyond the knowledge and the timely activation of the relational cultural codes – including that of an inter-ethnic transactional idiom composed of words borrowed from Ukrainian, Slovak and Rumanian – this ability includes having mobility between both transitory and permanent local links, and maintaining a scrupulous respect for pledges and engagements, which are always verbal. This "mestizo competence" (Losonczy 2002: 24), which is part and parcel of the masculine status, but not entirely inaccessible to women, consists of the permanent economic and social mobilization of inter-ethnicity, and of the constant strategic crossing of cultural, linguistic, religious, and state frontiers. It therefore constitutes the opposite of ethnicist isolationism, which is the domain of the local Hungarian political elites. In this trans-border economic game, the "Hungarianess" of the actors (or its negation) is but one asset amongst many resources to be mobilized in the transactions whose networks create a functional, "cultural intimacy" (Herzfeld 1997) among persons of various origins. This cross-border cultural intimacy does not invalidate the internal cultural intimacy particular to each group, but is instead a result of their partial intersection.

The KGST Market of Nyiregyháza

The black market appeared in Hungary in the 1980s, most notably through Poles who got into trading second-hand products after being struck by the economic crisis of their country. The impoverishment of large sectors of the rural Hungarian population as a consequence of the change of regime helped renew and increase demand for this trade. The ethnic recomposition of informal trade, particularly intense along the borders, led to a change in the designation of the black market: it was re-dubbed "the KGST market", the Hungarian initials for the now extinct Comecon organization.

In spite of the quick reshaping that affects the organization, size and the flow of goods, this market is still the place par excellence where both the ethnic complementarity and specialization are conspicuous and exploited in the informal trans-border circulation of goods and services. Initially, these activities were characterized by mobility, lack of organization, petty delinquency, and miserable sanitary conditions. By the mid-90s the municipal authorities had recognized their importance and attempted to organize and legalize them by assigning fixed spots to sellers of different products in the market place. Nyiregyháza, the major town of the northeastern department of Hungary, some 40 km from the Ukrainian border, is also relatively close to the Slovak and Rumanian borders. Consequently, it has one of the largest KGST markets of the whole country.

This market is held in a huge parking lot in a peripheral suburb. The spatial setting, layout of its retailers, and range of supplies were stabilized in the late 1990s. Different sections are assigned to the different groups of retailers and types of merchandise. A large section of Ukrainians – including Hungarians, Rumanians, and Roma – have a well-stocked amount of tools, cigarettes, and vodka placed under old bath towels. In the Hungarian sector, most merchants have a licence to sell specific goods, but actually trade products off licence, namely clothing from China or Turkey. Alongside them, a small group of Rumanian Roma sells second-hand goods and smuggled cigarettes and spirits. They instil fear and mistrust among their competitors and buyers because they are quick to react to alleged slights. They work in families, and are generally present in several markets in the area. Where the Poles once used to trade illicitly, the Chinese and Hungarian retailers now sell quality clothes on clean, well-arranged stands. There is also an ethnically mixed section of people from Transylvania – Hungarians, Rumanians, and some Ukrainians – who sell smuggled spare parts for agricultural machines, particularly for the Russian or Belarussian tractors used in Hungary. They also sell Rumanian-made products, such as kitchen equipment, tools, smaller electric domestic appliances and clothing. Next to them, a small group of Armenian Jews change money and sell Asiatic electronic gadgets. In the all-important food section, Hungarian retailers sell in bulk to Ukrainians and Rumanians, who pay a much higher price in their country for the same products. Next to this market, in a separate area, there is a small Chinese section, nicknamed "the Chinese Yard" by the locals. In the early 1990s, the Chinese supplanted the Polish and Hungarian merchants. Their aggressive commercial stance made them unpopular and caused them to be mistrusted by their colleagues; thus, they ended up separating their market space from the KGST market space. After some initial success due to their low prices, the poor quality of their products and their separateness made customers scarcer.

The profile of merchants has professionalized over time: most of them are either qualified workers, or graduates from technical schools who lost their jobs at the end of the communist period. After a period of itinerant trade, they settled into this market. Their type of commercial activity is basically illegal, since retailers do not pay taxes. Nonetheless, they abide by a strict rule where keeping one's word is fundamental. Thus, the verbal contract is superior to the written, and long-term financial engagements are scrupulously respected. Apart from this basic component of the system, the ability to react rapidly to changes in the tastes and demands of customers is also important: clothing fashions, innovations in electrical appliances, and new brands of cigarettes and vodka are carefully observed.

This market, along with smaller ones on the Ukrainian side of the border, fulfils a fundamental social function in a region where the middle-classes have been downgraded by the change of regime and the newly impoverished have proliferated. Non-Hungarian buyers in this market are often retailers from Slovakia, Ukraine or Rumania (mainly from areas inhabited by Hungarians) who buy in bulk and resell in their home countries. But Rumanian, Ukrainian, and Slovak sellers also come periodically to the KGST for a day or two either monthly or quarterly. Local buyers are mostly unemployed people, the recently impoverished former members of the communist middle-class; however, members of the economic and intellectual elite of the city also frequently visit the market. While the former categories typically buy food and clothing, the wealthier elites practice a kind of neighborhood tourism. They browse through an exotic world where they can find, with a bit of luck, interesting, decorative, or traditional popular objects from Hungarian-speaking regions of the neighboring countries.

The daily attendance at this market is between two and three thousand people on weekdays, but rises to almost twenty thousand before Christmas, when dozens of buses and coaches arrive from Poland, Slovakia, Ukrainian Transcarpathia and Rumania. During that period, the number of merchants is then over one thousand. Thus, the market contributes simultaneously to reinforce ethnic limits through commercial specialization and the inter-ethnic relations by facilitating interactions and strengthening a common interest in its permanency. Moreover, this continuous movement of goods and services will definitely enhance the survival and the regional ethnic prestigious status of those who successfully manage inter-ethnic commercial dealings and conflicts.

Yet smuggling activities are not limited to these stabilized "grey" zones where they have been channeled into markets now tolerated by the authorities. In spite of the Schengen process, smuggled goods from Transcarpathia are still distributed on the sly along smaller roads, out of car trunks, in farmhouse backyards, in private residences, and in small village pubs. In this flexible, informal trade, buyers and sellers are inter-dependent, and they switch their roles as they cross to either side of the Ukrainian-Hungarian border. Those involved in these grey and black areas of the economy are assured of the success, stability and reproduction of this mode of living. Reasons for this include the opportunity to pass quickly from one commercial role to another, to adapt immediately to changes in demand for diverse products, and to supplement their income through other activities that also rely on permanent, trans-border mobility.

Among these activities, the Transcarpathians have developed both formal and informal varieties of tourism, such as receiving tourists, organizing small-scale tours, and commercializing touristic products. In this activity, however, there is a clearer division of labor: Transcarpathians – typically Hungarian Transcarpathians – are the sellers, Hungarians the buyers.

Homeland and "Limes" as an Inter-Ethnic Heritage

The wider context of this incipient tourism is, obviously, the fall of communism in Hungary as well as the collapse of the Soviet Union, which has resulted in the resumption of trans-border mobility in the region. Yet one should not underestimate the important role played by the post-communist Central European cultural policies. These policies attempted to tie ideological bases with instruments of patrimony management, and national identity with tourism, in order to construct a "national" cultural capital which could be negotiated politically with neighboring countries having a Hungarian minority, while simultaneously promoting internal and external tourism. Whereas the main target of this policy "across the border" inspired by a kind of "transborder nationalism" (Brubaker 1996) was indeed Transylvania,[4] the extension of these identity premises toward all adjacent Hungarian speakers particularly by Duna TV – even before the fall of communism, this television station was conceived as the central voice of pan-Hungary – suggested a new economic perspective to the Transcarpathian Hungarians and provided an idiom which they could use to build up a virtual image of their region. Concurrently, it promoted a touristic demand for Hungarian identity within Hungarian borders. Moreover, as in most regions of Central and Eastern Europe, the rural character of Transcarpathia with its scant industry and weak infrastructure generated the emergence of small-scale, local tourist entrepreneurs offering urban and rural bed-and-breakfast services, along with organized tours of the symbolic sites of the region. In spite of local tourist associations in towns and villages (usually headed by female members of the local intelligentsia, such as schoolteachers, professors, and engineers finding employ in touristic activities), the trans-border, inter-ethnic networks of kin and affines still remain the main informal vehicle for "passing" tourists from hand to hand, and from place to place. Similarly, personal contacts, or contacts through relations (such as school or religious event organizers or tourist agents from Ukraine and Slovakia), allow these entrepreneurs to receive an increasing number of non-Hungarian families and groups.

The tourist associations operate the web pages and manage the sites of their localities, and often serve as intermediaries between the regional political elites, who promote and ritualize *lieux de mémoire*, and the small local peasant entrepreneurs, who set up activities in relation to the patrimonialized landscape (wild nature, hiking, horse cart riding, and fishing) as well as traditional crafts (weaving, cooking, farm-restoring, pastry, home distillery of spirits, and pig slaughtering).

Similar to other rural areas of post-socialist countries, rural tourism emerges in Transcarpathia as a gradual process whereby some local customs of family hospitality, traditionally intended for kin and affine, are progressively dropped from the system, which still regulates the private sphere. They are stylized according to a changing tourist demand, but also adopt the symbolic tourist images offered by the media. Thus, after the almost hermetic closure of borders, the first tourists, who arrived in the 1980s, were members of the German minority who had either been expelled or had fled following the annexation of Transcarpathia by the Soviet Union, and who had organized active memorial associations and communities in Germany (Ilyés 2003). After all those years away, they were returning to the village where they had been born, and to the friends and family long lost to them. Called *Heimattourismus* in German anthropology,[5] this tourism of the "lost country" is part of a memorial practice, a collective elaboration of mourning aimed at repairing the consequences of deportation from their native land. The associations created by this German population of Eastern and Central Europe began this form of tourism in the late 1970s, and the movement accelerated for a few years after the fall of communism. Around 1995–97, this tourism transformed into an alternative, recreational practice; one linked to the memory without remembrance of the new generations born in Germany.

Homeland and Passage: Identity Tourists and their Inter-Ethnic Reception

At the beginning of the 1990s, tablets, tombstones, and monuments were set up through the initiative and donations of local actors and ethnic organizations who actively mobilized allied politicians and Hungarian political parties. However, these external allies are now progressively appropriating and sacralizing regional *lieux de mémoire* – symbolic of a more distant Hungarian past – as if the *memory core* built around the Gulag had opened the way to the re-organization and re-territorialization of the entire commemorative landscape. Thus, at the onset of the political struggle to introduce and incorporate Hungarian history into the curriculum of Transcarpathian schools, more ancient *lieux de mémoire* were renovated and equipped with commemorative tablets. Some examples include those linked to the anti-Habsburg insurrection led by Prince Ferenc Rakoczi, a native of the region, or to the stronghold of Munkács (Munkasevo), where there was a protracted Hungarian resistance against a siege by the Turks; both have been ritualized through annual commemorations.

Yet the core of this localized narrative of Hungarian history seems to be one of the most symbolic locations in Hungarian national mythology: the Verecke Pass in the northeastern Carpathians. This pass, located in an area traditionally inhabited by Ruthenian shepherds and peasants, was reputedly the point of entry for the tribes whose sedentarization, coalition, and conversion to Christianity constituted the foundations of the millennium-old kingdom inaugurated by Saint Stephen in the Carpathian Basin. Later, in the thirteenth century, the Tartar-Mongol army invaded Hungary through the same pass. Still later, at the beginning of the First World War, the Austro-Hungarian and Russian armies fought another hard battle there. Finally, during the Second World War, the Hungarian defence line – called the "Arpad Line" against the Red armies – also included this pass. The original monument commemorating this place as the boundary between "historical Hungary" and the Russian empire was erected by Hungarian authorities in 1896 to celebrate the millennium of the Kingdom. However, by the end of the 1940s, the Soviets had destroyed the commemorative tablets, later dismantling the whole structure.

The new monument, built by the sculptor Peter Mati from Munkasevo, was erected in several stages, with work beginning as early as the late 1990s.

Though its construction was marked by polemics as well as several minor acts of vandalism, in 2008 it was jointly inaugurated by the Hungarian and Ukrainian authorities. The open monumental portal – a symbol for the passage between East and West according to tourist pamphlets – is composed of the vaulted superposition of seven massive stone slabs, each one representing the seven foundational tribes of the Hungarian nation.

By telescoping mythical and historical references in a majestic panorama, this place offers Hungarian tourists a sort of wandering passage through time and space. Such wandering is supposed to convert mythical history into identity memory centered around a symbolic founding frontier. This includes an outpost, facing the ever-menacing East, where the guides invite the tourists to deposit a commemorative bunch of flowers encircled with a tricolored band. Subsequently, the place has come to constitute the central, culminating focus of the tours offered by associations and travel agencies connected to local or Hungarian political elites, as well as by the local small-scale, informal touristic entrepreneurs. The "national" memorial interpretation of this ancient border – offered to and reinforced by this form of tourism (Dallen 2001) – erases the multi-ethnic and multi-secular character of this region, and obscures the complex web of inter-ethnic relations and conflicts.

Yet, as the tourist guides and brochures in Hungarian indicate, several landmarks co-exist on this *limes* that are in the process of becoming patrimony. Close to the commemorative portal there is a sober white pillar, topped with an orthodox crucifix and marked by a commemorative tablet, recently erected to commemorate the Ukrainian partisans executed by the Hungarian army in 1939, when the region was returned to Hungary. Every year, commemorative rituals are held there, including decorative wreaths made by Ukrainians from the region of Lviv. Behind the pillar, one can see a statue, erected during Soviet times to represent the stylized figure of a Ruthenian mountain shepherd. Thus, the Verecke Pass, sparsely inhabited by Ruthenians, has also been integrated into the Ukrainian memorial narrative. It symbolizes the process of nation-building, while simultaneously becoming a place of convergence for rival memorial and symbolic activities, as well as a contested object of conflicting interpretations between local religious elites, namely the Greek-Catholics, and the Calvinists.[6] This marking and ritualization of *inter-patriotic* places (Losonczy 1997), equally invested with symbolic value by other ethnic groups such as the Ruthenians or the "national" Ukrainians, then continues to feed political counter-rituals like vandalism, the dismantling of monuments, or the construction of rival insignia and monuments, accompanied by polemics in the media and the occasional diplomatic incident.

If local tourist activity builds up the commercial profile of these places by drawing generously from the stock of "national" memorial narratives while enriching them with selected local stories and anecdotes, it does so precisely by circumventing the rigid and conflicting identity frontier established and shaped by institutionalized memory. As is often the case with collective tourism (as with schools, associations, and religions), the logistics of certain stages of the tour compel the collaboration of Ruthenians, Rumanians, and Ukrainians in mixed-population villages. On these occasions, the organizers try to put forward tokens of identity labeled "Hungarian" in the presentation of culinary, choreographic, agricultural, or artisanal activities. These attempts feed "patriotic tourism", enacting a certain sort of secular pilgrimage by individuals, families and groups coming from Hungary, as well as Hungarians from other countries, to commune at places considered ethnic identity reservoirs beyond state borders. However, the desire to receive Ukrainian, Russian, or Slovak tourists also demands the co-operation of inter-ethnic allies and partners. In this effort, the same game switches identities, and Hungarians – who may speak Russian or Ukrainian – offer tourists an alternative reading of the commemorative portal, this time as a symbol not of the passage, but of the opening up between East and West. Their commentary includes other places to visit, typically centered around untouched nature, the diversity of local cuisine, the antiquity of *all* churches and monuments, and the shared experience of both communist repression and its ultimate demise.

Amongst the smaller-scale, local tourist entrepreneurs, conflicts are more suggestive of occasional commercial competition, rather than a rivalry over memorialization, which thereby legitimates regional political elites and their local delegates. According to their touristic audiences, whether they are Hungarians, Ruthenians, Rumanians, or Ukrainians, the promoters of local tourism will draw on the symbolic memorial reservoirs produced by rival elites whenever necessary. Furthermore, they will not hesitate to appeal to the relational network of their kin and allies belonging to other ethnic groups in order to widen the recruitment of tourists.

Yet the ethnographic observation of the daily and religious life in villages, towns, and peripheral neighborhoods – with a particularly close watch on the current practices that often tend to travel across borders – leads to an obvious conclusion: a large part of the local economy and social organization of the Hungarian area of Transcarpathia is deeply embedded in the economy and organization of other ethnic groups, both regional and trans-border, and activates family and local solidarities which have existed long before the polarized political networks. If these practices depart from the political logic of ethnic isolation, then the dominant set of norms of the latter serve to reinforce their ties to the sphere of the *informal*. Illegal as they are according to national juridical norms, these practices tend to be perceived by the ethnic elite as illegitimate, since they polarize the local social world between the beneficiaries of legitimate economic resources and the insecure actors attempting to capture illegal resources.

Conclusion: Borders and Crossings

The intense memorial elaboration around the deportation of Transcarpathian Hungarians to the Gulag, which emerged at the end of the Soviet regime in Transcarpathia, has been appropriated and politicized by the Hungarian-speaking elite over the years. It has been utilized in the construction of a Transcarpathian Hungarian ethnicity, entertaining complex and moving relationships between the Hungarian authorities and political parties and the Ukrainian government. This political ethnicity has generated new cultural frontiers with regard to other regional or external ethnic groups; it defends and favors the ethnic isolation of Hungarians in a region traditionally characterized by trans-border economic and family networks. At the same time, the opening up of state borders along with the reactivation, patrimonialization, and ritualization of ancient and recent *lieux de mémoire* has created new opportunities for informal trade and exchange across the border in this rather impoverished region. It has also contributed to new local symbolic capital which joins a Hungarian cultural policy heavily tinged with identity concerns and which feeds patrimonial tourism. The informal trans-border trade, smuggling, and small-scale tourism thus appear as privileged resources for survival, serving to rekindle and broaden local transactional skills whose inter-ethnic logic is contrary to that of the ethnicist cultural isolates. Yet, it is by staging the latter that new forms of nostalgic tourism are constructed via the institutional patrimonialization of an historical mountain pass posing as a frontier, but one that is unable to receive tourists without mobilizing inter-ethnic resources. Furthermore, supplying tourism based on the appeal of an ecological country life and fully intact natural resources, which reflects contemporary globalized sensitivities, seems to question the central symbolic role of ethnic singularity.

Despite the conception of an ethnic frontier that would form a dividing line between self-contained cultural entities, is promoted by an intellectual and political elite, and grounds political discourse as well as the constructed touristic image of the ethnos, the everyday life of villages, neighborhoods, and multi-ethnic networks of this region takes place in a zone of ethnic and social diversity. This "intersection area" (Losonczy 1997: 184) linking social spaces of diverse groups works as a membrane through which memories, techniques, skills, and local identity stories can mix, interbreed, and complement or correspond to one another. If it is the case that this ancient regional knowledge of border-crossers is precisely what allows the Transcarpathian Hungarians to circulate between the rigid world of political ethnicity and that of its various conversions into exchangeable goods, then the question raised here is more general. The models of ethnicity advanced by Central-European ethnographers of a folkloristic orientation and by the new actors constructing politicized ethnicities are readily borrowed by various ethnic political leaders. Yet they are not capable of accounting for the functionality of daily sociabilities or the reproduction, change, and autonomy of the social relative to the political in these societies. Furthermore, the ethnography of multi-ethnic regions on the margins of diverse national spaces susceptible to international dispute calls attention to the paradoxical inter-dependence between the durability of political ethnicities relying on the permanence of inter-ethnic solidarities and co-operation.

Notes

1 In Russian, a higher echelon bureaucrat.

2 Most of these cars are various types of diesel-powered Mercedes, especially equipped in Germany with extra-large tanks for taxi drivers, lest custom officials suspect makeshift tinkering with the vehicle.

3 Since 2000, the Transcarpathian press is replete with stories of threats and violence against customs and immigration officers, including Hungarians, typically following the confiscation of even small quantities of goods. Similarly, through the Hungarian language webnews *karpataljainfo.ua* and conversations with customs officers one can estimate the volume of this smuggling: hundreds of thousands of cigarette cartons, dozens of clandestine migrants – male and female – and hundreds of gallons of spirits per week. The silence of these actors becomes more eloquent when dealing with arms and drugs traffic, considering that they are caught between the pressure of EU regulations for border protection, a lack of means and personnel at the border – often with their families living nearby – and the intimidation of mafia actors in collusion with the Ukrainian central administration.

4 Some of the reasons for this centrality of Transylvania in the national imaginary are examined in Brubaker et al. (2006). See also Losonczy (1997).

5 This phenomenon has generated many studies in Germany; see Bausinger (1987), among many others.

6 A comparable process of patrimonialization of an ancient boundary in the Gimes region, in Transylvania, has been analysed in greater detail by Ilyés (2005).

References

Bausinger, H. 1988: *Népi kultúra a technika korszakában*. Budapest: Osiris-Századvég.

Bausinger, H. 1989: Párhuzamos különidejűségek. *Ethnographia* 100:1–4, 24–37.

Brubaker, R. 1996: *Nationalism Reframed: Nationhood and the National Question in the New Europe*. Cambridge: Cambridge University Press.

Brubaker, R., M. Feischmidt, J. Fox & L.Grancea 2006: *Nationalist Politics and Everyday Ethnicity in a Transylvanian Town*. Princeton: Princeton University Press.

Comaroff, J.L. & J. Comaroff 2009: *Ethnicity, Inc.* Chicago: The University of Chicago Press.

Dallen, Timothy J. 2001: Borders and Tourism. In: Th. Dallen (ed.), *Tourism and Political Boundaries*. London & New York: Routledge, pp. 1–11.

Eyal, G., I. Szelenyi & E. Townsley 1998: *Making Capitalism without Capitalists: The New Ruling Elites in Eastern Europe*. London: Verso.

Fedinec, C. & M. Vehesh (eds.) 2010: *Kárpátalja 1919–2009: Történelem, politika, kultura*. Budapest: Argumentum.

Fejős, Z. 1996: Kollektiv emlékezet és az etnikai identitás megszerkesztése. In: L. Dioszegi (ed.), *Magyarság-kutátás, 1995–96*. Budapest: MTA.

Fejős, Z. & Z. Szíjárto (eds.) 2003: *Helye(in)k, tárgya(in)k, képe(in)k: A turizmus társadalomtudományos magyarázata*. Budapest: Néprajzi Múzeum, pp. 40–50.

Hall, D. & L. Roberts 2001: Social Construction? In: D. Hall & L. Roberts (eds.), *Rural Tourism and Recreation: Principles to Practice*. London: Cabi Publishing, pp. 24–51.

Hann, C. 1993: Religion and Nationality in Central Europe: The Case of the Uniates. *Ethnic Studies* 10, 201–213.

Herzfeld, M. 1997: *Cultural Intimacy: Social Poetics in the Nation-State*. London & New York: Routledge.

Horváth, G.K. & I. Kovatch 1999: A feketegazdaság (olajkereskedelem és KGST piac) vállalkozói Keletmagyarországon. *Szociológiai Szemle* 3, 1999.

Ilyés, Z. 2003: Az emlékezés és az újratanulás terei- a "honvágyturizmus ", mint tér és identitásszervezés. In: Z. Fejős & Zs. Szíjártó (eds.), *Helye(ink), tárgya(ink), képe(ink): A turizmus társadalomtudományos magyarázata*. Budapest: Néprajzi Múzeum, pp. 51–58.

Ilyés, Z. 2005: A gyimesi "ezeréves" határ olvasatai. In: M. Feischmidt (ed.), *Erdély (de)konstrukciók*. Budapest-Pécs: Néprajzi Múzeum, PTE Kommunikáció- és Médiatudományi Tanszék, pp. 35–49.

Karas, G.D. 2008: *Politiques de l'ethnicité: Le cas des Hongrois de Transcarpathie*. Paris: Mémoire de mastère IEP, Politiques comparées.

Losonczy, A.-M. 1997: Les itinéraires de la patrie: De la construction de l'espace interpatriotique en Hongrie contemporaine. In: J. Hainard & R. Kaehr (eds.), *Dire les autres: Réflexions et pratiques ethnologiques*. Lausanne: Editions Payot, coll. Sciences humaines, pp. 177–193.

Losonczy, A.-M. 2002: Marrons, Colons, Contrebandiers: Réseaux transversaux et configuration métisse sur la côte caraïbe colombienne (Dibulla). *Journal de la Société des Américanistes* 88, 179–201.

Losonczy, A.-M. 2010: Ritualisation mémorielle et construction ethnique post-communiste chez les hongrois de Transcarpathie (Ukraine). Bruxelles, Institut de Sociologie. *Civilisations* 59:1.

Losonczy, A.-M. 2012: L'école amère et l'humour de Dieu: Deux Hongrois au Goulag. In: A. Blum, M. Craveri & V. Nivelon (eds.), *Déportés en URSS: Récits d'Européens au Goulag*. Paris: Editions Autrement.

Magocsi, P.R. 1997: Les Ruthènes de l'Europe du Centre-Est. *Revue des Etudes Slaves* 69:3, 417–428.

Magocsi, P.R. 2002: *Encyclopedia of Rusyn History and Culture*. Toronto: Toronto Univerity Press.

Rusinko, E. (ed.) 2009: *Committing Community: Carpatho-Ruzyn Studies as an Emerging Scholarly Discipline*. New York: Columbia University Press.

Sárkány, M. 2010: Etnicitás és gazdaság: Gazdasági antropologiai megközelitések az interetnikus viszonyok kutatásában. In: M. Feischmidt (ed.), *Etnicitás: Kûlönbségteremtö társadalom*. Budapest: Gondolat, MTA, Kisebbségkutato Intézet.

Verdery, C. 2003: *The Vanishing Hectare: Property and Value in Postsocialist Transylvania*. Ithaca: Cornell University Press.

Anne Marie Losonczy is *directeur d'études* at the EPHE, Sorbonne, Paris. She has taught and lectured in the universities of Barcelona, Brussels, Paris X, Neuchâtel, Budapest, Pécs, Florianopolis, Bogota, and Rio de Janeiro. Since 1991, she has studied popular and official reconstructions of *lieux de mémoire*, languages and rituals of patriotic belonging in post-communist Hungary, Transylvania and Transcarpathia. She has published *La «patria» como categoria en el postcomunismo: Ensayos sobre Hungria y Romania* (2008, Mexico: Nouvelle édition, CEMCA).
(alosonczy1956@gmail.com)

ANTI-BODIES
The Production of Dissent

Manuela Cunha and Jean-Yves Durand

Drawing on narrative interviews and ethnographic research in French and Portuguese settings, we examine a contemporary form of vaccine acceptability as it emerges in routine vaccination. Against a backdrop of manifestations that are circumscribed to particular cultural scenes or bounded systems of ideas, we focus on a diffuse tendency which resonates with wider contemporary transformations. Its analysis cannot be framed within the narrow limits of health and risk management. Health and the body are but one of the domains in which a same pattern of production of dissent arises. It is by exploring the political dimensions of such pattern that the production of consent and that of dissent stand in relation to one another as two sides of the same coin.

Keywords: immunization, vaccination, resistance, body politics, state

The Changing Landscape of Immunization

Michel Foucault (2004) once used vaccination as an analyser of society. As he had done before with the prison institution, he considered it to express the general economy of power prevailing at a given historical moment. Foucault (2004) thus identified a shift from a "disciplinary society" to a "security society". The disciplinary logic that produced docile bodies started to give way to – or to co-exist with – the actuarial logic of late modern societies, increasingly based on risk management (Simon 1998; Petersen [1997]2006). But this insight can be developed in yet other ways. If we are to consider not so much "mechanisms" of power, as the philosopher did, but the people who are their object, immunization can be an analyser of society inasmuch as it also reveals them in their agency, as political subjects. Vaccination is deeply anchored in relations of power and authority between the State, expert systems, and citizens (Moulin 2007). These relations however, are not limited to matters of health, trust and risk. They are connected to other areas of citizenship involving the body, personhood and individual identity. They form coherent patterns of political participation which are central for understanding the production of consent and dissent. We thus set out to approach current engagements with vaccination both as an object in themselves and as a window onto these processes.[1]

Immunization is one of the most globalized techniques of securitization used to address public health problems such as epidemics and infectious diseases, especially since the World Health Organization (WHO) launched the *Expanded Programme on Immunization* in 1974, and national vaccination programmes (hereon NVP) were implemented. People worldwide have been confronted with state-imposed or state-sponsored vaccination for themselves or for their children against an ever-growing range of medical insecurity concerns. The classic sextet that has characterized national vaccination programmes (diphtheria, measles, pertussis, polio, tetanus, tuberculosis) has not ceased to expand and vaccines are now expanding beyond their usual target of infectious diseases. Cancers, chronic disorders, and contraception all become part of their aim. The very idea of vaccine is redefined.

But even when considering strictly its traditional profile – the prevention of infectious diseases – vaccination today assumes increased complexity on the biomedical and the public fronts. At the same time that vaccine technology and infrastructure have gained increasing scope and sophistication, the unlimited confidence and political allure which the principle of universal vaccination benefited from has waned.

On the biomedical front, the emergence of new or rejuvenated pathogens and the need to update many vaccines due to the genetic drift of pathogens in relation to the original vaccine prototype have contributed to the decline of the optimistic model of eradication, predicated on the triumph over smallpox. A new, less ambitious but more realistic model is adopted, based on the constant monitoring of diseases, on international surveillance and on the notion of "preparedness" – as the response to the flu pandemic exemplifies (Moulin 1991, 2011). In addition to this postmodern development, the acknowledgement of the diversity of individual immune systems has recast mass immunizations and the manipulation of the collective immune system (i.e., "herd immunity") in a new light. Although on the one hand such strategies are advocated insofar as they aim to protect public health, on the other hand there is also a growing awareness that they are unable to take into account the uniqueness of individual biology, especially when the evolution of the immune system is considered throughout the course of a life span, or at critical stages such as early childhood and old age (Moulin 2011). Hence the claim for individually-tailored vaccines and emerging notions of personalized immunity or personalized immunization, which are now set in contrast with the principle of universal vaccination.

Besides the complexified landscape of vaccine science and vaccine policy, there is also a changing public engagement with vaccines that is destabilizing the model of universal vaccination in other ways. Social and cultural attitudes vis-à-vis vaccines are more diversified, and today they take on a variety of forms, especially in Euro-American societies. The way in which now part of the public questions the prevailing consensus around vaccination defies the grand narrative that presents vaccination as the result of the inexorable march of progress and reason (Moulin 1991). According to this narrative, instances of popular resistance to programs of mass vaccination tend to be located in the "third world" or the geopolitical "South", and they are explained in terms of "traditional" beliefs and incomplete scientific rationality (Poltorak, Leach & Fairhead 2004).[2] However, and despite perceptions that associate non-vaccination with an "exotic" location and an incipient scientific culture, the "North" itself has been witnessing phenomena of vaccine uptake decline which do not fit such an evolutionist framework. Far from being a residual anachronism expected to fade away, the emergence of non-vaccination practices is part of wider social transformations which include, but are not limited to, their relation to science and to the State.

Research Issues and Methodology

We intend to examine the meaning and the experiential basis for some contemporary forms of vaccine acceptability as seen through the perspective of parents and as they emerge in routine vaccination, that is, integrated in regular healthcare services and administered by the State at precise stages of life. Vaccination campaigns involving extraordinary circumstances and/or new vaccines are considered only inasmuch as they may provide additional feedback on the way people relate to ordinary vaccination. The term *acceptability* implies a perspective that considers acceptance and non-acceptance as facets of the same phenomenon rather than as two unrelated phenomena, thereby requiring an encompassing analysis to match both, instead of two separate approaches.

Between 2007 and 2010 we developed an ethnographic research in several French and Portuguese settings with different vaccination regimes (compulsory and non-compulsory, respectively) in order to identify the scope of variation in current engagements with vaccination, and try to understand how dimensions of consent and dissent can be traced to specific cultural locations and systems of ideas, or, on the contrary, resonate with wider contemporary transformations (cf. Cunha & Durand 2011). This paper will focus mainly on the Portuguese materials – and within these, on parents' detailed narratives and on observations in healthcare centres – complemented by the French case, which acts as a background comparative reference.

We conducted 19 in-depth, open-ended interviews with a range of actors, selected using "snowball" techniques. The number of major interviews was decided by "saturation", that is, recruiting continuously until no new themes emerged from interview data. Data were also derived from observation of ordinary vaccination practices and interactions between users and healthcare professionals as they routinely occurred in healthcare institutions. Finally, we conducted 5 focus-group discussions (with 10 to 15 elements each) in Portugal (Braga, Vila Real, and Lisbon) and in France (Forcalquier, Alpes de Haute-Provence) with frontline healthcare professionals, civic associations and participants in grassroots vaccinophobic movements. Whereas the dimensions of consent were mostly accounted for through the observations in healthcare institutions, dissent was for the most part registered through interviews outside these settings; focus groups confirmed both aspects of consent and dissent. As in any ethnographic investigation, in some cases observation and participation produce richer and more revealing data than interviews, depending on what its goals and purposes are. In other cases it is the opposite. The complexity and the multiple dimensions of dissent explored in this paper – including its experiential basis – were in this case more fully grasped through discursive data and outside clinical situations.

The project's general design was structured so as to diversify ethnographic settings and interlocutors along lines of region, ethnicity, and class. This diversification did not aspire to express statistical representativeness, but to identify the key themes that bear upon the acceptability of vaccination as they emerge in different contexts. We tried therefore to create different contact chains with a variety of entry points: schools and healthcare centres (leading to parents who decline to vaccinate their children), different social and professional milieus and social location in terms of generation, education, and income level. Some of these chains ended up intersecting one another, as the kinds of constraints that these parents face in light of their personal choices stimulate the onset of informal social networks enabling them to better deal with those constraints.

Interviews with parents who did not vaccinate their children were arranged and scheduled according to their preference and convenience, mainly in their homes, cafés and schools. They lasted on average between 90 minutes and 2 hours, but could also include previous or subsequent shorter conversations (e.g., following up on an episode, going over a specific point). The fact that interviews took place outside healthcare settings facilitated a conversational focus not restricted to health matters. Parents' responses spontaneously led to a variety of other experiential areas involving their children, themselves, or both. Allowing them to articulate their experiences in multiple spheres of life, from health to education, from childbirth to naming, this wide focus enabled us to connect these seemingly disparate domains into coherent patterns. The common link between these areas was our interlocutors' perception of their relation with institutional power and the State in light of notions of personhood and citizenry. Since we integrated new themes as they emerged, parents were invited to talk not only about vaccines and decision-making processes regarding immunization, but also about medication, health biographies and lifestyles; not only about their relationship with healthcare professionals, scientific information, and the mediation of family and friends in a variety of issues, but also about their relationships and experiences with other institutions that as parents they also had to deal with. However, in most cases these core themes were not elicited through questions. They unfolded out of parents' narratives on their own initiative. Questions were used to clarify points, redirect the narrative, and introduce issues that hadn't been approached.

Anthropology and other social sciences have looked into the history of vaccination and of immunology (e.g., Darmon 1984; Moulin 1991) and have also produced cultural analysis of the rich metaphors generated by the notion of immunity (e.g., Martin 1994; Napier 2003; Haraway 1991; Tauber 1994). They have approached vaccination as one of several aspects that can give access to social understandings about the workings of the immune system. Leaving aside instrumental researches that focus on the factors hampering the acceptance of mass immunization programs in developing countries, ethnographical comprehensive attention to ordinary vaccination or non-vaccination practices has been relatively scarce, especially in Euro-American societies (see Streefland, Chowdury & Ramos-Jimenez 1999; see Streefland 2001 for an overview of varieties of vaccine refusal that includes industrialized countries).

Among the most notable exceptions are studies addressing the pressing scientific controversies raised over particular vaccines in specific countries, such as the research led by Poltorak, Leach and Fairhead (2004; Poltorak et al. 2005), in the UK (Brighton), in a context marked by a public controversy about the safety of the MMR vaccine (measles, mumps and rubella). As documented in Brown's et al. (2010) systematic review, this controversy has also shaped parental attitudes to combination vaccines, generating concerns about the risk of combined shots, beliefs in the safety of separate vaccines, and fears of immune overload in a variety of other contexts. Poltorak's team ethnographic research has persuasively shown the need to go beyond approaches founded on too static and too generalized dimensions of risk perception, science-society relations, and trust in state and global institutions (see also Frykman et al. 2009 for a related discussion). It also showed that people's consideration of the trade-offs between individual benefits and risk is not only a matter of calculation influenced by information, but is mediated through cultural and experiential perspectives. Personal histories, notions of disease, infection, and immunity, personal and cultural perceptions of responsibility, parenting and parental reasoning concerning children, context-specific relations to health care providers, among other aspects, are all implicated in how risk enters people's practical reasoning in relation to immunization practices (Mills et al. 2005; Rogers & Pilgrim 1995; Serpell & Greene 2004; Streefland, Chowdury & Ramos-Jimenez 1999; Poltorak, Leach & Fairhead 2004; Poltorak et al. 2005).

Beyond Risk and Bounded Systems of Ideas

But even when considered in this light, that is, embedded in particular cultural and experiential worlds, risk may still remain an insufficient framework for capturing important dimensions involved in current engagements with vaccination. This is not to deny its analytical relevance as a structuring notion in contemporary societies (Giddens 1991; Beck [1986]1992; Caplan 2000; Douglas 1985). Risk may also be an adequate notion to characterize ethnographic realities such as the ones portrayed by Leach and Fairhead in the UK. Nevertheless, it may be too narrow as a comparative category applied to issues of vaccine acceptability in other contexts, such as the ones we have studied in Portugal and in France.

To begin with, public anxieties generated by controversies over specific vaccines vary in type and intensity across countries. While in the UK the object of a high profile controversy was the MMR vaccine (suspected of inducing autism), in France it was hepatitis B (suspected of inducing multiple sclerosis). In Portugal neither of them gave rise to a debate besides a few short journalistic pieces mentioning events witnessed in other countries. Our monitoring of this public non-debate is consistent with the country's relative imperviousness to other recent scientific controversies around other "new risks" reported by Gonçalves et al. (2007). The controversies over MMR and hepatitis B did not have an impact on the public acceptability of such vaccines, nor did they reflect on the way parents went on interacting with healthcare institutions or healthcare professionals. Our fieldwork and Saavedra's (2011) showed that this interaction is usually characterized by the near absence of questions regarding possible vaccine side effects. Concerns voiced by parents, or anticipated by frontline healthcare professionals trying to reassure them, are focused mostly on immediate and superficial consequences such as fever, local swelling, and rash.

Moreover, health professionals anticipate parents' anxieties almost exclusively in terms of the pain caused by the injection on the child. As one nurse put it, "it's for her own good, it will hurt a little but it will soon be over". Other concerns may be exoticized in terms of cultural differences, as in the case of immigrant parents. Another nurse summed up several cases of reticence towards vaccine administration with the following comment: "With immigrants we start to learn that, within each culture, concerns are always of the same kind." She was specifically referring to a Brazilian mother who preferred waiting to go to Brazil to vaccinate her 3-year-old daughter against rubella with a separate vaccine, rather than doing it in the combined variety of MMR; she also included an Eastern European father who did not allow the simultaneous administration of more than one vaccine per day – in her words, "here we usually apply two vaccines, but in Eastern European cultures they're not supposed to take more than one per day, nor take a bath that same day".

The compared examples of Portugal, France, and the UK regarding the effects of scientific controversies on the acceptability of vaccines suggest the need to take into account national differences which reflect – but are not necessarily limited to – different vaccination regimes, scientific literacy, and public engagement with scientific expertise. More importantly however, non-vaccination does not emerge exclusively within the context of episodic vaccine science controversies and involves other dimensions besides risk, like those expressed in the form of dissent that is analysed below.

Within Euro-American societies, the more visible refusal of dominant views on vaccination has been associated mostly with small groups of proponents of alternative immunological theories and therapeutic systems, or with adepts of specific religious views (cf. Streefland, Chowdury & Ramos-Jimenez 1999; Streefland 2001). While sharing this tendency, France nevertheless has a long history of resistance against vaccination even among physicians (at least since the nineteenth century, Darmon 1984), and currently there are quite a number of groups that actively fight public policies on vaccination, mainly through the organisation of public talks. The issue of vaccine mistrust has a diffuse visibility that cuts across specific cultural or religious backgrounds.[3]

The same does not happen in Portugal. Anti-vaccination is much less vocal, and it has been comparatively invisible. In addition to high rates of vaccine coverage (Direcção-Geral de Saúde 2009), just in the last three decades Portugal has gone from seriously problematic child mortality rates (80 per 1,000 children in 1974) to being one of the top four countries with best rates in the world (the third within Europe): 3 per 1,000 (Direcção-Geral de Saúde 2009). Not surprisingly, extensive vaccine coverage takes an important part in the public narrative of this evolution.

Some breaches or specific nuances in this wide consensus around vaccination are connoted with particular groups, such as Roma communities (Casa-Nova 2011) and adepts of alternative dietary systems like macrobiotics, insofar as their attitudes towards vaccination – whether or not uniformly shared within the group – tend to be informed by specific and relatively bounded systems of ideas about health and the body, and/or by symbolic strategies that are fairly specific to a social scene. The system of practices and perceptions about the body involved in macrobiotics leads to a type of questioning which promotes vaccine avoidance, although resistance to vaccination is not extensible to all of its practitioners. Considering health as a process, and as the natural capacity to overcome disease, the macrobiotic social scene studied by Virgínia Calado (2011) singles out food and lifestyle as the fundamental aspects for having a strong immune system. This is perceived in terms of a particular balance in blood chemistry. Diseases could thus be naturally prevented, as well as defeated, by means of a diet providing this balance. Nonetheless, some diseases, such as measles, would ultimately be beneficial by triggering "elimination processes" considered essential for building a resistant organism. From this point of view, biomedicine blocks these processes and vaccines are a damaging aggression, since they prevent the body from spontaneously creating its own natural defences. This system of ideas is also often combined with an atmosphere of suspicion towards biomedical knowledge and the profits of the pharmaceutical industry, thereby fostering general doubts and mistrust directed at the global institutions' securitization policy.

However, whether expressed in attitudes of reticence, ambivalence, or active rejection, a distinct and more diffuse tendency of vaccine avoidance is emerging beyond the cultural locations or systems of ideas described in this section.

Lay Reflexivity and "Pluralistic" versus "Alternativist" Practices

Although in Portugal vaccination is not compulsory by law, there is a widespread assumption that it is. It is fed both by healthcare authorities that deliberately let the ambiguity linger on, and the combined workings of several institutions (e.g., government institutions, civil service, schools). They create a pressure in favour of vaccination, for example by requiring vaccine certificates for purposes of school enrolment, to obtain a driver's licence, or apply for a job as a public servant. In the case of schools, parents who refuse to vaccinate their children have to sign a declaration supported by a medical doctor. Since there are not many doctors who will easily stand by this choice, those who do, find themselves being sought out by several parents, who rapidly circulate the information about them through informal networks. The same happens with the information about schools that accept unvaccinated children without further requirements.

Such parents usually belong to highly educated middle-class urban (mostly professional and art) milieus: they are teachers, psychologists, engineers, computer experts, lawyers, doctors, actors, painters, post-graduate students, and researchers. This does not necessarily imply that they are wealthy. Even though all our interlocutors have a college degree, many have unstable and precarious job situations and an irregular income, which is a combined effect of their relative youth (most are in their early or mid-thirties) and the eroded, highly dual Portuguese job market.[4] This will be a relevant aspect for framing their agency as political subjects. The emerging trend expressed by these parents in relation to vaccines is not coterminous with a specific social scene, nor is it predicated on a pre-given particular philosophy like macrobiotics. Although some features may coincide with the latter, such as concerns about the aggressiveness and allergenic effects of an excessively precocious, massive, and concentrated administration of vaccines in early age, they are not articulated in the same way, as the contrast between the following two cases illustrates.

Isabel, a macrobiotic 33-year-old mother of an unvaccinated child tells us how she immediately adhered to the anti-vaccination philosophy that she came across in lectures taking place within the macrobiotic social scene.

> The normal theory of disease doesn't make sense to me. Now, this theory of disease as a cleansing, a kind of balance – and not the other way around, as a virus that attacks us ... It's we who have to be healthy in the first place, because the viruses are out there anyway. That made every sense to me. And I was confident. I felt that my decision. ... I was not afraid. If I was afraid I would vaccinate. (...) At the time it was not even a decision, I listened and I felt: OK, this is what I want to do. I didn't even think. It was something that just made sense to me. When I got pregnant, I began to look for books, information (I met homeopaths, naturalists...). But for me it was more a matter of showing it to people, to justify myself, than to make a decision. Because for me it was like ... like those things that just make sense to you. (...) There was a book by an American doctor who helped me a lot. For me that book was like a Bible.

In this case, the adoption of an anti-vaccination stance was part of an entire, direct, and almost identitarian adherence to a philosophy on health and disease (*the* theory of disease, referred to in the singular) that was originated as a revelation (*I was not afraid. At the time it was not even a decision, I listened and I felt: OK, this is what I want to do. I didn't even think*). The search for specific information on vaccination was instrumental afterwards, that is, not so much as the basis of her decision, as to justify it before others. The almost "biblical" use of a medical book is consistent with this disposition. This narrative clearly matches the bounded system of ideas described in the precedent section. However, it is not the one that predominantly informs the diffuse tendency focused in this paper.

Another mother (30 years old) presents quite a different narrative about the decision not to vaccinate her two daughters. Even though both narratives share some vaccinophobic themes besides a general objection to vaccination, she particularizes the circumstances, contexts and risks of each vaccine.

> It just troubles me that a newborn baby takes vaccines against hepatitis B, tuberculosis ...[5] These were things that I read. The immune system of a baby is formed during the first two years of age, so until then the body is not ready for this. Apart from exceptional cases, up to two years there is no reason for this.
> [So the problem is that it is too soon?]
> Too soon, too many at the same time – in the MMR the body has to react to three vaccines simultaneously – (...) and also unjustified vaccines. The one for tuberculosis is obsolete, that strain no longer exists, and the one for hepatitis B is controversial, it makes no sense to give it to people who are not at risk. So we must ponder. Not to vaccinate is a risk, but to vaccinate can also be a risk. If it is justifiable, yes. A vaccine for AIDS, when my daughters are teenagers, I'll probably go for it... The papilloma I don't know yet. I consider vaccine by vaccine. For example, we are considering going for the meningitis one, because it can be a fast and deadly disease. Tetanus, we're also thinking of perhaps doing it. I know that this leaves us [me and my husband] in a position of anxiety, we're never relaxed, permanently having to decide. I'm not against vaccines; I think it is an advantage for public health. Vaccines were a fantastic discovery. What I don't agree with is the way vaccines are administered in the NVP, the lack of public debate about it, that no information is provided for people to base their decisions on.

The reflexive trajectory followed by another couple (Luis, a teacher, and Susana, a researcher) regarding vaccination decisions was marked by a long and cautious consideration of the risks and circumstances involved. It started with a "foreign" scientific controversy over the MMR vaccine.

> At first we had decided not to vaccinate our elder [son]. My husband is American and at the time there was this big controversy over the MMR there. It then spilled to the UK and there was that thing about Tony Blair not having his child vaccinated. Then we decided not to. He had taken the first dose, he didn't take the second. The younger one didn't get any. But we went on mulling over it, reading, researching, trying to follow the information, because we wanted to vaccinate according to the NVP. And last year came out a study that said there was no connection with autism after all. So we talked to the pediatrician to see if there was a problem with giving the vaccine out of schedule. And meanwhile other studies came out on the seriousness of some diseases prevented by the MMR, and we decided to vaccinate. And that's it; after this long process, the boys now have all the vaccines.

Although in this case questions about vaccination have stemmed from doubts about the safety of a particular vaccine, the type of reticence prevailing in most cases is of a more general nature. It is anchored in notions about the immune system and about a multiplicity of pathogens against which the number of existing vaccines would not provide enough guarantee anyway. Says another mother:

> Take for example, the 12 vaccines in the NPV. People think: there are 12 diseases, if I vaccinate my child against these diseases, he is protected. But there are thousands of diseases. The kids are protected from those, but then they are less able to resist the others. Then comes a little flu and that's it, they are immediately ill. And they become prone to lots of things, allergies, asthma...

Following the rationale that vaccines cannot protect against everything, and that while protecting against a limited range of problems, they could undermine the ability to withstand a variety of many other, these parents feel themselves obliged to manage a stake that resonates with the effects of the dissemination of knowledge about pathogens pointed out by Herring and Swedlund (2010: 1). As this knowledge increases and enters public consciousness, so would the sense of vulnerability and uncertainty grow in individuals as an intimation for the responsibility of choice: how and from what to protect themselves and their children. This also resonates with the ambivalence generated by the widespread presence of expert systems in everyday life, whether producing trust, or on the contrary, skepticism and uncertainty (Giddens 1991).

As to the parents we interviewed, it would be hasty and misleading to assume from the outset a connection between non-vaccination choices and alternative lifestyles or systems of ideas impervious to biomedicine. Unlike Isabel, the macrobiotic mother mentioned previously, whose "alternativist" stand tends to be highly coherent in terms of therapeutic ideologies, expert systems, and types of consumption, for example circumscribed to the "natural" and excluding the "pharmacological", the latter's practices express instead an eclectic and pluralistic pattern in which different therapeutic logics coexist. This pattern is not dissociated from a wider reconfiguration of therapeutic worlds of lay health management, increasingly characterized by a plural combination of therapeutic models and resources (Lopes 2010). This includes the relationship with expert authority. Instead of being a matter of choosing an alternative authority over an instituted one, these parents adopt an active questioning before *any* authority. They subject it to a personal scrutiny according to their specific situations. Complemented by the reflexive use of expert information, they ponder the suitability of the different options at hand. As Lopes pointed out (2010: 79), one of the effects of this therapeutic pluralism has been to increase lay autonomy in the management of health resources. But while this autonomy may be emancipatory, it can also be the source of increased anxiety and insecurity.

Even though certain "pluralistic" health practices appear similar to "alternativist" ones when considered separately (vegetarianism, the consumption of healthy/organic food, the preference for the "natural" over the "chemical"), as a whole they differ in the degree of systematicity and internal coherence. Moreover, if we include vaccination choices (but we could also include, for example, choices regarding a more or less medicalized childbirth), the combinations are more open, varied, and unpredictable in the "pluralistic" variety: in one family every member is vegetarian, vaccinated, and "follows conventional medicine, but in a critical way" – as one mother put it; in another, children are not vaccinated, but dietary concerns are limited to the avoidance of "processed food, canned food and too much sugar. Otherwise, outside home we eat everything."

Diffuse Dissent: A Process

Moreover it is important to compare not only patterns, but also processes. Decision-making has been characterized as a processual and distributed phenomenon, that is, an ongoing event that evolves and is shaped through multiple encounters with medical and non-medical others, print media and Internet-based knowledge (Rapley 2008). In the case of vaccination choices, their meaning is best captured by taking into account not merely the decisions per se, but also a retrospective examination of the trajectory leading up to them. In other words, giving more consideration to the dynamics through which a decision takes shape, than reading into its affirmation as being grounded in a static or polarized position. This can be illustrated by the complex process that preceded the decision made by Tiago and Maria (both artists, in their early fifties and mid-thirties respectively) against vaccinating their two daughters. They started to choose health care professionals, mainly doctors and paediatricians, as their first interlocutors.

> We were abroad when our eldest daughter was born. And there were plenty of people that did not vaccinate (...). Then we read books and information and we began to question a little. But when we came back to Portugal it was hard. Not with the Dutch side of Maria's family. They took it the Dutch way: "if they studied the subject and reached a decision, then they know what they're doing". But the others... The doctors didn't give us any support and just wanted to wash their hands of the problem. We wanted to know things, ask questions. What if she catches measles? One of them said, "Well, you don't need to vaccinate against everything. I myself decided not to vaccinate my daughter. But it's different with me, I'm a doctor." We hesitated a long time, we had many doubts, but we were alone in this. The doctors only wanted to impose things upon us. We wanted to discuss things, but no. All they did was simply to scare us [instead of] explaining things. We are treated as minors. People have this attitude that the doctor always knows best. Doctors don't have a tradition of explaining their reasoning, their decisions.

Lay reflexivity may induce a higher insecurity. The self-management of information flows may expose individuals to potential contradictory messages stemming from different expert sources (Lopes 2010: 31). The autonomy it expresses is not self-sufficient, but relational and embedded in social relations (Rapley 2008: 434). Given its requirement of a co-production of understanding, the importance of the doctors' role was recognized by our interlocutors. They sought the advice of physicians in the first place.[6] While some doctors (Helena's, one of Adriana's, as mentioned below) adopted a collaborative role typical of shared decision-making, that is, one that tried to combine patients' active questioning with the promotion of decisions that refer to evidence-based and research-based knowledge (ibid.), other health care practitioners did not seem open to forming a consensus based on such a combination.[7] Unable to find in health care professionals a communication channel capable of contextualizing, mediating, and assisting them in navigating the information they possessed, or to cope better with their questions and concerns, the parents above eventually looked for support on their own and they found it in the only channels left available to them: an anti-vaccination league based in Spain and a France-based vaccinophobic site. Thus, what had started as a *negotiated convergence* with one instance of biomedicine, ended up in a general alienation from it. Further on we will observe how this same pattern was reproduced in shaping parents' decisions about schooling and education.

Adriana, a 30-year-old school teacher, mother of two unvaccinated children, also uses the Internet as a source of vaccine information and a forum of discussion. But the way it impacts on her choices is mediated by networks of friends, peers, and health-care professionals.

> I often look for advice with this doctor, she gives me lots of information, but I also look for information online, on sites from other countries, associations... I don't always identify with these sites because they have this very dichotomous way of putting things, either you're for or against vaccines. And if you're against, it's in a very radical way. I understand; it's a strong opposition because if something is blind, the reaction ends up being blind too. Sometimes in these blogs, it is as if vaccines were the devil. But things aren't so. I make up my mind in light of the information I have. I also have some friends with whom I discuss this. They belong to an older generation, they have kids. We support each other, we share the same concerns; we talk about it, influence one another: "Look, read what I found." Each shares the information they find. A couple of friends hadn't immunized their child, but now they have decided to give him the tetanus vaccine.

Given the strong reactions that non-vaccination choices tend to elicit, peers are also important in providing a supportive backdrop without which it would be difficult to avoid feelings of isolation or marginality. Yet Adriana, whose own parents had also decided not to vaccinate her and her brother, noted that attitudes had softened – an evolution equally pointed out by other parents in the changes occurred between their older and younger children:

> Peer support is very important. Otherwise, we couldn't take the pressure. From other people, doctors... When the issue is vaccines, reactions are very strong, even from friends. People start fighting immediately – "Oh, but that'll kill them [these parents' children]."
>
> Things are changing, though, in comparison to what my parents had to put up with. Lots of paediatricians refused to treat us. I remember me and my mother being expelled from a doctor's office – and he had been in medical school with my grandparents', who were physicians. They thought my parents were loonies. When one of my daughters almost had pneumonia, one doctor said "nobody will want to treat this child because she is not vaccinated, nobody will take the responsibility". But today you can find doctors and people who support you ... Even healthcare officers have become more sensitive. Just the other day a woman from the health centre called to say that my daughters were not vaccinated yet and that she had to remind me that they had to be, otherwise they were unprotected. But she was very polite. Also at school, we are required to sign a standard statement, but it's nothing like what my parents went through. Every year they had to explain it to the school in writing. One year, the school was being especially punctilious, and my mother decided to say it was for religious reasons. It worked, they immediately stopped bothering her. There were no more problems, they accepted right away because religion is something untouchable.

The strategic use of the religious argument by Adriana's mother was successful in that it did not challenge the reluctance and the suspicion against an expression of individuation typical of late modernity (Giddens 1991), that is, a greater autonomy vis-à-vis the tutelage of instituted forms of knowledge-power and values. In the case at hand, personal choices were not accepted – or even comprehended – while they were perceived as being assumed by an individual in a position of self-regulation. They were tolerated only from the moment they could be related to some tutoring system. Alluding to how attitudes towards vaccines can be socially stratified, a nurse speculated on the reaction adopted by health professionals in the face of vaccine refusal:

> People think that those who do not vaccinate their children typically come from bottom of the [social] ladder, but no. Those worry a lot, as soon as the kid is 5 years old they come here right away to take the vaccine [necessary to enter school at 6]. Most of those who don't vaccinate are way up the ladder. It is they who study the subject, seek information. Except the extreme cases of total alienation, like drug addicts, those with less education comply, and spend huge amounts of money on vaccines that are not even included in the NPV. If necessary they don't eat in order to purchase those extra vaccines for their kids, they don't want to deprive them of anything. I usually don't bring them up because they are very expensive; if they're not in the NPV it's for some reason. And I try to assuage feelings of guilt expressed by parents for not being able to give these vaccines to their children.
>
> Those who don't want any vaccine, well, I have learned to accept that. They refuse, OK, it's their right, they're entitled to their beliefs. We have to resist this habit of judging them: "you have to do it because I say so, I'm the one who knows what's best for you".

This nurse is therefore also acknowledging the growing complexity of the relationship between parents and the health-care providers with regard to immunization decisions.

Frames of Communication

Using the concept of "biocommunicability" to describe the communication process of information about health – whose authority it is to assess this information, manage it, and speak about it – Charles Briggs (2010: 49) mentions different "cartographies of biocommunicability". The biomedical cartography, which tends to organize practices of institutions and health professionals, is unidirectional. It is characterized by "a flow from specialized, knowledge-rich sectors to sectors lacking this information or possessing erroneous beliefs, undertaking inappropriate behaviours and misguided actions" (Briggs 2010: 49; see also Fainzang 2006; Ong et al. 1995). In contrast with the classic opposition "medical authority/patient passivity", other cartographies centre on active patient-consumers and public-sphere citizen debates (Briggs 2010: 49). Like the middle-class subjects in Briggs's study, who did not identify with the biomedical cartography in the same way as lower social strata did (for the Portuguese case see Cabral, Silva & Mendes 2002), our interlocutors also distance themselves from it and do not relate passively with biomedical authority. They actively tap multiple sources of information and they derive their own evidence from their personal experience – for example, like Briggs's subjects, almost all parents spontaneously observed the absence of allergies in their unvaccinated children compared to others in their own immediate environment.

However, unlike Briggs and Hallin (2007), who consider these new cartographies as "neo-liberal" expressions of an "active consumerist orientation", we contend that the form of agency tried out by both our Portuguese and French interlocutors is more adequately characterized by situating them not as "consumers", but rather as "political subjects" (see also Fainzang 2011). Likewise, it is not to be equated with "healthism", a phenomenon Greenhalgh and Wessely (2004) associated with "Western middle-classes" and stereotyped as "demanding and manipulative behaviour by individuals for whom 'health for me' takes precedence over any notions of equity, fairness or citizenship" (ibid.: 207). Although some characteristics are similar (health-awareness, information-seeking, self-reflection), our interlocutors' conduct bears little resemblance to the "conspicuous consumption" orientation aligned with "healthism" (e.g., escalating demands for unnecessary tests, referrals and treatments). It tends to be rather the opposite (see Lopes 2010). In the specific case of vaccines, as the nurse above suggests, a consumerist orientation going well beyond NPV vaccines tends instead to be a characteristic of low-income, less-educated users. In terms of citizenship, the political orientation also far from matches the 1980s and 1990s free-market ideologies and the "cult of the individual" that defined the historical context out of which "healthism" arose (Crawford in Greenhalgh & Wessely 2004: 200). Firstly, the political ideological alignments of these interviewees are as heterogeneous as their lifestyles;[8] secondly, and despite this ideological heterogeneity, political agency often converges into forms of neo-cooperativism and neo-mutualism that transcend the usual dichotomy between the public and the market provision of services; thirdly, it does not break with the wide consensus existing in Portugal around the importance of the welfare State.[9]

We will return to this point later on. In any event, the issue in bio-communicability in some cases does not even pose itself as the opportunity to discuss information flowing from knowledge-rich professionals to a presumably all ignorant public, but as the possibility of actually obtaining from the former *any* kind of information at all, like the following mother (Helena, 36 years old) implies:

> We have been really lucky with our doctors, they explain everything to us. But we react badly to doctors who don't. We don't accept that they treat us like we're idiots. They provide an essential service, it is our health. But people accept it as if it were a divine thing. We're all human, we cannot relate to people as if they were infallible. We can only do our best and we have to trust them, but doctors should not feel upset by our questions. Both sides are responsible for this.

One might say that these parents relate to the NVP in the same way they relate to doctors, that is, as active, vocal interlocutors who do not delegate the power of decision over their bodies to higher authorities without critical scrutiny. They thus expect to be informed of the medical options adopted. Likewise, they relate to vaccines and vaccination in the same way as they relate to medication. The acceptability of vaccines shares many features with, and is accompanied by, the kind of compliance they express regarding medication and prescribed drugs. In this sense, the "biocommunicability" mentioned by Briggs (2010) is indeed a central dimension of self-regulation, that is, of the way individuals structure self-surveillance of health and the body – as the following mother exemplifies:

> I usually discuss a lot with doctors. [My daughter] is prone to ear infections, they want to give her antibiotics. But I know that if it's a virus, antibiotics won't help. They don't tell you that, this is something I know. They say, ah, but it's OK, it's a preventive measure (...) I don't want to do self-medication, I want to follow what doctors say, because I'm aware that they know more than me. And it's much easier to trust and go home without thinking about it anymore. But at the same time I also know that this doesn't give you any guarantee, because doctors have different opinions, and there are things that they don't know either.
>
> With children this is more difficult to manage, what to decide, because it is what you hold dearest. Take fever, for instance. When do we take the child to the hospital? Where do you draw the line? Sometimes it's not good to go there with the sick child. I rely on intuition, but intuition is something you train, it's an educated guess. To wait, to evaluate, to see if it comes down or not, whether it's constant or has cycles, whether the kid's behaviour is normal or not, but act. There's always this anxiety. When she had pneumonia, I saw immediately that something was wrong, I didn't even wait. I have no problems with antibiotics. Bless them when they're needed; But not in every situation. But dialogue with the doctors is very difficult. They deal with people as if they were ignorant, they often do not even bother to explain.

However, as far as these parents are concerned, their conduct seems to be less about defying the official cartographies of communication than about repositioning themselves as subjects within them and ceasing to be "interpellated" in the subject positions that they project. We use the notion of interpellation as proposed by Briggs (2010: 48), that is, as "the act of assuming the social position in which one is located by virtue of being designated as the 'receiver' of a particular discursive act". By disturbing the expected categories, subjectivities, and discursive relations of classic schemes of communication, this repositioning may generate a series of misunderstandings. The following example involves attempts reported by Adriana to escape what she considered to be an excessive medicalization of childbirth.

> Medicine is so hyper-preventive these days... It wants so much to control everything and to interfere with natural processes that it becomes aggressive. I had a hard time with doctors just because I wanted a natural childbirth. I didn't want them to induce it according to a pre-defined schedule; I didn't want an epidural (...). One of them said, "How can one possibly want to give birth in pain in the twentieth century? That is totally outdated." But this is not a matter of masochism. The epidural also anesthetizes the baby (...). With my youngest, the head nurse said "So, you don't want the epidural? But what is that, some kind of cult? Is it your husband who won't let you?" They really humiliate you, because they think you're ignorant.
>
> After the dilation, she comes in with a syringe this size [makes a gesture] to burst the water bag, which is an absurd procedure, totally outdated. It was used in the nineteenth century to speed up deliveries, but it's no longer done. So we were there arguing, I said I wouldn't let her do it. And she said: "But do you believe the baby will be born with the bag intact?" They don't give you any credit whatsoever.

The misunderstandings surrounding this interaction seem to stem from the fact that the social position presupposed by healthcare professionals within a traditional scheme of biocommunication no longer matches the one this mother assumes and identifies with. In a disagreement where both parties mutually locate themselves in an evolutionary scale of progress and end up relegating each other to "the past" (the nineteenth century), the misunderstanding is even more pronounced when a position that is presumed to be backward in the eyes of one party, is considered advanced by the other.

This negative experience took place in a private clinic, after which Adriana decided to "never go back to a private hospital again". Benefiting from health insurance,[10] she tried this option for the first time not because she found it more trustworthy in terms of medical competence and quality, but because she presumed she would find an environment more attentive to her preferences in what she deemed to be a special moment for her – only to find herself trapped in a cartography of communication even more rigid than the ones she sought to avoid.[11] Indeed the type of doctor–patient communication schemes is not so much contingent upon the division public vs. private sector as upon other factors, such as health care professionals' perception of patients' autonomy/dependency, and changing social attitudes towards the medical profession and authority in general (cf. note 11).

Diffuse Dissent: Patterns

It is important to stress that the trend expressed by these parents is not necessarily articulated in terms of health and disease. It would be too limiting to try to make sense of it within the frame of particular therapeutic ideologies or lifestyles. It is rather an instance of dissent whose form and meaning are better captured when put in a wider framework, together with claims of control over the body and the person in other spheres besides health. It includes negotiations of power vis-à-vis the State, authority, and the workings of institutions regarding processes and decisions that concern critical areas of life, citizenry, and individual identity. In the same way that these parents actively confront biomedical power in order to have more bearing on child delivery (a more or less medicalized childbirth, with or without an epidural, at home or at the hospital), they confront state bureaucracy – and they challenge it in court, if necessary – to have more freedom of choice over naming their children. In Portugal, the choice of names is strongly regulated by the State. These have to be selected from an official list of authorized first names. Since name is deeply constitutive of the person and of individual identity,[12] the ability to decide on this matter is not experienced as trivial. Two couples report their naming experience as follows:

> We had a problem with [the first daughter's] name, they wouldn't allow it because they said it was a male name [it is gender neutral]. Then with the [second daughter] they wouldn't allow her name either because it was not on the list of approved names. We have a lawsuit running so that we could register the name officially. I searched on the Internet and found an article by a professor who claimed that this [limitation] is a problem, that favouring mostly the legitimacy of religious names as traditionally Portuguese was a creation of Salazar's dictatorship. He [i.e., the professor] said that there was no basis for denying parents the liberty to choose, because there are thousands of exceptions anyway and today there is a big cultural mix, so it no longer makes sense in a multicultural society. I felt oppressed by not being able to make decisions about the small important things in our life, which concern us, not others.

> There were problems with the names of the two [children]. But we were lucky because they were born abroad, so we used that to name them as we wanted. When we came back to Portugal, we had to register them, and then another problem was the hyphen in the family name. We wanted to join the surname of the mother and father. We had no problem with that abroad, but here we had to make a request because it was not considered part of the Portuguese tradition.

A similar pattern arises in choices regarding schooling and the education of children. Again, these parents actively confront what they experience and perceive as rigid, opaque, and impermeable institutions, unable to respond adequately to parents' requests. If their attempts to have a stronger participation in school processes, or simply become better informed of them, are not reasonably satisfied, they may give rise to innovate varieties of informal education and care.

> I wanted to see the public school in my area of residence. I wanted to speak with the school principal, but there was no way to get to her, they told me that it was not usual to receive parents. I asked to speak with the coordinator. No use, I was always told that they didn't know for sure when she would be there. I asked to see the school, but they said it was impossible; I had to make a written request first. Then I asked whether they thought it was normal not being able to see the school where I was considering putting my daughter. I asked if it was a high security prison: you cannot see it, cannot speak to anybody. (34-year-old mother of two)

It was in the aftermath of this unfruitful attempt, while searching for other options, that this mother discovered not only another type of school, but also places where unvaccinated children were easily accepted. Like some of our other interlocutors, she took part in new schooling experiences. This process is not to be equated with a typical elite trajectory that buys its way out of public schools into private ones. Some of these parents (regardless of whether they could afford that trajectory or not) associate in informal "horizontal" structures that work as an alternative to both – in fact receiving children who were previously registered in public or private sector structures. They create small-scale trustful childcare environments and schools through mutualistic, non-profitable grass-root structures, associations or cooperatives.[13] They aim to have a higher degree of participation and choice regarding methods, pedagogy, diet, activities, and guidelines. Not incidentally, these are also schools where non vaccinated children are accepted without a medical certificate, or exempt parents from that requirement.

We asked the parents involved in these schools how they dealt with the daily co-existence of children with different immunization statuses. Those with (totally or partially) unvaccinated children answered along the same lines as a founding member of one of the schools. That is, parents who had chosen to vaccinate their offspring took certain precautions in order not to endanger non-immunized children.

> Some parents initially raised the issue of unvaccinated children, whether they could represent a risk to others. We explained that if there was a risk, it would be the other way around: it's those who are not vaccinated that would be at risk, the others are protected. We also warn parents not to bring kids to school for some time in case they are immunized with active viruses, because there could be a risk to others.

> My son had the polio vaccine when it was still given with the active virus. I didn't take him to school for a week because I knew there were unvaccinated children, they could become infected.

In weighing individual immunization choices, the issue of co-existence may arise for these parents on three specific levels. Firstly, it is considered (by vaccine-acceptors, vaccine-decliners and vaccine-undecided or partly decliners) in terms of concrete collectivities, such as the schools attended by their children. As the excerpts above suggest, co-existence is negotiated (in some cases with the mediation of school boards) by reversing the subject positions of danger: it is not unimmunized children who are a potential threat to immunized ones, but the other way round. Secondly, it is considered at the level of public health, weighing notions of personal freedom and the security of others in terms of concrete individuals. The following reasoning in connection to social responsibility exemplifies this:

> Nowadays there are vaccines for such trivial problems, things we all caught when we were children

– chickenpox, whatever – that one really wonders. But then on the other hand... Sometimes it is a question of social responsibility... For example, rubella. We have a neighbour who is pregnant. If an unvaccinated kid was to be around, and if she got it... If I were pregnant, I wouldn't like that either, to have a kid next to me with rubella... Damned... That was one of the things that made us change our mind and to eventually vaccinate our kids. (Mother, 36, two children)

Thirdly, also at the level of public health, the principles of individual freedom and collective security are considered in wider and more abstract terms. However, as shown by the following two couples, who opted for non-vaccination, the social narratives of risk in which those two principles come to play are diverse; moreover, even at this level the negotiation of such principles remains for these parents context specific, dependent on circumstances such as exceptional disease outbreaks or the evolution of herd immunity. The parents we interviewed are used to be confronted with the "free ride" argument (others vaccinating give them the possibility to enjoy herd immunity and avoid personal risks). But they present their option as innocuous for others while not risk-free for themselves in the present; also, they present it as reversible in the future, as an ongoing negotiation with collective circumstances.

There was a doctor who told us, "Yeah, you benefit from the umbrella of others' [children], who protect yours". Another guy told us: "But yours endanger others." ... Then we said it's not like that, on the contrary. Others are immunized; it's ours who may catch something.

In case of epidemics, then of course we must see things differently. Because this option of not vaccinating is only viable as long as other children are. So you cannot be against vaccines unconditionally or indefinitely. This has to be a dynamic thing. But people should not be required to vaccinate themselves in all circumstances. If suddenly it is necessary for public health reasons, then OK.

Overall, most of the interviewees who were vaccine-decliners and partial vaccine-decliners held less polarized and more provisional views on vaccine issues than the "alternativist" ones such as Isabel's. They seemed more open to reconsider them on the basis of collective changing circumstances, in the same way they seemed more open to advice from individual health professionals consulted in the first place. Vaccinating for the benefit of society, however, is not a primary driver of such reconsideration, any more than it is a driver of uptake for vaccine acceptors (Brown et al. 2010). Moral judgements and imputations of selfishness are therefore not only misplaced as promoters of vaccine acceptance, but are actually counterproductive in that they may induce or crystallize a defensive anti-vaccine stance. This potential counterproductive effect runs parallel to the authoritarian frames of communication we have identified, alienating rather than fostering parents' trust.

Concluding Remarks

Focusing on the variation of practices and perceptions that shape vaccine acceptability, we have addressed a tendency whose form and meaning are best described when put in the wider context of contemporary social and cultural transformations. This tendency is not confined to a particular social scene, nor circumscribable to a bounded system of ideas, an "alternativist" lifestyle or a "healthist" orientation. Unlike what has been reported for other countries (see Poltorak, Leach & Fairhead 2004), it is also not constituted specifically in relation to concrete vaccine controversies or vaccine issues – that is, the vicissitudes, uncertainties, and risks that this technique may entail for specific bodies with specific health biographies. Moreover, although this tendency is part of the current reconfiguration taking place within the lay management of health and the body, as well as an aspect of the eclectic reshaping and pluralization of therapeutic worlds that have created more leeway for personal autonomy (Lopes 2010), it may not even be articulated strictly in terms of risk, health and disease. Health and the body are but one of the realms in which a same pattern arises. This common pattern does more than simply provide the background or set the context for understanding the meaning and the form of the diffuse tendency we have approached here. Rather, it is at its very core and it is precisely what makes *this variant* of vaccine acceptability specific in relation to others. It would therefore be misleading to frame its analysis within the narrow limits of health and risk management.

In this case, it is by positioning these parents as political subjects that the views, conducts, and practices sketched out by them can be captured more accurately, whether relatively to health, education, care, or pertaining to the very idea of person, like naming issues. In several domains, they feature a more active agency vis-à-vis bureaucratic authorities, experts systems, and instituted cartographies of communication. They thus try out a different political participatory framework. The relationship with biomedical institutions is but one of these domains. And the relationship with vaccination is but one aspect of this pattern within the biomedical domain.

Changing engagements with immunization in Portugal are thus coherent and tend to go hand in hand with emergent forms of assertive citizenry that challenge what is experienced as a distant, opaque, and overbearing state regulatory power over the person and the body. However, this should not be confused with neo-liberal claims implying for example State withdrawal from health or education. On the contrary, there is no ideological stake on the private sector and more often than not these parents are actively engaged in confronting state institutions with inadequacies and insufficiencies which they thereby seek to attenuate. Public services in health and education are prized and would, by rule, be a first choice. What is claimed instead is more leeway for individual choice, agency, and participation *within* the state-regulated realm. When "opting out" occurs (which does not preclude the co-existence with, or the return to that engagement), it tends to take the form of a pragmatic neo-cooperativism that creates horizontal varieties of solidarity and interdependence.

For this reason, just as we have avoided positioning these parents as "consumers" in order to underline instead the specific *political* character of their agency, we also prefer to avoid the current ambiguity contained in the notion of "empowerment" and the instrumental connotations within its semantic scope. Although this notion was initially shaped in the context of civil movements and civic struggles for citizens' rights and emancipation, its extension to health has increasingly connected it with a discourse imparting – if not altogether transferring – health responsibilities to citizens themselves. Within this discourse, the increased power that results from possessing more information is to be promoted insofar as it potentiates personal control over the factors that influence health and a healthy lifestyle (Nogueira & Remoaldo 2010: 27). As follows from the description above, the notion of power that is at play in the conduct of our interlocutors has a wider scope and cannot be reduced to this instrumental aspect.

If indeed vaccination is deeply anchored in relations of power and authority between the State, science, and citizens, then this form of dissent is entirely coherent with predominant forms of consent in Portugal (see Saavedra 2011) in that it is built along the same lines, but as a symmetrical opposite. The consensus around vaccination is based not so much on a pro-active adherence and commitment to its principle, than on tight instruments of control, registration and monitoring dispersed through society. Moreover, the users over whom medical power and disciplinary action are exerted more fully and authoritatively in healthcare institutions are those more deprived of educational and economic capital, and positioned more unfavourably in the class structure. These are the ones who express a more passive acceptance of the norm and its administering agents. As Saavedra (2011) showed, hegemony in such consensus is dynamic and incomplete in that it does not imply a total homogenization of practical compliant behaviour. It hides a myriad of nuances, meanings, motivations, conveniences and personal priorities. The fact that these users juggle with the NPV schedule according to their daily priorities, and to how they assess their children's contextual vulnerability, expresses a practical negotiation of the limits of hegemony and of institutional power.

Yet, even if the concrete modalities, schedules, and circumstances in which vaccination occurs may be challenged, such irregularities in immunization practices are not articulated as a critique, nor cease to express a passive acquiescence before vaccination in its biomedical definition.

In the case of our interlocutors, they may contest vaccination not because they are more "enlightened" than the users above, or because they are in possession of more or better information from the outset. It is rather because they actively question themselves about vaccines and, in doing so, they do not find in healthcare institutions an environment that is receptive to such questioning, or willing to help them navigate other information they have obtained by themselves. Likewise, it is not necessarily because they have endorsed an alternative lifestyle beforehand that their children are sent to schools outside official circles. Instead, it is because such official circles were not open to their attempts at greater participation and were impervious to them. Dissent is thus more a point of arrival than a point of departure, more a process than a stance, more the result of a relationship than the expression of an individual trajectory. This is crucial for any attempt at understanding the production of contemporary forms of dissent.

At a wide analytical level, resistance or hesitation in relation to vaccination can therefore be considered as the reverse of consent. This is so even if consent, when considered at a more specific level, may reveal a variety, irregularity, and inequality, which also characterize dissent. Be that as it may, in their forms and meanings the production of consent and that of dissent seem to stand in relation to one another as two sides of the same coin. This is not without implications for policy. Despite the highly complexified landscape both in vaccine science and vaccine public acceptability, the case for routine vaccination has not ceased to be strong from an epidemiological point of view, as it has been historically. Declining vaccination rates have consequences, even in the absence of the major epidemics of the past.[14] But, precisely because of this importance and complexification, it is crucial not to presume that a consensus around vaccination may stand indefinitely on passive and unquestioning forms of citizenry. That consensus is now more fragile and uncertain. A renewed candid approach to dissent (e.g., Willrich 2011) in its diffuse contemporary variety may be a way to foster it.

Notes

1 This paper is based on the research project Vaccination: Society and Body Management (PTDC/HAH/71637/2006), FCT / "Vacinação e cuidado, poder e incerteza", CRIA; PEst-OE/SADG/UI4038/2011. We are grateful for the insightful comments of two anonymous reviewers.

2 Research has nevertheless shown that resistance is often less to vaccines than to vaccinators or to vaccination processes (e.g., Pereira 2002; Greenough 1995).

3 In French bookstores, the shelves with non-professional medical science books hold titles divided for the most part between two themes: the main one is ageing and dying (with many books on palliative care), and the other group deals with the dangers of vaccination.

4 Together with Spain, Portugal is the European country with the greatest job insecurity in the 25–49 age group (Oliveira & Carvalho 2008).

5 The vaccines mentioned by this mother are part of the Portuguese NPV.

6 As Brown et al. (2010) have suggested, personal advice from health professionals may be more powerful than generic information materials, thus the importance of a trusting relationship with parents.

7 A recent national study on compliance (Cabral & Silva 2010) showed that well beyond a "gratitude bias", Portuguese doctors inspire in patients high levels of trust and satisfaction in terms of prescribed treatment and "technical" competence. However, satisfaction is much lower in other aspects, such as doctors' ability to take patients' opinion into account, to present them with therapeutic alternatives, and to make room for them to ask questions and to express themselves. On the other hand, most patients show low levels of autonomy and tend to adopt a passive attitude during consultations, abstaining from dialogue and leaving the initiative to doctors. This pattern of communication is thus co-constructed; it does not arise out of the doctor's conduct only. Moreover, it has to be put in the wider context of Portuguese history. The very idea of health as a right pertains to a welfare state that saw its inception only after the democratic revolution of 1974. The long authoritarian regime to which this revolution put an end was not without leaving its marks on the political culture of everyday citizenry (Cabral 2000). Question-

ing (medical) authority – and accommodating that questioning – is also part of changes in that culture.

8 These alignments range from right-wing conservatism to the socialist and radical left.

9 According to the last European Social Survey (2008), Portuguese widely value the welfare State; they are among the less neo-liberal Europeans in this regard (Carreira da Silva, forthcoming).

10 Health care in Portugal stands on three systems: public (National Healthcare Service, NHS), parapublic (e.g., for civil workers, military, bank employees), and private. The overwhelming majority of the population is covered by the NHS (circa 85%), followed by parapublic services (circa 12%–13%), and a residual minority by private health insurance (Cabral, Silva & Mendes 2002; Cabral & Silva 2009). Private services are mostly used as a complement to public ones, and in specific situations (mainly for ophthalmic and dental care).

11 In a compared assessment of public perceptions about both sectors, surveys (Cabral, Silva & Mendes 2002; Cabral & Silva 2009) have shown that private services are deemed to be more attentive, better organized and provide faster access; however, irrespective of the demographic and socio-economic characteristics of respondents, public services are considered to offer high quality and better prepared health care professionals. This perception is reinforced among middle-class respondents and those with a higher education degree: they deem the quality of human and technical resources in the public sector higher than in the private one – a counter intuitive survey result in the light of often media vilified public services.

12 For the nominative resonances, emotional implications, and references involved in the choice of names, see Pina Cabral (2008).

13 Officially, parents may declare their children to be home-schooled when such establishments are not legally recognized as schools. These informal neo-cooperativist arrangements differ from some of the forms that preceded them in the 1960s and 1970s in that they are not informed by a coherent philosophy or alternativist ideology (Cunha 2006).

14 See for example Mieszkowski (2010).

References

Beck, Ulrich (1986)1992: *Risk Society: Towards a New Modernity*. London: Sage.

Briggs, Charles L. 2010: Pressing Plagues: On the Mediated Communicability of Virtual Epidemics. In: A. Herring & A.C. Swedlund (eds.), *Plagues and Epidemics: Infected Spaces Past and Present*. Oxford & New York: Berg, pp. 39–59.

Briggs, Charles & Daniel Hallin 2007: Biocommunicability: The Neo-liberal Subject and its Contradictions in News Coverage of Health Issues. *Social Text* 25:4, 43–66.

Brown, K.F., J.S. Kroll, M.J. Hudson, M. Ramsay, J. Green, S.J. Long et al. 2010: Factors Underlying Parental Decisions about Combination Childhood Vaccinations Including MMR: A Systematic Review. *Vaccine* 28:26, 4235–4248.

Cabral, Manuel V. 2000: O Exercício da Cidadania Política em Portugal. In: M.V. Cabral, J. Vala & J. Freire (eds.), *Trabalho e Cidadania: Inquérito Permanente às Atitudes Sociais dos Portugueses*. Oeiras: Celta.

Cabral, Manuel V., Pedro A. da Silva & Hugo Mendes 2002: *Saúde e Doença em Portugal*. Lisbon: Imprensa de Ciências Sociais.

Cabral, Manuel V. & Pedro A. da Silva 2009: *O Estado da Saúde em Portugal*. Lisbon: Imprensa de Ciências Sociais.

Cabral, Manuel V. & Pedro A. da Silva 2010: *A Adesão à Terapêutica em Portugal: Atitudes e Comportamentos da População Portuguesa perante as Prescrições Médicas*. Lisbon: Imprensa de Ciências Sociais.

Calado, Virgínia 2011: 'Vacinas, só em caso de epidemia ou de risco grave!' Macrobiótica e Resistência à Vacinação. In: M. Cunha & J.Y. Durand (eds.), *Razões de Saúde. Poder e Administração do Corpo: Vacinas, Alimentos, Medicamentos*. Lisbon: Fim de Século, pp. 161–180.

Caplan, Pat 2000: Introduction: Risk Revisited. In: P. Caplan (ed.), *Risk Revisited*. London: Pluto Press, pp. 1–28.

Carreira da Silva, Filipe (ed.) forthcoming (2012): *Os Portugueses e o Estado Providência*. Lisboa: Imprensa de Ciências Sociais.

Casa-Nova, Maria José 2011: Vacinação e Percepções em Torno do Corpo e da Doença em Contextos de Etnicidade. In: M. Cunha & J.Y. Durand (eds.), *Razões de Saúde. Poder e Administração do Corpo: Vacinas, Alimentos, Medicamentos*. Lisbon: Fim de Século, pp. 181–196.

Cunha, Manuela P. da 2006: Formalidade e Informalidade: Questões e Perspectivas. *Etnográfica* 10, 219–231.

Cunha, Manuela P. da & Jean-Yves Durand 2011: A Dissensão Vacinal Difusa: Corpo, Pessoa e Sujeitos Políticos. In: M. Cunha & J.Y. Durand (eds.), *Razões de Saúde. Poder e Administração do Corpo: Vacinas, Alimentos, Medicamentos*. Lisbon: Fim de Século, pp. 197–230.

Darmon, Pierre 1984: Les Premiers Vaccinophobes. *Sciences Sociales et Santé* II:3–4.

Direcção-Geral de Saúde 2009: Elementos Estatísticos: Informação Geral, Saúde/2007. Direcção-Geral de Saúde, http://www.dgs.pt/. Accessed October 3, 2010.

Douglas, Mary 1985: *Risk Acceptability According to the Social Sciences*. New York & London: Russel Sage/Routledge.

Fainzang Sylvie 2006: *La relation médecins-malades: information et mensonge*. Paris: Presses Universitaires de France.

Fainzang, Sylvie 2011: Automedicação: Entre Escolha Terapêutica e Conduta Política. In: M. Cunha & J.Y. Durand (eds.), *Razões de Saúde. Poder e Administração do Corpo: Vacinas, Alimentos, Medicamentos*. Lisbon: Fim de Século, pp. 29–38.

Foucault, Michel 2004: *Sécurité, Territoire, Population, Cours au Collège de France, 1977–1978*. Paris: Seuil/Gallimard.

Frykman, Jonas et al. 2009: Sense of Community: Trust, Hope and Worries in the Welfare State. *Ethnologia Europaea* 39:1, 7–46.

Giddens, Anthony 1991: *Modernity and Self-Identity: Self and Society in Late Modern Age*. Cambridge: Polity Press.

Gonçalves, Eduarda et al. (eds.) 2007: *Os Portugueses e os Novos Riscos*. Lisbon: Imprensa de Ciências Sociais.

Greenhalgh, Trisha & Simon Wessely 2004: 'Health for me': A Sociocultural Analysis of Healthism in the Middle Classes. *British Medical Bulletin* 69, 197–213.

Greenough, Paul 1995: Intimidation, Coercion, and Resistance in the Final Stages of the South Asian Smallpox Eradication Campaign, 1973–1975. *Social Science and Medicine* 14:D, 345–347.

Haraway, Donna 1991: *Simians, Cyborgs, and Women: The Reinvention of Nature*. London: Free Association Books.

Herring, Anne & Alan C. Swedlund (eds.) 2010: *Plagues and Epidemics: Infected Spaces, Past and Present*. Oxford & New York: Berg.

Lopes, Noémia Mendes 2010: Consumos Terapêuticos e Pluralismo Terapêutico. In: N. Lopes (ed.), *Medicamentos e Pluralismo Terapêutico: Práticas e Lógicas Sociais em Mudança*. Porto: Afrontamento, pp. 19–85.

Martin, Emily 1994: *Flexible Bodies: The Role of Immunity in American Culture from the Days of Polio to the Age of AIDS*. Boston: Beacon Press.

Mieszkowski, Katharine 2010: Areas of Low Vaccination Rates Poses Risk to Students, NYT: http://www.nytimes.com/2010/09/12/us/12bcvaccines.html. Accessed November 9, 2010.

Mills, E., A.R. Jadad, C. Ross & K. Wilson 2005: Systematic Review of Qualitative Studies Exploring Parental Beliefs and Attitudes towards Childhood Vaccination Identifies Common Barriers to Vaccination. *Journal of Clinical Epidemiology* 58:11, 1081–88.

Moulin, Anne-Marie 1989: The Immune System: A Key Concept for the History of Immunology. *History and Philosophy of the Life Science* 11, 221–236.

Moulin, Anne-Marie 1991: *Le Dernier Langage de la Médecine: Histoire de l'Immunologie de Pasteur au Sida*. Paris: Presses Universitaires de France.

Moulin, Anne-Marie 2007: Les Vaccins, l'État Moderne et les Sociétés. *Médecine Sciences* 23:4, http://www.medecine-sciences.org/reserve/print/e-docs/00/00/0A/B4/document_article.md. Accessed December 10, 2007.

Moulin, Anne-Marie 2011: O Ponto de Viragem da Saga Vacinal: De Ferramenta de Governo a Instrumento de Saúde Individual? In: M. Cunha & J.Y. Durand (eds.), *Razões de Saúde. Poder e Administração do Corpo: Vacinas, Alimentos, Medicamentos*. Lisbon: Fim de Século, pp. 125–136.

Napier, David A. 2003: *The Age of Immunology: Conceiving a Future in an Alienating World*. Chicago & London: The University of Chicago Press.

Nogueira, Helena & Paula C. Remoaldo 2010: *Olhares Geográficos Sobre a Saúde*. Lisbon: Colibri.

Oliveira, Luísa & Helena Carvalho 2008: A Precarização do Emprego na Europa: Dados. *Revista de Ciências Sociais* 51:3, 541–567.

Ong, L.M.L., J.C.J.M. de Haes, A.M. Hoos & F.B. Lammes 1995: Doctor/Patient Communication: A Review of the Literature. *Social Science & Medicine* 40:7, 903–918.

Pereira, Leonardo 2002: *As Barricadas da Saúde: Vacina e Protesto Popular no Rio de Janeiro da Primeira República*. São Paulo: Editora Fundação Perseu Abramo.

Petersen, Alan (1997)2006: Risk, Governance and the New Public Health. In: Alan Petersen & Robin Bunton (eds.), *Foucault Health and Medicine*. London & New York: Routledge, pp. 189–206.

Pina Cabral, João 2008: Outros Nomes, Histórias Cruzadas: Apresentado o Debate. *Etnográfica* 12:1, 5–16.

Poltorak, Mike, Melissa Leach & James Fairhead 2004: *MMR "Choices" in Brighton: Understanding Public Engagement with Vaccination Science and Delivery*. Brighton: Institute of Development Studies.

Poltorak, Mike, Melissa Leach, James Fairhead & Jackie Cassell 2005: "MMR Talk" and Vaccination Choices: An Ethnographic Study in Brighton. *Social Science and Medicine* 61:3, 709–719.

Rapley, Tim 2008: Distributed Decision Making: The Anatomy of Decisions-in-action. *Sociology of Health & Illness* 30:3, 429–444.

Rogers, Anne & David Pilgrim 1995: The Risk of Resistance: Perspectives on the Mass Childhood Immunization Programme. In: J. Gabe (ed.), *Medicine, Health and Risk: Sociological Approaches*. Oxford: Blackwell.

Saavedra, Mónica 2011: O Consenso Vacinal Revisitado: Hegemonia Dinâmica. In: M. Cunha & J.Y. Durand (eds.), *Razões de Saúde. Poder e Administração do Corpo: Vacinas, Alimentos, Medicamentos*. Lisbon: Fim de Século, pp. 137–159.

Serpell, L. & J. Greene 2004: Parental Decision-making in Childhood Vaccination. *Vaccine* 24:19, 4041–46.

Simon, Jonathan 1998: The Emergence of a Risk Society: Insurance, Law, and the State. In: Pat O'Malley (ed.), *Crime and Risk Society*. Darmouth: Ashgate.

Streefland, Pieter 2001: Public Doubts about Vaccination Safety and Resistance against Vaccination. *Health Policy* 55, 159–172.

Streefland, Pieter, A.M.R. Chowdury & Pilar Ramos-Jimenez 1999: Patterns of Vaccination Acceptance. *Social Science and Medicine* 49, 1705–1716.

Tauber, Alfred I. 1994: *The Immune Self: Theory or Metaphor?* Cambridge: Cambridge University Press.

Willrich, Michael 2011: Why Parents Fear the Needle, http://www.nytimes.com/2011/01/21/opinion/21willrich.html. Accessed January 20, 2011.

Manuela Cunha holds a Ph.D. in anthropology and is a member of CRIA-UM (Portugal) as well as IDEMEC (France). She is a professor at the University of Minho. Her research interests centre on prisons, total institutions, and moral economies, on informal processes, the compared structure of drug markets, and on intersection between crime, gender and ethnicity. Together with Jean-Yves Durand she edited *Razões de Saúde. Poder e Administração do Corpo: Vacinas, Alimentos, Medicamentos* [Health Reasons. Power and the Body: Vaccines, Foodways, and Medication] (Lisbon: Fim de Século).
(micunha@ics.uminho.pt)

Jean-Yves Durand holds a Ph.D. in anthropology and is a member of CRIA-UM (Portugal) as well as IDEMEC (France). He is the Director of the ethnographic museum Museu da Terra de Miranda in northern Portugal. He is interested in various types of "knowledges" (water-dowsing, ethnobotany, traditional handicrafts, immunology) and in objects associated to techniques of mobility (traffic-circles, GPS). Together with Manuela Cunha he edited *Razões de Saúde. Poder e Administração do Corpo: Vacinas, Alimentos, Medicamentos* [Health Reasons. Power and the Body: Vaccines, Foodways, and Medication] (Lisbon: Fim de Século).
(jydurand@yahoo.com)

THE CULTURAL PARADOX OF PREDICTIVE GENETIC TESTING FOR HUNTINGTON'S DISEASE

Niclas Hagen

The aim of this article is to perform a cultural analysis of the effects and implications of predictive genetic testing for individuals who have undergone predictive genetic testing for Huntington's disease (HD). Moreover, the analysis aims to relate these effects and the implications of these tests to current initiatives that advocate a large-scale incorporation of genetics and genomics into mainstream health care. The abstract and elusive character of our genes is found to generate a liminal space wherein the affected individuals are situated between normality and abnormality. This juxtaposition of cultural classifications is in turn found to constitute a cultural paradox that might create disagreement in the relations between medical expertise and lay people as genetics and genomics is put to use within mainstream health care.

Keywords: predictive genetic testing, paradox, liminal space, Huntington's disease

I meet up with Jimmy, who is in his early thirties, in his apartment for an interview about his experiences of Huntington's disease (HD)[1], a fatal genetic disease that primarily affects the brain. Jimmy lives in one of the larger cities in the southern part of Sweden. He has a long-term relationship with his girlfriend. His mother has been diagnosed with HD, and as a consequence of the genetic laws that direct the inheritance of HD, the disease and its effects mark the family history on his mother's side of the family. The disease has been traced all the way to his grandmother's mother. Jimmy's mother has now reached that stage of the disease in which the affected individual shows clear signs and symptoms. In order to exclude other possible diagnoses, Jimmy's mother went through a diagnostic genetic test for HD that confirmed that her signs and symptoms were in fact due to Huntington's disease. Genetic testing is used partly as a diagnostic tool to differentiate between diagnoses, and partly as a predictive tool that gives information on carrier status and individual risk for future disease. As a diagnostic tool, the genetic test is performed in relation to more or less clear and visible signs and symptoms. A clear set of these signs and symptoms is usually not present in relation to predictive genetic testing, since the first appearance of the disease might lie several years, or even decades, in the future. The predictive genetic test for HD provides knowledge on the genetic status of those who choose to go through with taking the test. It does not however offer any knowledge about when those who are found to be gene-carriers for the mutated HD gene will develop the disease (Kristoffersson 2010: 67–75, 89–98). Apart from confirming that his mother's signs and symptoms were HD, the genetic test and the subsequent diagnosis also put Jimmy at a 50% risk for having inherited the mutant HD gene.[2] Hitherto, Jimmy's own risk for inheriting the gene had more or less been something that resided in the back of his mind. The confirmation of his mother's HD-diagnosis comprised a transition point (Tibben 2007) that made the potential consequences of the mutant HD-gene obvious for Jimmy:

> That's when you'll get it, it's like a punch straight in your face. When you really understand that it's bloody serious. And that I'm in a fix here too...

At this point, Jimmy could choose to wait and see what the future might hold for him. However, he could also choose to undergo a predictive genetic test that would disclose if, or if not, his genome contained the mutant HD-gene. If that were the case, Jimmy would be a genetic carrier or pre-symptomatic patient whose genome contains the mutated gene, even if clear signs and symptoms of HD are not visible at the time when the genetic test is carried out. Due to the scientific development within genetics, the different forms of genetic testing that are available have increased during the last decade and now encompass a range of conditions (Lock & Nguyen 2010: 330–331). In parallel with this increased medico-technological possibility, the prospect for disease prevention has been acknowledged. For example, a discussion article in one of the major Swedish newspapers from 2010 featured three biomedical researchers and experts writing strongly in favour for a wider use of genetic testing within the Swedish health-care system:

> A DNA-test would not necessarily make people more worried than other tests within the health-care system. Instead, they can give people an increased knowledge and tools that will enable them to reduce the risk for developing disease. (Björkegren, Nilbert & Syvänen 2010. My translation.)

Similar arguments can be found in the official report from the British Human Genomic Strategy Group on the use of genomics within the British health-care service:

> Genomic technologies have the potential to transform the delivery of healthcare in the UK, providing vital insights to support more accurate diagnosis of disease and inform therapeutic decisions – so that more patients get the right treatment at the right time. They can enhance preventive care and enrich our understanding of disease risk, as well as enabling outbreaks of infectious diseases to be controlled faster. (Human Genomics Strategy Group 2012)

These three "snap-shots" convey different viewpoints and different experiences of the ability to make various predictions of future disease in the absence of clear signs and symptoms. From a cultural perspective, these "snap-shots" raise a number of questions. What happens to those individuals who find themselves to be at risk for a genetic disease, and who choose the option of a predictive genetic test in order to receive knowledge about their genetic status? What salient issues can be discerned in conjunction with predictive genetic testing? How can these issues be understood from a cultural perspective? And what implications do these issues have in relation to the use of genetics and genomics as a predictive and preventive tool within mainstream health care?

Consequently, the aim of this article is to perform a cultural analysis, based on ethnographic interviews (see below), investigating the effects and implications of predictive genetic testing on individuals who went through predictive genetic testing for HD. The analysis also aims to relate these effects and implications to current initiatives advocating a large-scale incorporation of genetics and genomics into mainstream health care.

The analysis is guided by concepts obtained from studies in anthropology, ethnology, sociology, as well as science and technology studies. Victor Turner's concept of a liminal space is used as the main analytical perspective. This captures a situation of being in between, as he terms it betwixt-and-between, stable and recognized cultural classifications (1979, 1977). Other important analytical perspectives are Åkesson's notion of the gene as an invisible "alien" inside the body (1999), as well as Nikolas Rose's idea of a somatic individuality (2007). Moreover, in relation to the notion of the gene as an "alien inside", the concept of embodied risk or danger also guides the analysis (Lock & Nguyen 2010: 303–329; Kavanagh & Broom 1998). Monica Konrad's notion of a cultural paradox that arises in relation to predictive genetic testing is employed in conjunction with a juxtaposition of normality and abnormality that was observed in the ethnographic interviews (2005: 82). Brian Wynne's investigations of relationships between experts and lay people are used for the section on effects and implications in relation to the utilization of genetics and genomics within mainstream health care. According to Wynne's standpoint, expert notions too often omit emotional and cultural aspects in favour of a more rational and calculative approach on important issues (1996). The concluding remarks of the analysis are built upon this standpoint when they state a necessity for mutual frameworks between experts and lay people in order to make predictive genetic testing sustainable when put to use in mainstream health care.

Regarding the aim mentioned above, HD functions as an illustrative case, as it represents a large group of devastating chronic diseases for which there are currently no cures available. The choice of HD as an illustrative case is a well-established research strategy, since the disease, despite the relative low number of affected individuals, has come to function as a "model disease" within the medical sciences, as well as within the social and cultural sciences. Within the medical sciences, HD shares clinical features with more common brain disorders such as Alzheimer's disease and Parkinson's disease for which there is no clear explanation concerning the causes of these disorders. Within the cultural and social sciences, HD has served as a "model disease" in relation to social and ethical issues, particularly in relation to predictive genetic testing, as HD was among the first genetic diseases where this form of genetic testing became available within the clinical setting (Tibben 2007; Brouwer-DudokdeWit et al. 2002). The predictive genetic test for HD has been available in the clinical setting since early 1993, following the discovery of the mutated HD gene. In Sweden, an informed consent is required to perform pre-symptomatic or predictive genetic investigations on HD. This means that the provider of the predictive genetic test, which in Sweden is provided by the national health-care system at a genetic clinic, has to be reassured that the individual who is taking the test has been given adequate genetic counselling. The provider must also ensure that the person undergoing the test understands the implication of taking the test. The testing process includes both a consultation with a clinical geneticist, as well as several meetings with a genetic counsellor. The process is designed to provide the individual with enough time to think through his or her decision and it is possible for the individual to withdraw from the testing process at any time. The result is given by a clinical geneticist and followed up at a meeting with a genetic counsellor even if the individual is found not to be a gene-carrier. The individuals undergoing testing and their family members should be offered psychological support suited to their needs. Results are usually followed up for a set period and according to a fixed schedule (Kristoffersson 2010: 95; Socialstyrelsen 2012).

The structure of the article is as follows. The article proceeds with a section on the methods employed in order to obtain the empirical material for this article. The next section will analyse the situation that faced the affected individuals as they discovered that they were at risk of inheriting the HD gene. After this, the consequences of predictive genetic testing upon this situation will be analysed. Finally, the analysis of the ethnographic interviews will be related to the use of genetics and genomics as a predictive and preventive tool in mainstream health care.

Method

A central concern in ethnography is the interpretation of matters that are at stake for particular participants in particular situations (Kleinman 1997: 98). In order to understand the way people experience these particular situations, the ethnographic approach often displays a commitment to the particular; this is achieved by using small representative samples instead of larger samples resulting in quantitative generalizations (Smith, Flowers & Larkin 2009: 29–32). This approach will direct the ethnographer to collective (both local and societal) and individual (both public and intimate) levels of analysis of experience-near interests (Kleinman 1997: 98). This strategy within ethnography and ethnology has been employed in a number of studies that investigate different kinds of issues within the context of health (e.g., Alftberg 2012; Browner & Preloran 2010; Lock & Nguyen 2010; Hanson 2007; Konrad 2005; Lundin 1997; Klein 1989).

The ethnographic material for this article was obtained in southern Sweden in 2009–2010 as part of the Basal Ganglia Disorders Linnaean Consortium (Bagadilico) (http://www.med.lu.se/bagadilico). Bagadilico is an interdisciplinary research consortium at Lund University focusing on Parkinson's and Huntington's diseases. The study was performed with individuals who in various ways are affected by HD.[3] The empirical material mainly consists of in-depth interviews with the participants, whereas observations (which were recorded in the author's field diary, directly after the completion of the interviews) were used as an additional source of knowledge employed in the subsequent interpretation of the interviews. Following Alftberg (2012), it has to be acknowledged that the in-depth interview at times might be seen as a combination of verbal reports and ethnographic observations. The totality of the situation, not only what is verbally reported by the informant, forms the basis for the knowledge produced through the in-depth interview. Here, Alftberg uses the concept "ethnographic interview" as a way to capture this combination of verbally reported material and ethnographic observations (Alftberg 2012: 22). In relation to this article, the ethnographic interview provided an in-depth explorative and detailed knowledge of the experiences reported by the affected individuals. Apart from the knowledge reported verbally, it also included other aspects that came forward in the interview situation (for example in relation to emotional expressions such as crying at certain points in the interview). The names of the participants have been anonymized in order to protect their privacy. The study was approved by the regional ethical committee at Lund University.

An Invisible "Alien" Inside

Those things and aspects of our existence that, for different reasons and within different contexts, are considered unfamiliar or "alien" have always carried a powerful cultural charge (Åkesson 1999: 121). Arranging different phenomena into cultural classificatory systems is a well-known strategy to create order and control in a world that otherwise would stand out as chaotic and incomprehensive (Åkesson 1991: 57; Lundin & Åkesson 2000: 11). Within the cultural and social sciences, the importance and function played by different classificatory systems is a thoroughly investigated topic (e.g., Foucault 2002; Bowker & Star 2000; Frykman 1993; Åkesson 1991; Douglas 1966).

Within medicine, albeit with a great cultural diversification, classificatory systems are employed in order to diagnose illness and normalize health (Kleinman 1997: 22). These medical classifications split up the world of signs and symptoms into useful categories and models; this became crucial in conjunction with the growth of the modern state (Bowker & Star 2000: 101, 111). For example, the origin of the International Classification of Diseases (ICD) can be traced to the development of the welfare state and its concern with large-scale public health measures and programmes (Bowker & Star 2000: 111, 139–140). And, as noted by Michel Foucault and numerous others, these classifications can also be seen as entwined with the exercise of power within modernity (Hacking 2002: 99–114; Foucault 2000; Lupton 1995; Nelkin & Tancredi 1994).

Traditionally, these "alien features" of our existence were located externally, through such obvious visible criteria as skin colour or sex, which made them easy to incorporate within cultural categorizations. In conjunction with the context of disease, this aspect can be exemplified by breast cancer. During the eighteenth and nineteenth centuries predisposing causes of breast cancer were traditionally understood in terms of outside influences, like injuries, childbearing, ethnicity or belonging to a certain age group (Schlich 2004: 212). Yet, during the twentieth century, heredity factors became increasingly important as a predisposing factor in relation to disease, often with reference to the developing field of genetics (e.g., Fox-Keller 2010; Nelkin & Lindee 2004; Petersen & Bunton 2002). Disease hazards and predispositions, these "alien features" of our existence, are relocated from various outside influences to the internal aspects of our body; this represents a process wherein these dangers and hazards become embodied (Lock & Nguyen 2010: 303–329; Kavanagh & Broom 1998). Epidemiologist Anne Kavanagh and sociologist Dorothy Broom consider that these embodied predispositions, these internal "aliens inside", are different compared with external hazards and predispositions because "they impose their threat from within – a person both has and is a body" (Kavanagh & Broom 1998: 442).

Today, genetics and genomics are to a large extent centred on the molecular constitution of the human body; DNA, RNA, proteins and various types of other molecules interact with each other and build up the body. New knowledge on our molecular constitution is seen as having profound implications, since it offers a greater understanding of the finest details of disease processes. Moreover, the impact of this development might also be seen within the context of diagnosis and prevention of disease, as it offers a more precise measurement of disease processes and even a reconceptualization of disease classifications (Shostak 2010: 251–254; Rose 2007: 13). According to Nikolas Rose, this development has the potential to reorganize the relations between individuals and biomedical expertise through a reshaping of the way in which human beings relate to themselves. Increasingly, we see and describe ourselves as "somatic individuals", as beings "whose individuality is, in part at least, grounded within our fleshy, corporeal existence, and who experience, articulate, judge, and act upon ourselves in part in the language of biomedicine" (2007: 6, 25–26). However, the anthropologist Monica Konrad points out that this picture might be too simplistic, as individuals are not "simply passive recipients of information given to them by clinical professionals" (2005: 63). The ethnographic interviews made within this study involving the experiences among the participants of being at risk, indicated that the participants evaded the idea of the statistical 50% ratio, which only gives a general depiction of the pattern of inheritance concerning this embodied danger that the participants faced. Instead of this general statistical notion, the participants tried to make sense of this potential and abstract "alien inside" by invoking various perceivable aspects within their everyday life.

Patricia is in her thirties and lives in a medium-sized town in the south of Sweden. She has no children and at the time I met her, she lived on her own. Patricia's situation resembles Jimmy's, as she came to understand the significance of HD and what it meant for her own future when Peter, her father, was diagnosed with the disease, who in turn inherited the mutated gene from his mother. At the point of her father's HD diagnosis, Patricia found herself at risk for having inherited the mutant HD gene and she came to the conclusion that she wanted to go through predictive genetic testing in order to find out if she carried the mutant HD gene. However, before she did the test, she tried to make sense of the circumstance of her being at risk by thinking in a way that was tangible for her:

> Yeah, you know... when you start adding up on things, you can't really put your finger on it, but if you ransack yourself, if you really look at the whole picture, you do feel, in some sort of way, that: Yes, that's the way it is. Of course, I have it. And then I told my mother and the rest of the family: Yes, I have it. Because I did get poisonous goitre from my grandmother, and I... if something strikes... something strange, then it strikes me.

At this point in time, Patricia did not have any knowledge of whether she in fact was a gene-carrier for the mutated HD gene, but despite this ambiguity of her genetic status, Patricia pinpointed herself as a gene-carrier for the HD gene. She came to this conclusion on the basis of a perceived resemblance (the poisonous goitre) with her grandmother who had already developed HD. Jimmy's reaction on his mother's HD diagnosis provides an additional illustration:

> I was completely convinced that I was carrying the gene. So, I went around and checked, planned what I wanted to do during my last ten years alive. What I wanted to do before I was afflicted, that is. Whatever you do, you'll notice a symptom; you spill something, you drop something. Yes, it's symptoms all the time.

As a consequence of his mother's diagnosis, perceived signs and symptoms of the mutant HD gene mentally dominated Jimmy's everyday life. This aspect was also illustrated by a remark made by Carla, who is in her late fifties and is affected by HD through her husband. At the time of the study, he had recently passed away due to the disease. Carla has two children and they both decided to go through with the predictive testing to resolve their genetic status. They were both found to be non-carriers, but before they were tested, their everyday life was also very much dominated by the prospect of being a gene-carrier: As Carla puts it: "Before they were tested? Oh, yes! Every time something happened... oh, now I've got it."

When the participants learnt that HD ran in their family, their everyday life became filled with perceived signs and symptoms of HD; seemingly random accidents, like dropping something, were taken as palpable signs of the mutant HD gene. Likewise, perceived resemblances, like a shared history of coming down with the same diseases, were also taken as palpable signs of an abnormal genetic status (cf. Shostak, Zarhin & Ottman 2011; Konrad 2005: 61–86). At this point, no knowledge of the participant's genetic status existed, apart from the 50% ratio that constitutes a general and statistical description of the inheritance pattern of the HD gene. Nevertheless, from a cultural perspective, the experiences of the participants were that of being situated between the cultural classifications of normality (being out of danger) and being abnormal (being a gene-carrier). It should also be highlighted that these experiences of being situated between normality and abnormality also included an element of time. As shown in the citations above, the participants fluctuated in time between their present status of being at risk but not yet tested, and an eventual future status of actually being afflicted with HD. The participants seemed to move directly from the present into an anticipated future on the basis of perceived signs and symptoms of an abnormal genetic status, which they come across in their everyday life.

These unclear and indistinctive conditions can be understood, as mentioned above, through Victor Turner's term "liminal space". The term conceptualizes an existence betwixt-and-between different stable and recurrent conditions that are culturally recognized (1979: 467, 1977: 36–37). Inspired by folkloristic research on rites of transition and ritual processes, Turner discerns three phases in these rites. The first phase constitutes a separation, when the subjects who go through the ritual process are detached from their old places within the society. The intermediate phase occurs when the subject is betwixt-and-between recognized cultural classifications. In the third phase of re-aggregation, the subject returns to a new place or position within the community or society (1977: 36–37). Turner characterizes the intermediate phase as a liminal space within which ordinary cultural and cognitive classifications do not apply. Subjects who are situated within this liminal space cannot be understood and categorized through clear-cut cultural classification as they, being "betwixt-and-between" are "neither-this-nor-that, here-nor-there, one-thing-not-the-other" (1977: 37).

The ethnographic interviews indicated that the response of the participants could not be seen in terms of a passive reception of the 50% risk of inheritance of the mutant HD gene. Instead, an active and highly emotional response could be seen among the affected individuals that could be understood in terms of a juxtaposition of normality and abnormality that involved a fluctuation between being at risk and being afflicted with HD. In other words, the everyday existence of these individuals can be understood as being betwixt-and-between normality or abnormality. Monica Konrad considers that this juxtaposition of normality and abnormality can be seen in terms of a cultural paradox (2005: 82). Thus, to enter this liminal space means that you are forced to manage this cultural paradox and the emotional responses that arise as a consequence of an existence betwixt-and-between these two recognized cultural classifications. The ethnographic interviews indicated that this management came to rely upon aspects that were perceivable within the everyday life of the affected individuals. As a way to rework the unclassified betwixt-and-between character of this liminal space into something that was manageable and possible to categorize as either normal or abnormal, they ascribed accidental events or resemblances with an HD-affected relative as a sign of the mutant HD gene.

What happened then when individuals went through with predictive genetic testing for HD? What impact did the knowledge of whether the affected individuals did or did not carry the mutated HD gene have upon their situation? Were they still situated within this liminal space?

The Impact of Predictive Genetic Testing

Both Jimmy and Patricia decided to go through with taking a predictive genetic test for HD. Here their paths start to diverge, because Jimmy's test revealed that he did not carry the mutated gene. Patricia however, was found to be a gene-carrier and will eventually develop HD. As a consequence of her test result, she obtained a status as a gene-carrier or a presymptomatic patient but, as will be shown below, this status did not alleviate Patricia's uncertainty as she struggled to cope with the result of the predictive test. This was also the case for her mother, Emma, who now had to face the difficult fact that the disease would definitely not stop with Peter, her husband, but would also affect her daughter as well.

For Emma, who is in her late fifties, Peter's diagnosis spelled out a future marked by a possible continuation of HD in her family, but Peter's diagnosis also involved a relief as the family got an answer explaining Peter's irritability and at times aggressive behaviour:

> Now I have the answer, you know. And now I know why certain things happened. Because he was… I did come in for a lot of physical stuff, you know. And it could be about such a thing that I'd cooked the wrong kind of dinner for him.

The psychiatric symptoms of HD include personality changes, irritability and aggressive behaviour, as well as disturbances in a person's state of mind, such as depression. The loss of cognitive functions includes deficits of memory and attention, which progresses to dementia in the later stages of the disease. For the affected individual and the family, the psychiatric and cognitive disturbances more than often constitute the most difficult and distressing features of HD, even though these signs and symptoms may appear as less striking compared with the more visible motoric signs (Ross & Tabrizi 2011; Petersén 2001: 16).

Carla's HD-stricken husband also displayed behaviour that at times was troublesome, which nevertheless struck Carla as being part of his personality up until genetics provided a confirmation of HD:

> Yes, when we came to know [about HD] I understood certain things that were present already when we met, like his urge to be in control (---) He wanted to know everything about what I did and things like that. But at that point, I thought that this was part of his personality.

Carolyn, who is of the same age as Carla and Emma, and has children who at the time of our interview had not undergone the predictive genetic test, also reports the same kind of thoughts. Carolyn's husband was diagnosed with HD at quite an old age, and in our interview she also talked of the diagnosis in terms of a disclosure that gave an explanation of past experiences: "With all the answers in my hand, I can see a lot of symptoms going on many, many years back in time. Today I can connect this to Huntington but at that time I didn't, of course."

The crucial point in the cases above resided in the presence of clear and visible neurological signs, which a diagnostic genetic test confirmed as being HD. Therefore, within the context of diagnostic genetic testing for HD, the affected families were able to incorporate the result of the test into a cultural classification that permitted the affected individuals to review past events as a consequence of a disease and thereby being of an abnormal kind. This, however, did not necessarily seem to be the case for those who went through predictive genetic testing, when clear and visible signs were more or less absent. For Jimmy, predictive testing showed that he did not carry the abnormal HD gene within his genome. However, despite the test result, there still resided a small but lingering uncertainty in Jimmy's mind weather he was carrying the HD gene or not:

> No, but it is just that I don't know anything about all this; I was not present during the [analysing] process. I haven't seen all those machines that do the work. I don't really know how... how it works. The only thing I know is that they got my blood. That's all I know.

This was illustrated by the uncertainty reported by Carla's response to the test result of her two children, who were found not to be HD-gene carriers: "And just this; somebody telling you that you will not be afflicted, or that you will come down with it. Ok, but what does that really mean? That I will develop it. Or that I will not get it?"

Due to the abstract and invisible character of our genes, the result of the predictive test could not be attached to something obvious and concrete. This basic condition, which is an intrinsic aspect of predictive genetic testing, made it difficult for the affected individuals to create a stable and coherent understanding of their test result and of their genetic status.

Carla's thoughts are significant in those instances when the test result showed that the genome did contain the mutant HD gene.

The first meeting that I had with Patricia took place at the public library in her hometown, and there was nothing in her appearance that gave away that she was a gene-carrier for HD. For me she seemed to be perfectly healthy, with no trace of anything near HD. However, when we later met for conducting an in-depth interview Patricia told me about the symptoms that she in fact could perceive. These symptoms resembled those she had encountered during her childhood and her adolescence, when she and the rest of the family were faced with Peter's mood swings:

> Yes, it's this... exactly. These somewhat unbalanced [mood swings]; I can get really, really angry. But that's it, as I said previously and today I can say the same, I can get really angry but there's people who become furious and can get wild without having HD (...). But there's this extra dimension, it's hard to explain but it's this extra dimension, so to speak.

In this quote, Patricia identified her own mood swings as abnormal. She could perceive a difference, an extra dimension, which set apart the way she reacted and what she saw as a normal type of reaction. However, in relation to the presence or non-presence of symptoms there was also ambivalence in her experiences; this became apparent at a later stage in the interview when Patricia talked about the test result and about things that were actually happening to her. Things that might be clear signs of the disease:

> I feel both relieved and afraid. Yeah, I'm relieved because I feel just like anybody else, I feel energetic and... well, no problems at all. But at the same time I'm really scared because I feel and sometimes I can think: Oh, shit there's actually something that is happening with me.

Up to this point in the interview, I noticed how Patricia had been composed when she talked about HD and her difficult situation. I knew from our initial meeting at the public library that she was quite used to talking about the disease, but at this point the emotions were coming through and she started to cry slowly. Something was happening to her. Despite the fact that she felt healthy, she also sensed that something was actually going on inside her body. Ambiguous bodily signs that she had not been able to grasp up to this point were now marking their presence in her everyday life. Patricia's experiences might also be associated with Jimmy's statement about not being able to really fathom the abstract process whereby his genome was found to be free from the HD gene. The only experience that Jimmy had about this process was his blood sample from which his DNA was extracted. For Patricia, the discovery that her genome did contain the HD gene was similarly a knowledge that had its origins in the same abstract and remote technological process. This remote technological process revealed that she sooner or later would develop a disease with a pathological appearance that was still quite intangible with her appearance of being a healthy individual.

The two quotes showed that Patricia, despite the knowledge she had about her genetic status, still experienced her situation as being betwixt-and-between normality and abnormality. A similar observation is made by Konrad who means that "the classificatory line between the categories of the pre-symptomatic and the symptomatic resists unambiguous differentiation as separate diagnostic entities" (2005: 81). This kind of collapse of classificatory lines is also observed in conjunction with other medical conditions, where Forss, Tishelman, Widmark, and Sachs report that women who are notified of having cellular abnormalities when screened for cervical cancer are projected into a "liminal state" where "neither health nor disease was confirmed or excluded" (2004: 307). Undergoing predictive genetic testing offered no direct possibility for the affected individuals to clarify themselves as normal or abnormal with respect to HD. Instead of a clarification of their classificatory status, it seemed that both carriers and non-carriers stayed within the liminal space despite the knowledge offered by the predictive genetic test.

To be exposed to this liminal space with its cultural paradox may not only have caused an emotional effect on those who are situated within the liminal space. It may also pose a radical challenge to the Western biomedical notion of the patient as someone who demonstrates a clear and unambiguous cluster of detectable signs and symptoms (Konrad 2005: 82; Sachs 1995: 504). This later aspect came forward in the ethnographic interviews, and it did so mainly in relation to the diagnosis of HD. Currently, the formal HD diagnosis is made when clear motor symptoms appear, a circumstance that Patricia objected against:

> Ok, now they're calling me a gene-carrier. But who is saying that? And who has the right to say that, you know? Saying that from now on you're unwell. From now on, although up to that day when somebody says that you're afflicted you're only a gene-carrier. It kind of feels like that I'm not included.

Despite the situation of being betwixt-and-between normality and abnormality, Patricia still made a claim for the power over those classifications that ultimately define her as afflicted or not afflicted with HD. According to Patricia, this power was not to be held by the medical expertise alone, but should also be granted to the affected individuals. Patricia's reaction illustrates how this cultural paradox not only has an impact on the everyday life of the affected individuals, but how it also contains a struggle over definitions and interpretations between those who are situated within this liminal space and various experts.

In the previous sections, I have shown how the abstract and elusive character of our genes give rise to a liminal space within which the affected individuals are situated as a consequence of being at risk for developing HD. To be situated within this liminal space give rise to intuitions, emotions and actions among the affected individuals that include fluctuation between the present and an anticipated future in their everyday life. From a cultural perspective, these responses and actions on behalf of the affected individuals are seen as a result of a cultural paradox that arise from a juxtaposition of normality and abnormality within this liminal space. Undergoing predictive genetic testing does not appear to resolve this situation. Despite the knowledge of their genetic status, revealed through the predictive genetic test, the affected individuals are still situated within this liminal space with its juxtaposition of normality and abnormality. As a consequence of this juxtaposition, the boundaries that separate the categories of being at risk for HD, being a pre-symptomatic gene carrier or being symptomatic and afflicted with HD are dissolved in the everyday life of the affected individuals.

As the possibilities of making various disease predictions on the basis of genetic and genomic knowledge expand, the issues that have been investigated above might apply to a far greater number of individuals than those who are affected by HD. In relation to this expansion, the proclaimed right on behalf of those who are situated within this liminal space to define the boundaries of normality and abnormality raises questions regarding the relationship between lay people, medical expertise and the health-care system.

Genetic Preventions in Mainstream Health Care

Currently, genetics is partly transformed from being a diagnostic tool, used in the presence of clear and visible symptoms, to a predictive and preventive tool. When this predictive tool is implemented in mainstream health care, the cultural paradox that was accounted for in previous sections can become relevant in relation to other diseases as well. Preventing a disease might of course imply finding a cure, but today prevention has also taken on another meaning, which according to Nikolas Rose aims at making the future "the subject of calculation and the object of remedial intervention" (2007: 19). A central point in this undertaking is to clarify the consequences of a harmful lifestyle, as well as to provide behavioural choices for people so that individuals can make informed decisions on matters of health and health-related behaviour. Here, the growing understanding of genetics and genomics is seen as a significant contribution (Human Genomics Strategy Group 2012: 34). The two citations given in the introduction showed how the prospect of genetic prediction is framed by medical expertise in terms of offering the individual citizen access to a powerful source of information in order to maintain or restore health. This desire for a future, open for calculation and medical intervention, can also be seen in economic terms, as the state tries to release itself from some of the responsibilities of the consequences of illness and accident that it acquired during the twentieth century (Rose 2007: 19, 63). In this cultural and political setting, every citizen is required to take an active role for securing his or her well-being (2007: 63).

An increased knowledge about the role of genetics and genomics in relation to disease offers great potential for alleviating suffering in various conditions. For a number of these diseases, such as cancer, preventive efforts and early detection is crucial in order for medicine to be applied to save lives. However, a realization of this potential depends, as noted by the Human Genomics Strategy Group, on "public trust in the application of technologies in diagnosis and treatment" (Human Genomics Strategy Group 2012: 79). An important measure in order to safeguard public engagement and trust in the use of genetics and genomics is education of the public on issues relating to genetics and genomics (Human Genomics Strategy Group 2012: 79). However, the relationship between scientific expertise and lay people also depends upon the acknowledgement of interpretative differences between the two groups. Sociologist and STS-scholar Brian Wynne makes the critical remark that expertise of all sorts often "tacitly and furtively impose prescriptive models of the human and the social upon lay people" and that these prescriptive models are "implicitly found wanting in human terms" (1996: 57). The critique of Wynne is directed towards conceptions of lay people in which their response towards expertise is seen in terms of a rational-calculative model. The main critique made by Wynne towards this model concerns the way it put too much emphasis on cognitive dimensions at the expense of the cultural dimensions of public response to expertise (Durant 2008: 7). Instead, all prescriptive models on the relationship between lay people and expertise have to acknowledge the "need to recognize hermeneutical differences" (Wynne 2008: 22) which might arise and even diversify the relationship between scientific expertise and lay people.

Predictive genetic testing for HD harbours, as shown by the ethnographic interviews, a cultural paradox in relation to classifications where the invisible "alien" inside give rise to intuitions, emotions and actions that are quite far removed from those rational and calculative approaches that are envisioned in the citations in the introduction. The ethnographic interviews reported in this article also showed that knowledge about whether the participants did or did not carry the mutated HD gene did not totally resolve these hermeneutical differences. Even though the knowledge provided by the predictive test resolved the issue of the participants' genetic status, there still seemed to exist a hermeneutical difference in relation to the question of normality and abnormality. This difference points towards the challenges that reside in conjunction with a large-scale implementation of genetic tests in the health-care system, since notions of genetic risks and genetic status seldom contain neutral aspects. This absence of neutrality continued to mark its presence in the empirical material on HD, despite the fact that the predictive genetic test itself provided a clear-cut answer about the genetic status of the participants. Furthermore, these challenges concern not only those who are directly involved, patients and medical expertise, but also those social and cultural scientists who study the scientific development within genetics and genomics from various disciplinary viewpoints.

In relation to these differences between lay people and scientific expertise, the importance of an establishment of a mutual framework becomes a crucial measure in order to avoid a diversification and alienation on behalf of those affected. These mutual frameworks have to acknowledge the multiplicity of meanings, viewpoints and practices that exists in relation to predictive genetic testing, as well as the informational requirements generated by this multiplicity (Bowker & Star 2000: 297). The establishment of such a common framework between lay people and scientific experts would make predictive genetic testing and disease prevention sustainable if it is to become part of future mainstream health care.

Notes

1 Huntington's disease is caused by a mutation in the HD gene and the pattern of inheritance is autosomal dominant, which means that a child of an affected parent has a 50% risk of inheriting the mutated gene (Huntington's Disease Collaborative Research Group 1993). In Sweden, the prevalence of HD is about 1/17,000 individuals (Kristoffersson 2010: 94), which means that there is about 1,000 individuals who are diagnosed and afflicted with HD. The disease is characterized by a combination of neurological, psychiatric and cognitive symptoms. In general, the onset of the neurological symptoms appear at an age of between 35 to 45 years, and the progression of the disease always leads to death within 15–20 years after the onset of the neurological symptoms (Ross & Tabrizi 2011). The formal clinical diagnosis is based on the presence of unequivocal signs of motor dysfunction (Huntington Study Group 1996). These neurological symptoms include disturbances in the movements of the afflicted person, mainly causing involuntary movements. The psychiatric symptoms of HD, which most often are present before the onset of the neurological symptoms, include personality changes, irritability and aggressive behaviour, as well as depression (Johnson et al. 2007; Julien et al. 2007). HD also includes cognitive disturbances including deficits in attention that progress to dementia in the later stages of the disease (Stout 2010).

2 The concept of risk has been crucial in relation to genetic diseases; it has been investigated from a wide range of disciplinary approaches (e.g., Shostak, Zarhin & Ottman 2011; Lock & Nguyen 2010; Etchegary 2009; Hallowell et al. 2004; Cox & McKellin 1999; Kessler & Bloch 1989).

3 Eligible participants in the study were those who in various ways have come in close contact with HD. Participants were recruited through advertisements on the Internet, as well as through personal visits made by the author to various meetings for HD affected individuals held by patient organizations. HD is a sensitive and difficult topic for many of those who are affected. Consequently, the decision was taken to let the number of participants included in the study be based only upon those individuals who the author came in contact with as a result of these advertisements and personal visits. These individuals were then sent additional information (including the form for informed consent) and

were also given time to further reflect on their participation and on the informed consent. Semi-structured interviews were performed with eleven participants at a place of their choice, and the interviews lasted between 1.5 and 2.5 hours. An interview guide was employed for the interviews, but used in such flexible way that the interviewees could go into various aspects regarding their experiences of HD on their own terms. All interviews were recorded by the use of a digital voice recorder, and all interviews were subsequently transcribed *in verbatim*, and each transcript was then read and re-read until a number of themes were identified in the transcript. All citations from the interviews used in this article have not been altered into grammatically correct English, but kept in their original format.

References

Åkesson, L. 1991: *De ovanligas betydelse*. Stockholm: Carlssons bokförlag.

Åkesson, L. 1999: Selection and Perfection – Modern Genetics and the Alien Inside. In: S. Lundin & L. Åkesson, *Amalgamations – Fusing Technology and Culture*. Lund: Nordic Academic Press.

Alftberg, Å. 2012: *Vad är det att åldras*. Lund: Lund University, Department of Arts and Cultural Sciences.

Björkegren, J., M. Nilbert & A.-C. Syvänen 2010: Avdramatisera DNA-testerna. In: *Svenska Dagbladet*. www.svd.se/opinion/brannpunkt/avdramatisera-dna-testerna_5521935.svd. Accessed January 16, 2012.

Bowker, G.C. & S.L. Star 2000: *Sorting Things Out – Classification and its Consequences*. Cambridge: MIT Press.

Brouwer-DudokdeWit, A.C., A. Savenije, M.W. Zoeteweij, A. Maat-Kievit, A. Tibben 2002: A Hereditary Disorder in the Family and the Family Life-Cycle: Huntington Disease as a Paradigm. *Family Process* 41:4, 677–692.

Browner, C.H. & H.M Preloran 2010: *Neurogenetic Diagnoses, the Power of Hope, and the Limits of Today's Medicine*. London: Routledge.

Cox, S.M. & W. McKellin 1999: There's this Thing in our Family: Predictive Testing and the Construction of Risk for Huntington Disease. *Sociology of Health & Illness* 21:5, 622–646.

Douglas, M. 1966: *Purity and Danger: An Analysis of Concepts of Pollution and Taboo*. London & Henley: Routledge & Keegan Paul.

Durant, D. 2008: Accounting for Expertise: Wynne and the Autonomy of the Lay Public Actor. *Public Understanding of Science* 17, 5–20.

Etchegary, H. 2009: Coping with Genetic Risk: Living with Huntington Disease (HD). *Current Psychology* 28, 284–301.

Forss, A., C. Tishelman, C. Widmark & L. Sachs 2004: Women's Experiences of Cervical Cellular Changes: An Unintentional Transition from Health to Liminality? *Sociology of Health & Illness* 26:3, 305–325.

Foucault, M. 2000: *Essential Works of Foucault, 1954–1984. Vol. 3 Power*. In: J.D. Faubion (ed.). New York: The New Press.

Foucault, M. 2002: *The Order of Things: An Archaeology of the Human Sciences*. London: Routledge.

Fox-Keller, E. 2010: *The Mirage of a Space between Nature and Nurture*. Durham: Duke University Press.

Frykman, J. 1993: *Horan i bondesamhället*. Stockholm: Carlssons bokförlag.

Hacking, I. 2002: *Historical Ontology*. Harvard: Harvard University Press.

Hallowell, N., N. Foster, R. Eeles, A. Ardern-Jones & M. Watson 2004: Accommodating Risk: Responses to *BRCA 1/2* Genetic Testing of Women who have Cancer. *Social Science & Medicine* 59, 553–565.

Hanson, K. 2007: *I ett andetag – En kulturanalys av astma som begränsning och möjlighet*. Stockholm: Critical Ethnography Press.

Human Genomics Strategy Group 2012: *Building on our Inheritance – Genomic Technology in the Healthcare*. www.dh.gov.uk/prod_consum_dh/groups/dh_digitalassets/@dh/@en/documents/digitalasset/dh_132382.pdf. Accessed January 25, 2012.

Huntington Study Group 1996: Unified Huntington's Disease Rating Scale: Reliability and Consistency. *Movement Disorders* 11:2, 136–142.

Huntington's Disease Collaborative Research Group 1993: A Novel Gene Containing a Trinucleotide Repeat that is Expanded and Unstable on Huntington's Disease Chromosomes. *Cell* 72, 971–983.

Johnson, S.A., J.C. Stout, A.C. Solomon, D.R. Langbehn, E.H. Aylward, C.B. Cruce, C.A. Ross, M. Nance, E. Kayson, E. Julian-Baros, M.R. Hayden, K. Kieburtz, M. Guttman, D. Oakes, I. Shoulson, L. Beglinger, K. Duff, E. Penziner, J. S. Paulsen & the Predict-HD Investigators of the Huntington Study Group 2007: Beyond Disgust: Impaired Recognition of Negative Emotions Prior to Diagnosis in Huntington's Disease. *Brain* 130:7, 1732–1744.

Julien, C.L., J.C. Thompson, S. Wild, P. Yardumian, J.S. Snowden, G. Turner & D. Craufurd 2007: Psychiatric Disorders in Preclinical Huntington's Disease. *Journal of Neurology, Neurosurgery & Psychiatry* 78:9, 939–943.

Kavanagh, A.M. & D.H. Broom 1998: Embodied Risk: My Body, Myself? *Social Science & Medicine* 46, 437–444.

Kessler, S. & M. Bloch 1989: Social System Responses to Huntington Disease. *Family Practice* 28, 59–68.

Klein, B. 1989: Ett eftermiddagssamtal hos Elsa. In: B. Ehn & B. Klein (eds.), *Etnologiska beskrivningar*. Stockholm: Carlsson.

Kleinman, A. 1997: *Writing at the Margin*. Berkeley: University of California Press.

Konrad, M. 2005: *Narrating the New Predictive Genetics*. Cambridge: Cambridge University Press.

Kristoffersson, U. 2010: *Genetik och Genteknik – nya utmaningar för hälso- och sjukvården*. Lund: Studentlitteratur.

Lock, M.M. & V.-K. Nguyen 2010: *An Anthropology of Biomedicine*. Chichester: Wiley-Blackwell.

Lundin, S. 1997: *Guldägget – Föräldraskap i biomedicinens tid*. Lund: Historiska Media.

Lundin, S. & L. Åkesson 2000: Arvets kultur. In: S. Lundin & L. Åkesson (eds.), *Arvets kultur – Essäer om genetik och samhälle*. Lund: Nordic Academic Press.

Lupton, D. 1995: *The Imperative of Health: Public Health and the Regulated Body*. London: Sage.

Nelkin, D. & L. Tancredi 1994: *Dangerous Diagnostics: The Social Power of Biological Information*. Chicago: The University of Chicago Press.

Nelkin, D. & S.M. Lindee 2004: *The DNA Mystique: The Gene as a Cultural Icon*. Ann Arbor: The University of Michigan Press.

Petersen, A. & R. Bunton 2002: *The New Genetics and the Public's Health*. London: Routledge.

Petersén, Å. 2001: *Effects of Dopamine and Excitotoxicity in Experimental Models of Huntington's Disease*. Lund: Wallenberg Neurocenter, Faculty of Medicine.

Rose, N. 2007: *The Politics of Life Itself*. Princeton: Princeton University Press.

Ross, C.A. & S.J. Tabrizi 2011: Huntington's Disease: From Molecular Pathogenesis to Clinical Treatment. *Lancet Neurology* 10, 83–98.

Sachs, L. 1995: Is there a Pathology of Prevention? The Implications of Visualizing the Invisible in Screening Programs. *Culture, Medicine and Psychiatry* 19, 503–525.

Schlich, T. 2004: Objectifying Uncertainty: History of Risk Concepts in Medicine. *Topoi* 23, 211–219.

Shostak, S. 2010: Marking Populations and Persons at Risk: Molecular Epidemiology and Environmental Health. In: E.C. Adele, L. Mamo, J.R. Fosket, J.R. Fishman & J.K. Shim (eds.), *Biomedicalization – Technoscience, Health and Illness in the U.S.* Durham: Duke University Press 2010.

Shostak, S., D. Zarhin & R. Ottman 2011: What's at Stake? Genetic Information from the Perspective of People with Epilepsy and their Family Members. *Social Science & Medicine* 73, 645–654.

Smith, J.A., P. Flowers & M. Larkin 2009: *Interpretative Phenomenological Analysis: Theory, Method and Research*. London: Sage.

Socialstyrelsen 2012: http://www.socialstyrelsen.se/rarediseases/huntingtondisease. Accessed September 8, 2012.

Stout, J.C. 2010: Neurocognitive Signs in Prodromal Huntington Disease. *Neuropsychology* 25:1, 1–14.

Tibben, A. 2007: Predictive Testing for Huntington's Disease. *Brain Research Bulletin* 72, 165–171.

Turner, V. 1977: Variations on a Theme of Liminality. In: S. Falk & B.G. Myerhoff (ed.), *Secular Ritual*. Assen, Amsterdam: Van Gorcum.

Turner, V. 1979: Frame, Flow and Reflection: Ritual and Drama as Public Liminality. *Japanese Journal of Religious Studies* 6:4, 465–499.

Wynne, B. 1996: May the Sheep Safely Graze: A Reflexive View of the Expert-Lay Knowledge Divide. In: S. Lash, B. Szerszynski & B. Wynne (eds.), *Risk, Environment and Modernity: Towards a New Ecology*. London: Sage.

Wynne, B. 2008: Elephants in the Rooms where Publics Encounter "Science"? A Response to Darrin Durant, "Accounting for Expertise: Wynne and the Autonomy of the Lay Public". *Public Understanding of Science* 17, 21–33.

Niclas Hagen is a Ph.D. student of ethnology at the Department of Arts and Cultural Sciences, Lund University. His research is focused on cultural and social aspects of biomedicine, with a particular interest in genetics and neuroscience. He is the co-author (with Bo Isenberg) of *The Manifestation of Modernity in Genetic Science* (2011).
(Niclas.Hagen@kultur.lu.se)

SENSING POST-FORDIST WORK LIFE
Recent Perspectives in the Ethnography of Work

Irene Götz

The article discusses the transition from Fordism to post-Fordism in the world of work and at the same time pleads for a critical reflection on the use of these concepts. It presents three German case studies conducted under the supervision of the author, which examine how this transition is experienced very differently: by mothers using managerial techniques of parenting, independent financial advisers, and manual workers in a picture-frame factory. The mothers see the changes as a challenge, the financial advisers as an opportunity, and the manual workers as a threat. Thus, ethnographic case studies in this field highlighting the diversity of work in the post-Fordist era enbable us to go beyond discourses that treat Fordism and post-Fordism as clearly separated and holistic entities.

Keywords: transformation of work, Fordism, post-Fordism, work ethnography, economization of work and life

All spheres of present-day society are affected profoundly by the post-Fordist world of work and the economization and commodification of social relationships. Arlie Russell Hochschild (2003) has demonstrated how commercial considerations have been shaping the modes of action and the patterns of feeling characterizing "private" life for some time. This has contributed to the fusion of the "private" and the "public" sphere: The "coaching" of families by professional advisers increasingly resembles the management strategies pursued in the world of business. For example, it is quite common for "coaches" to ask families to carry out "team-building exercises" and "evaluate" the behavior of individual family members. Conversely, corporations are adopting "pedagogic and therapeutic discourses" originally developed in closed, personal, therapeutic settings. In doing so, they transform intimate aspects of personhood into instruments of leadership (cf. Illouz 2006: 43).

The following case study illuminates this state of affairs. It presents the work of Petra Schmidt, a Munich-based European Ethnologist, who has interviewed German working and non-working mothers from middle-class, liberal milieus.[1] Schmidt's work represents one of the three case studies presented in this paper. They emerged out of a Munich-based research project on "Spätmoderne Arbeits- und Lebenswelten" that examined the great variety of attitudes and practices of different groups of workers trying to cope with the challenges resulting from recent changes in work organization.[2] Informed by the complexity and ambiguity of the three cases, I will discuss both the key characteristics of the transition from Fordism to post-Fordism in the world of work and the shortcomings of the debates in the social sciences around this issue. If focused on the perspectives of actors on the shop floor and linked up with macro-contextual "structuring structures" in the sense of Pierre Bourdieu et al. (1997), ethnographic work can serve as an important research tool that allows us to reflect critically on and transcend dichotomous understandings of Fordism and post-Fordism. Starting with Schmidt's case study allows me to highlight some of the key characteristics ascribed to "post-Fordism".

On "Total Quality Mothers", the "Family Team", and "Training for the Job" from the Start

"Do your best!" – this is how Carla tends to challenge her six-year-old when he "once again 'deviates' from the social norm". She is a Munich-based mother of two boys, who are of pre-school age. Due to the recurring conflicts with her older son, Carla has decided to seek advice and practical help. Once a week, she is taking part in a "coaching program for parents" (Schmidt 2012: 160).

The market for parenting advice and education is currently expanding; the program in question is based on an elaborate regime of knowledge contributing to the optimization and professionalization of motherhood and parenthood. It relies on a system of rewards derived from "total quality management", a corporate strategy from Japan based on quality assurance and self-management[3]: There are constantly recurring demands for improved work ("continuous improvement"), which are meant to motivate the employees to perform at the highest level and to create a feeling of community. This strategy is based on a behaviorist system of rewards aimed at making the employees internalize management guidelines and motivate themselves.

The corresponding parenting program aims at implanting the principle of "continuous improvement" in the actions and thoughts of a child. As Schmidt puts it:

> The feedback provided has a supporting function. Vinzent gets it from his parents in the form (...) of small daily rewards, for example star-stickers and gummi bears. Once a week, there is also an "extensive evaluation" based on a "stars chart". These evaluations are reminiscent of the weekly meetings held in corporations dedicated to quality assurance. This approach to parenting also focuses on the improvement of *social skills*; it governs everyday actions and thoughts. The weekly feedback (...) creates a feeling of unity in the family – of having achieved something together. It mobilizes a "family team" that constantly operates in the spirit of "wanting improvement and optimization". In particular, Carla's attempt to constantly optimize both her son's behavior and her own, knowledge-based parenting strategies reveals the socially dominant ideals and expectations concerning the "right" way of parenting. (Schmidt 2012: 160f.)

The program promises that the acquisition of social skills pays off in the long run. It turns parenting into the targeted promotion of *soft skills,* and into an activity providing "training for the job" from the start.

> In this context, a technology of government is at work that aims at activating the self of children, or – as Bröckling (2000: 131) puts it – at engaging in acts of "total mobilization", which are meant to use mental and physical resources the optimal way. Besides, the example reveals what kind of strategies of self-regulation, self-disciplining, self-rationalization and self-mobilization are influencing both the physical and the mental aspects of the conduct of life today. (Schmidt 2012: 162)

Schmidt's case study demonstrates how mothers (and sometimes fathers if they take an appropriate responsibility for family matters) have become health experts, dieticians, coaches dedicated to the advancement of the offspring, and mediators preserving peace in the family (cf. Schmidt & Götz 2010). This development began during the Enlightenment: it was declared the primary task of bourgeois women to engage in the parenting and the moral education of her children; they were seen as being better equipped than uneducated wet nurses and nannies to prepare the children for their future careers (cf. Rosenbaum 1982). Today, the work of mothers involves providing their children both with a warm shelter for their regeneration and a training camp for career instruction. In the knowledge society, this is a highly complex task: Mothers with upper middle-class backgrounds are required to continuously learn more and optimize their performance at work, but they are also responsible for the monitoring and active coaching of their children.

Post-Fordist Realities of Work: The Blurring of Work and Life

Some of the most important issues of post-Fordism are highlighted by this case study: the ever more acute *blurring of work and life*; the *economization of all areas of life* including children's rooms; the importance of *self-activation* and *knowledge work*; and the *transformation of life into a project* based on *independent re-training* and the *permanent optimization* of the use of resources. I will further elaborate on these issues by drawing upon work research in the social sciences and, primarily, in European ethnology.[4] The key terms informing the academic discourses – *flexibilization, subjectification, mobilization, and precarization* – can be seen as seismographs of the zeitgeist and the current social climate. And yet, as they are only broad and undifferentiated categories for complex processes of social transformation, they tend to produce simplistic interpretative patterns. This sometimes obstructs our view on the underlying, more differentiated worlds of experience. The categories can thus only be used as preliminary "holding concepts" with a heuristic function: They direct us towards research questions, which, however, have to be fleshed out with reference to each specific case.

If such a context-sensitive and casuistic approach is chosen, the categories help us decipher the practices, attitudes, values and conflicts of the individual actors entangled in the discourses and politics of the "new" world of work. This then reveals that "the" transition from Fordism to post-Fordism is not a linear process. People interpret and tackle the challenges arising due to the transformation of work in different ways depending on factors such as biographic experiences; education and qualification; class and gender; and professional habitus (cf. Schönberger 2007).

The article seeks to outline the contribution of ethnographic approaches to the inter-disciplinary field of work research and to critically reflect on some of the issues that public debates on the transformation of work refer to when they make implicit comparisons between "past" and "present", which are often presented as holistic entities without internal differentiation. In doing so, I will shift the focus of the debate and point out the challenges that we have to tackle: first, we have to develop a more differentiated understanding of periodization overcoming the strict separation between Fordism and post-Fordism; second, we have to move beyond "national" perspectives, which are often informed by the views of the "old" middle classes and the established, educated milieus.

Post-Fordism – both in its "objectified" essence and its meaning ascribed by the public and scientific discourses – is a comprehensive transformation project shaped and propelled by an aspiring middle class which promotes a new type of a "creative" and individualistic "entrepreneurial self" (Bröckling 2007). Post-Fordism is characterized by knowledge work, the ability to use the new information technologies efficiently, international corporations, transnational mobility, and an increasing number of freelancers working without the social protection and benefits offered by companies. As a result, there are profound changes to the prevalent conceptions of work: wage labor no longer creates communities and identities in the same way. Work and free time, work and non-work, blur and mix in terms of their contents, times, spaces and functions (Gottschall & Voß 2005; Herlyn et al. 2009).

Table soccer in an IT firm, the provision of massages and yoga classes in the workplace through the employer – these are examples of how feelings formally linked to free time such as well-being, recreation and relaxation have become constitutive elements of a new culture of work in and beyond the creative industries. In the designer offices of the professionals, spaces of autonomy, originally gained through worker resistance, overlap with the incentives provided by the company on the grounds of economic calculations. There is an *informalization* of work, which covers up its character of being work at all – at least in the ads of the companies (cf. Barth 2009). In many sectors of the expanding creative industries, circles of friends, customers and colleagues have become interwoven and now form new, productive networks.

Knowledge-based society needs and produces "immaterial labor" (Lazzarato 1998) more than ever; the creative workers, the PR agencies, the web designers and communications experts all become part of a new ensemble of leading industries. Certain characteristics of the subject – such as interpersonal skills, expertise in communication, and the independent development of ideas – become essential aspects of a new type of labor power. One example of this development is that the knowledge worker represents a new role model for mothers: they are supposed to keep on learning about ideal ways of boosting the career chances of their children; and to see their children as projects requiring the active investments of time and energy. Similarly, private companies and public institutions demand from their employees that they invest in personal traits and their "soft skills". On the other hand, employees – both skilled manual workers and service workers – increasingly demand that they be treated as independent actors with a stake in the business process.

This demand of a new type of labor power reflects a process of "dual subjectification" (cf. Kleemann, Matuschek & Voß 2003): on the one hand, subjectification is desired by the employees; on the other hand, it is molded by the company-owners according to their own goals. In any case, it is accompanied by the expansion of economic strategies into all areas of everyday life; the boundaries of wage labor become blurred, and work is increasingly separated from the firm. This is demonstrated by the example provided at the start of this article: the "total quality" mother. Günter Voß and Kerstin Rieder highlight another instance of this development: Online customers of retail companies (e.g., IKEA and Amazon) become unpaid "members of staff". They are "working customers" designing construction kits, or in other cases, compiling books or mixing organic mueslis online; they (are invited to) contribute to product marketing; and they participate in quality assurance for free by evaluating the services provided (Voß & Rieder 2005).

The separation of work from the firm can be observed everywhere; it is propelled, governed and shaped by the labor market policy of the welfare state in transformation (Lessenich 2008): the emergence of "enterprises of the self" (the official German category "Ich-AGs") (Witte 2007) and the state-driven expansion of temporary and precarious work are processes informed by a new role model: the "entrepreneur in labor power" (in German: *Arbeitskraftunternehmer*) (Pongratz & Voß 2004). This entrepreneur offers all the resources and capacities in his/her possession on the market – and does so without benefiting from the security provided by labor contracts. The most important capital of such precarious start-ups of "activated" freelancers, which are usually born out of poverty, is not a qualification obtained through formal education. It is a set of ideas and capacities that conform to the zeitgeist, can be presented in an alluring manner, and can be converted into a service. In the process, creativity is commodified in many different ways and becomes a business factor (cf. Löfgren 2003).

It seems that being such a creative "flexible human"[5] – and internalizing principles such as being mobile, taking risks, being service-oriented and constantly available for others – comes with a price. It becomes increasingly difficult (and, in some cases, less desirable) for people in the Western world to achieve the security of clearly defined, long-term careers and of relatively stable living conditions.

But what is the temporal and spatial horizon, the vantage point of the discourses of post-Fordist mobilization and precarization (Castel & Dörre 2009; Götz & Lemberger 2009)? This question is relevant no matter how we see the transformation of work

– whether we speak of a "corrosion of character" (Sennett 1998) or greet this transformation enthusiastically as a liberation from the shackles of Fordist routine and alienation (see, e.g., Friebe & Lobo 2006). In other words, it is necessary to reflect on some of the values and institutions that characterized the "golden age" of the welfare state in the West and greatly influenced the habitus of employees with a middle-class background and their families (as well as working-class people to some extent). According to this habitus, certain achievements of Fordism and the conveniences of modern life are taken for granted, and they have given rise to a value system that has informed the common sense of the middle classes for decades. This value system forms the backdrop against which the transformation of work life is examined most of the time.

Assessing the Transformation of Values and Life Courses: Fordism as a Vantage Point and a Background of Analysis

Concerning the ideological basis and the vantage point of current evaluations of post-Fordism, there is one issue that should be considered first: Up until the 1980s, it was still possible for large parts of the male population to build on a biographical narrative based on the breadwinner model and the principle of working permanently in a single job – of having a career without ruptures. In the post-Fordist era, the dominant forms of work and life and the corresponding narratives on work biographies have changed. According to Ulrich Beck (1986), "risk society" is characterized by processes of detraditionalization and precarization, as well as by a tendency for the economization and rationalization of work and life. As a result, the traditional notion of a "normal biography" characterized by three phases becomes questionable. As long as the standardized, disciplinary system of Fordism[6] dominated, large parts of the population could expect "conventionalized" biographical transitions and a certain degree of upward social mobility. The first phase of the "normal biography", childhood and adolescence, was marked by the suspension of learning (the German "Bildungsmoratorium"). This was followed by a long phase of waged work and rearing children. The final phase was the pension age, which roughly coincided with the last third of life. Of course, it needs to be stressed that this was a male biography.

The predominance of a *gendered labor market* equating the "normal family" with the breadwinner model was another hallmark of Fordism. It centered the work biographies of women on motherhood. Accordingly, female occupational profiles resembled domestic work, were badly paid, and offered no opportunities for training and career advancement (cf. Beck-Gernsheim 1976). We all know that this has not changed much, as is demonstrated, for example, by the occupational profiles of nurses (Schweiger 2011), shop assistants (Götz 1997; Krohn 2008) and hairdressers (Braun 2013). In the decades before the cultural revolution of 1968, the breadwinner model required middle-class women to refrain from "working for real"; it was deemed unsuitable to work outside the family home. Undoubtedly, this model had (and still has) certain attractions for some parts of the population.

Historically speaking, the post-war period marked the first time when even manual workers could orient themselves towards this model – at least in some of the European welfares states of the late 1950s to the 1970s. This Fordist era was characterized by a relatively high level of productivity, and the "social integration of the working class in terms of wages, work hours and prices" (Schönberger 2007: 66); affluence and the new opportunities for consumption had strong, integrating effects. In this context, some people speak of "Deutschmark nationalism" in relation to West Germany. Considering the anti-national mood in the country after the war, this was the only real form of national identification in everyday life – maybe with the exception of sports (Götz 2011).

However, the traditional order of gender-specific "normal biographies" characterized by a three-phase life cycle has eroded in the post-Fordist era, even if it still informs current debates and personal career expectations to a certain degree. "Normal biographies" are now marked by the increased importance, in quantitative and qualitative terms, of its two extremes: the phase of adolescence has become longer, and the same applies to old age (it takes longer, but if "employability" is considered, it also starts earlier). The changes in the labor market and the corresponding role models, which prescribe and consolidate these changes, are responsible for this state of affairs.

Due to the labor market strategies of business and increasingly shorter working lives, the middle phase of life is transformed – consider old-age part-time working and the complete de-valuation of people over 50 in some branches, who end up in permanent unemployment. And yet, the dominant economic and labor-market policies suggest that this is not affordable over the medium-term due to demographic change and the resulting lack of suitable workers. As a result, the pension age is raised gradually.

In sum, work continues to determine and to structure the life cycle. But in contrast to the Fordist era, it is no longer certain how exactly this happens, and what the effects are. Long-term plans are increasingly surrounded by uncertainty, which also affects the middle classes; the qualifications, occupations, careers around which people used to develop personal plans become unstable. The identities, plans (including family planning[7]), and social ties of the "flexible human" (Sennett 1998) are challenged through forms of work that require dealing with multi-level mobility, the threat of redundancy and the according biographical ruptures. Many of the people whose habitus was shaped in the Fordist era are ill-prepared for these changes – at least according to the cultural pessimists contributing to this discourse (see, e.g., Sennett 1998; Schultheis 2007; Voß 2009).

Along these lines, Richard Sennett displays a deep discontent with the inhumane nature of "flexible capitalism". According to him, the "defensive community" sought by "the flexible human" as a shelter against the trials of insecure labor relations has nothing in common with the Fordist communities, which were characterized by production and creative resistance. Sennett (1998) remarks pointedly that late modern capitalism has cut people's ties to the location. He comments, in a slightly stern and pessimistic manner, on the changed meaning of the relationship between space and work in the global economy, which is characterized by fluid movements that are driven by financial markets. The mobilities related to jobs, commodities, and humans – as well as the processes of deterritorialization linked to them – are both a precondition and a by-product of globalization. However, they exist alongside new personal strategies of striking roots and multiple forms of becoming part of a community; there are plural practices of constructing and combining old and new homelands (see Seifert 2010). And the so-called "normal (nuclear) family", whose death has been announced frequently, has simply changed its shape. The traditional family is replaced by plural forms; multi-locality and blurred gender roles have – to a certain degree – become a manageable, "normal" pattern.

Importantly, my line of argument should not be understood as contrasting the "inhumanity" and "cruelty" of post-Fordism with an idyllic, sheltered pre-industrial world or with a safe, predictable, and affluent work and family life under Fordism. It is common knowledge that the rigid community of the village shackled the life of the individual, and that monotonous work in fixed groups can be straining. However, in one respect, Sennett is right: The precarization of work and the corresponding processes of disembedding and exclusion may lead to defensive, even destructive forms of community-building that (re-)produce oppressive ideologies and violence: Empirical studies on East Germany reveal the link between the rise of neo-Nazi organizations and processes of precarization and social disintegration. The people in the areas affected are immobilized; and they compensate for this state of affairs by creating communities that exclude "foreigners" (cf. Dörre 2006).

There is a second aspect of current debates in the media, which confirms Richard Sennett's verdict that there is a *change in the dominant norms*. According to him, dependency and routines are de-valued in the moral sense of the word. Undoubtedly, terms like "activation", "mobilization", "flexibilization", "responsibility", "risk" and "creativity" act as contemporary strategies of "self-government and the government of others", in certain situations, they are producing a type of rationality that then becomes hegemonic (cf. Bröckling, Krasmann & Lemke 2004: 9f.): the imperative of "activation" serves to legitimize and justify the transformation of the welfare state into an "activating" state (Lessenich 2008); according to this discourse, dependent people are "redundant people" (Bauman 1997) – they are not just weak but also "parasitic". Recipients of "Hartz IV" (a benefit recently introduced in Germany providing a basic income) are time and again attacked as "benefit scroungers" (cf. Lehnert 2009). This is the flipside of the existence of a young, creative, urban milieu enthusiastically embracing the "end of jobs for life" (Friebe & Lobo 2006) and transforming it into a new, possibly temporary freedom. On the macro-level of discourse, a narrative of independence and mobility prevails. According to Sennett (1998), this narrative undermines two of the foundations of social ties: mutual trust and the commitment to a common goal, which result from the recognition of reciprocal dependence and the ability to enter conflicts. Due to the existence of trans-local companies and the changing places of business, flexible practices of power prevent the creation of productive forms of trust, which also means that human beings become more vulnerable.

In her work from the early 1980s, Arlie Russell Hochschild pointed out another aspect of this vulnerability – even deformation of the personality – associated with post-Fordism. She enquired into the psychological cost of a new and very subtle form of alienation affecting people's character traits by studying the work of "flight attendants" and "bill collectors" (Hochschild 1983; see Götz 2013). In particular, this type of alienation is experienced by people working in post-Fordist, service sector jobs. In interactions with customers, they have to marketize their feelings, conduct, and entire outward appearance. In other words, they have to shape their emotional display and physical appearance according to certain "feeling rules", and to ensure that the customers are not able to decode this "marketized" version of the self and the business interests behind it. The potential consequences of working on an "authentic" demeanor, in particular the alienation experienced in this process, have to be covered up.

In this context, "alienation" refers to the fact that the service workers have to repress stress and "unsuitable" feelings like anger when they are interacting with customers – under conditions of an extreme intensification of work. The extraction of labor power becomes a permanent process without limits. If we use traditional images of the body, this process of extraction today targets the *inside*, the feelings and, importantly, the immaterial field of knowledge – and not so much the *outside*, the "routinized" body movements that used to be associated with industrial work. Accordingly, the symptoms of work-related medical conditions change. The "exhausted self" (Keupp 2010), the burn-out as a stage on the long way into depression, increasingly affects service workers and mothers of young children. It can be kept secret for some time – in contrast to the physical strain of industrial work, which quickly imprinted itself on the bodies of the workers and hence was visible at a young age.

An Ethnographic Approach: The Munich Case Studies on Work Life

In the last sections, I have sketched some characteristics of Fordism and post-Fordism that are ascribed to these "eras" at the level of discourse. However, these characteristics infiltrate different contexts of work and life in profoundly different ways. Ethnographic case studies allow us to depict the perspective of individual actors and their positions in the social space (cf. Bourdieu et al. 1997), and to relate the practices, strategies, and values of individual actors to the structural conditions of a certain regime of work. They demonstrate in how far this particular regime creates a work culture that fuses Fordist and post-Fordist elements in new and surprising ways. It may very well be that young, educated, and creative networkers can turn the imperative of activation into something positive. However, there is also a differentiated, constantly changing panorama of novel activities in the expanding service sector that are precarious and only exist temporarily. In this context, the threat of an "end to permanent employment" (Friebe & Lobo 2006) is accompanied by economic and emotional crises: the blurring of work and life and the corresponding forms of self-management are experienced as a burden – and they trigger resistance.

Case studies also have the advantage that they provide deep insights into such strategies and practices of individual *commitment* or (situational) *resistance* against the demands created by post-Fordist processes of workplace restructuring. In doing so, case studies are an appropriate heuristic means of assessing the validity and relevance of the "master narratives" of precarization, flexibiliziation and subjectification with regard to particular sectors, vocations and milieus. Moreover, ethnographic fieldwork also allows us to learn about how individuals are still bound by the Fordist habitus and value system and therefore get into conflict with the new work conditions. And they draw our attention to other cases and milieus where the processes of subjectification and flexibilization as well as the blurring of work and life are experienced as a challenge. Here, case studies potentially work as a kind of "laboratory" enabling us to observe the emergence of a new habitus and type of worker.

The question how the new work-related role models affect different industries and milieus was addressed by the Munich-based ethnographic research project mentioned above (cf. Götz, Huber & Kleiner 2010). For several months, twelve young ethnographers carried out interviews and participant observations in different fields – in agencies and task forces; in offices and companies; in welfare services catering for the "primary" and for the "secondary" labor market. Everywhere, the transformation of labor markets was visible – and so was the current economic and financial crisis.

The case studies were about understanding the logics of action produced by milieu, gender and occupation, and about revealing habitual orientations and practices contributing to the cultures of post-Fordist work. Accordingly, the following case study focuses on the professional habitus of independent financial advisers. It brings to light the mental dispositions, evaluations, rationalities and practices specific to this field, which informed the reactions of the advisers to the emergence of the current financial crisis.

The "Trust-Building Work" of Financial Advisers

Thomas J. Heid produced portraits of a number of independent financial advisers. He examined how they informed their customers about the financial crisis, how they coped with the damage to the reputation of their occupation, and how they saw their own future. In the interviews, the advisers treated him like a customer, informed and convinced him regarding their services, which enabled him to reflect on their conventional practices of interacting with their clients. In order to find out about the professional habitus of the advisers, Heid examined the self-stylizations of the advisers and the contradictions emerging in interaction, taking in account their dress style, the design of their offices, and the glossy leaflets provided to the customers.

Heid's portraits revealed the strategies, practices and ingredients of *trust-building work*. In times of a loss of trust in financial investments, trust literally had to be "produced" – it had to be tailored to the personal needs of the individual customer: "In relation to the emotion work carried out, it can be observed that Mr. Kaiser actively works on his attitudes. His aim is to appear convincing for his customers (and the interviewer), and to create positive feelings and trust" (Heid 2010: 104). Kaiser admitted that after the stock market crash in 2009, some customers were in need of more frequent contact, i.e., "telephone calls, e-mails and face-to-face meetings aimed at exchanging information and offering advice and reassurance". Nevertheless, his rapport with the customers was mostly "unchanged and relaxed", "friendly" and characterized by "a great deal of contentment and trust". Interestingly, he did not address the contradiction between the two statements.

He seemed to separate between the anxieties of his customers caused by abstract events in the financial markets and, as he put it, the unbroken

> trust in his person and his professional attitude. His openly displayed ease and his professional demeanor, which was created by body work (gestures, facial expressions, speech, clothes), seemed to be the product of work that had to be carried out over and over again. Both appeared to be the basis of making deals – at least since the onset of the crisis. (Heid 2010: 104f.)

Against this backdrop, I would like to provide some more detailed observations by Thomas Heid on the *genesis* of trust-building work in the financial consulting sector:

> Mr. Kaiser never gives the impression that his "merchant's honor" is insulted, or that he has made a mistake. Quite the contrary: throughout the conversation with the interviewer, he oozes self-confidence. He proudly announces that he does "a very good job" for his customers, and that he can offer products or broker deals based on his *business portfolio* with a clear conscience. (…) In conversation, it is noticeable that Mr. Kaiser has the ability to gently guide conversations towards targets. Mr. Kaiser's rhetoric is characterized by his cautious, adequate, and precise choice of words; he uses the extensive specialist vocabulary of his profession carefully and in a matter-of-fact way. His evident ability to negotiate and his eloquence are supported by his gestures, which involve handling an expensive biro. The air of confidence exuded by Mr. Kaiser is underlined by his correct sitting posture and his choice of clothes (…). The consultation is pervaded by his subtle attempt to convince customers – with the help of many practical examples and in an understated yet vigorous manner – of the financial service offered. For this purpose, Mr. Kaiser even presents his own online current account as a case in point. (Heid 2010: 114)

Thomas Heid experiences, in his own skin and in a prototypal manner, how Mr. Kaiser interacts with customers. In this situation, Heid becomes the focal point of cultural analysis: he acts as a projection screen for the adviser, who does not even abandon his professional conduct and his work of persuasion in an interview with an ethnographer. Despite the damaged reputation of financial services (or in an act of defiance?), the advisers portrayed by Heid appear to trust in themselves and their investment strategies. They rely on the discursive logic and the apparent plausibility of individually calculated life risks, which they first calculate and construct, and then pretend to fight with customized security schemes. Due to the general decline in trust in financial investments, it is more important than ever that there is a "trustworthy" adviser whose personality serves to alleviate such concerns. In other words, the consultant acts as a concrete, accessible, locally materialized personalization of a regime of security. Yet in reality, this regime is based on incomprehensible, incalculable investments evading controls and vanishing in the opaque space of financial capitalism.

The trust-building work described here is based on a rationalized and empathetic manner of speaking, which was apparent in conversations with customers, the advisers' clothes and bodies, and the "props" on display. Independent financial consulting relies on such symbolic practices of personalization that compensate for the lack of transparency in the financial markets – and the importance of this mechanism is amplified in a situation of crisis. This explains why the advisers portrayed do not just have to act in a manner exuding security, but also to *feel* and embody it. In times of crisis, the value of personal traits, in particular empathy, leadership and the skill of trust-building, is increasing – and it is remunerated exorbitantly (think of bonuses!). This also reveals how far the economization of psychotherapeutic techniques of guiding conversations and, by this means, of human emotions and attitudes has advanced. Eva Illouz (2006, 2009) has demonstrated that this process is a characteristic trait of "emotional capitalism".

In sum, post-Fordism is characterized by the simultaneous creation and professional management of insecurity. A market for advice and training has emerged that governs the body and the psyche, feelings of security and success. It turns such feelings into the objects and also the instruments of work.

In the post-Fordist landscape of knowledge, the dominant guidelines, insights and practices have become more differentiated. In the case of the financial advisers, this relates to the diversification of financial investments and the privatization of provision measures for one's old age and medical care in a deregulated state; in the case of the "total quality" mothers, it refers to the fact that childcare and education are increasingly being a privatized matter of ambitious knowledge-based monitoring and training. The creation and management of this knowledge and its incorporation into people's habitus have become complex forms of work, which require extra time – in particular in fields close to domestic work like child- and eldercare[8], where labor is governed by a strict regime of time and economization.

A final case study was conducted in the milieu of factory workers. It reveals how workers experience the transition from a Fordist regime of work to newer, more subjectified forms of work. In contrast to the financial advisers and the professionalized mothers, the factory workers do not simply comply with the new, post-Fordist regime of work and use the techniques of self-management expected from them. In their case, tensions and acts of resistance are not transformed into productive powers; rather, they become a nuisance and a source of fear.

A Picture Frame Factory in Munich – The Worker's Habitus and the Resistance against a Subjectified Regime of Work

In the role of a worker, Olga Reznikova (2010) conducted participant observations in a Munich workshop. The firm had been producing picture frames for generations; it was now facing tough competition from China in the form of "cut-price frames". The new boss had lain off some of the workers in order to prevent bankruptcy. When the fieldwork took place, no one knew whether there would be further job losses.

The workers had been employed by the firm for a long time; on the grounds of an internal reorganization, the new boss had demanded for some time that they engage in practices of self-organization and take more responsibility for the work process. However, the new order was at odds with the worker habitus[9] and created acts of resistance. The workforce, already deeply upset by the redundancies, experienced the introduction of a new, subjectified regime of work as a dual crisis: a personal jobs crisis and crisis of work organization according to unfamiliar forms of governance which forced the workers to be pro-active, take initiative, and replace surveillance through self-control.

Reznikova's ethnography demonstrates how narratives of the workers can be interpreted in a context-sensitive fashion. In her work, such narratives emerge out of single episodes, in which individual workers explain their conceptions of a legitimate regime of work with reference to the past of the company.

The old, Fordist regime of production was characterized by the distribution of clearly-defined tasks and the existence of obvious temporal-spatial and social boundaries. After several decades of employment, it had inscribed itself in the habitus of the workers, who were mostly of Italian origin. The legitimacy of this order had partly resulted from the fact that it had helped the workers to integrate into German society. It was tied to a single person: the old boss, who acted as a patron offering the workers protection and helping them to acquaint themselves with their new social environment.

> "The new boss, Franz, is not seen as the legitimate boss (...): He doesn't want to do things the way we've always done them, the way Gregorie [the foreman; O.R.] has done them, the way the old boss [has done them]. He wants to go in a different direction. But that's not on!"
> "What's the other direction you're talking about?"
> "Well, for instance, he takes a form: 'Marie, I'll give you this form [an order form containing deadlines, models etc.; O.R.], and you'll have to know when these tasks will be done.' Then you move on – and you're supposed to pass this form to the person next in the production line. But that person has a look at the form and leaves it somewhere. And then someone else shouts: 'where is

> the form?' And nobody has got a clue. Because I'm not responsible for the form! We've told him at various points that he should do it the way Gregorie did it. But instead of telling me what I have to do first, and [what I have to do] after that, he tells me that he has sold everything [the frames] already. I have to think about how to do this, I have to take care of this form. But [I say:] no, thank you! It's not my shit, I'm not the boss. And everything continues to go wrong. I'm not keen on working longer hours; all this isn't mine." (Reznikova 2010: 45)

This episode is centered on the order form, which acts as a symbol that demonstrates what kind of attitudes and experiences cause the workers to perceive the subjectified practices of work as unreasonable, inadequate and a threat to their existence. From the vantage point of the "worker habitus" (Wittel 1998), the new freedom demanded by the new boss, which entails taking responsibility and forming a team involved in the planning and the logistics of production, appears to be an expression of confusion and bad organization. It seems that work has to be divided up and distributed in a clearly defined fashion, and it has to be straightforward.

The workers accept the boundaries between those "at the top" and those "at the bottom" as long as the activities of the "boss" conform to two criteria: the projections concerning his role in terms of protection and responsibility, which are a reflection of the workers' socialization, and the clear limits placed on work activities and working time that are a product of the Fordist class compromise. The workers put up with capitalist control and the fact that "all this isn't theirs" (as the worker quoted puts it vigorously) as long as the responsibility for certain decisions is not delegated to them. Reznikova concludes:

> A sheet of paper can symbolize the new hegemonic demands, which force the workers to include planning and administration in their "proper tasks" (...). But the order form passed on from position to position also represents an anonymous type of leadership lacking presence: the boss walking around and giving orders (...) is replaced by the duty to regulate oneself and to operate as a self-reliant team. The circulating order form becomes the symbol for a new technology of leadership and discipline aimed at establishing self-government, which is contested (...) by the workers. (Reznikova 2010: 47)

The new demands do not only contravene the embodied habitus of Fordism (work as a means of earning money and a physical activity marked by routine and subordination; a clear separation between work and free time), but they also have no rational and practical justification for the actors. Quite the contrary: "The new social order does not offer advantages to the workforce examined here; in reality, it is accompanied by the threat of redundancies" (Reznikova 2010: 47).

Post-Fordist Regimes of Work: Crises and Opportunities

The Munich project gives diverging answers to the question how post-Fordist, subjectified regimes of work are lived, experienced, justified, subverted and rejected. The cases reveal what different developments at the macro-level mean for certain actors and occupational groups affected, for example the current financial crisis, the processes of rationalization resulting from globalization, and the unfamiliar, subjectified regimes of work.

The examples, which to some degree give conflicting accounts of the developments in question, demonstrate how responsibility – as well as the capacity to actively address risks, the consequences of economic downturns, and the effects of subjectification – is distributed unevenly across different social groups. Those who created the risks were also those most capable of dealing with the crisis: By providing "calming" advice, the financial advisers were able to partly turn their customers' fear of financial losses into a positive force and an economic strategy for themselves; they delegated the responsibility for the trouble in the financial markets to other financial advisers (and consultancies) with "worse" investment products. Of course, the people employed in the "real economy" – those working on the "shop floor" and in the sphere of production – are as dependent on the developments in the world market as the financial advisers. The advisers, however, suggest that they are capable of actively and successfully managing the crisis – and they benefit from it.

Research based on individual case studies explains in a graphic manner how a range of social factors determine whether people are able to cope with post-Fordist forms of work or not. These factors include class, gender, age, occupation, and education, but also (and increasingly) lifestyle and networks of family, friends, and work contacts. In other words, it is negotiated along these lines whether subjectified, post-Fordist conditions of work are perceived as a state of insecurity or as an extension of autonomy and creativity – as a burden (in the case of the factory workers) or as an improvement and a challenge (in the case of the professionalized mothers). In some of the "younger" lines of business, a new habitus based on the "homo oeconomicus" (Schultheis 2007) has become dominant, and this seems to have been a smoother process than elsewhere. This new habitus concerns in particular IT, the network-based creative industries, and financial consulting – i.e., sectors where people use their lifestyle and the milieus they inhabit in order to market their services.

In contrast, there is very little room for older workers, unskilled manual workers and migrants. Members of these groups are stressed or upset because they are suddenly expected to become people with a subjectified and flexible habitus (cf. Reznikova 2010). It is not a coincidence that women with medium or low qualifications predominate in sectors where a permanent link between subjectification, rationalization, and customized standardization is emerging. Examples are eldercare and healthcare (Schweiger 2011), as well as the "lower" segments of the service sector such as retail: shop assistants have to do interaction and emotion work, but they are still located in standardized work environments, which are characterized by assembly-line practices involving the moving and selling of goods (Götz 1997; Krohn 2008).

"Sedentariness" vs. Mobility: Further Reflections on a Simplistic Dichotomy

A good standard of living and "sedentariness" thanks to life-long employment in a single firm, a clear separation between different tasks at work and clear hierarchies, a clear distinction between work and non-work – for the majority of workers, these principles were only realistic goals during the relatively short era of Fordism. The picture frame factory can be regarded as a typical Fordist workspace. Yet, even under the Fordist regime of work, the boundaries between work and non-work blurred in some respects – especially in family businesses (cf. Lemberger 2007): the old boss of the picture frame factory, for example, acted as a patron and supported his immigrant workers in their attempts to become integrated in German society. It appears that the notion of "Fordism" is a construction; next to the Fordist realities of work, pre-industrial life worlds continued to exist – for example in agriculture, where industrialization remained limited for a long time, and where holistic lifestyles and gendered practices of work predominated (see Konvalinka 2013).

Nevertheless, in a Western, industrialized nation such as Germany, the post-war era of Fordism – even if its characteristics did not apply everywhere – had a profound effect on people's consciousness. For several decades, the Fordist regime formed an important and fixed part of state policies and business strategies, of public discourses, and of the habitual orientations of many workers.[10] The values and modes of work of Fordism and the principles of a "normal biography" and a "normal family" with a male breadwinner became commonly held ideas. Today, these ideas are still dominating political and academic debates on "work in new times" (see Götz, Huber & Kleiner 2010). It is necessary to critically reflect on them and to point out that they emerged under specific *historical and regional conditions* – a fact that is often neglected in the current debates on "modern" principles of work and life.[11] Such a critique of the historical and regional biases of current narratives of post-Fordism should address the fact that new developments in the world of work cannot be grasped adequately if the label of *post*-Fordism is applied too quickly, and if these developments are simply related to a narrow and one-dimensional understanding of Fordism. The developments in question often do not conform to a linear logic and to pre-fabricated dichotomies.

Assessing case studies, I suggest that there is in particular one problem at stake within the frequently used opposition between a sedentary/immobile past and a present characterized by spatial and social mobility as well as "patchwork biographies" marked by ruptures. It seems necessary to deconstruct this view because many contributors to the debates on transformation processes (often implicitly) use such simplistic dichotomies. It is often overlooked that permanent employment and sedentary work lives were only a guiding principle in the relatively short Fordist era.

More than 30 years ago, Hermann Bausinger (1978) warned, in an article on identity, that we should not use under-complex generalizations and dichotomies when we distinguish between the pre-industrial and the industrial/post-industrial modes of work and community building. The often assumed social, spatial and temporal homogeneity, the closeness and immobility of pre-industrial, rural communities needs to be qualified: the pre-industrial, peasant population was indeed mobile, and there were "patchworks" of work activity. In urban market places, it encountered different life worlds and horizons, so that the intergenerational assumptions guiding rural life were changed through new experiences.[12] Along these lines, Orvar Löfgren (1995) has argued that terms fashionable in certain academic discourses such as *post*-modernity and *post*-traditionalism cover up the fact that Swedish peasants in pre-modern times spent more time on the road trading than at their farms working and being "rooted". Similarly, Katrin Lehnert, a Ph.D. candidate at LMU Munich, is currently conducting a historical and archival micro-study on short-distance mobilities in the Saxon-Bohemian-Silesian border area during early industrialization. She argues that the principle of a sedentary working population only became dominant when the (border) regime of the nascent national state emerged (see Lehnert 2012). Moreover, she observed a kind of anachronism: capitalism was even in rural areas increasingly based on mobile workers while state control needed settled and disciplined workers.

On the one hand, people had the opportunity or were forced to settle after having moved to urban places where labor was being concentrated, and this process can be regarded as a by-product of the formation of modern, national labor markets. On the other hand, there is no doubt that industrialization entailed new forms of spatial and social mobility and the differentiation characteristic of modern job markets: the field of wage labor became more multifaceted, and work increasingly took place outside the home. The imperatives of effort and social advancement became dominant. They were linked to the rise of the bourgeoisie, the leading class of so-called "first modernity" (cf. Beck & Bonß 2001). This was accompanied by the constant creation of new jobs and niches. As we all know, "first modernity" was characterized not just by industrialization and the consolidation of the bourgeoisie as a political and economic power, but also by the emergence of a social order based on the national state. Both became guiding principles and social realities in Europe: "national economies" emerged, and the modern national state increasingly regulated labor markets and qualifications with the help of social, educational and work-related institutions. Besides, it created clear-cut communities along the lines of class and milieu and ensured that its members remained immobile to a certain extent: In this world of production halls and offices (cf. Lauterbach 1998) everyone was disciplined and formed through a permanent job, a clearly defined role. As Max Weber already recognized, the organization of the military lived on in the world of work (cf. Sennett 1998): there were chains-of-command, military-style careers, and clear-cut, pyramid organizational structures, which entailed rigid occupational identities.[13]

In sum, approaches should be questioned that operate with a dichotomy between a relatively immobile era of pre-modernity marked by homogeneous, stable communities and identities and a highly mobile era of (post-)modernity characterized by relatively fluid, hybrid identities. The prevalence of this bias is also a result of the agenda of historical migration research, which has mostly been looking at long-distance movements of migration.[14] In other words, the short-distance mobilities of traders, seasonal workers, and commuters working in the new factories have so far been neglected. As Lehnert's dissertation will show, both historical work studies and migration research should examine the mobilities in early capitalism – especially those of people mobilized due to poverty, who had to sell their labor power in the emerging labor markets and were self-dependent, precarious workers.[15]

Beyond the Fordist/Post-Fordist Paradigm: Transcending National and Middle-Class Perspectives

Today, the achievements of Fordism discussed no longer represent guiding principles and social realities for an increasing number of people, among them members of the middle classes.[16] Academics and journalists have argued time and again that this is the product of at least three developments: the decline in the power of the national state, which has been deregulated; the substantial transformation and the neo-liberal restructuring of the world of work, which has been globalized; and the emergence of "shareholder capitalism", which is driven by the expansion of financial markets.[17]

Despite of these powerful developments: As the case study on the picture frame factory showed, the Fordist habitus has remained significant in some sectors of industry – despite re-structuring within firms and processes of technification and de-regulation (see, e.g., Müske 2010; Wittel 1998). In other contexts, for example in the much-discussed field associated with the "Digital Bohemia", the "end of permanent employment" (Friebe & Lobo 2006) is celebrated as a liberation of creativity. The new, "flexible human" (cf. Sennett 1998) subscribing to the "post-Fordist conduct of life" (Schönberger 2007: 81) does not just seem to have become a new guiding principle, but part of a new habitual arrangement concerning work. The cases of the financial consultants and the "total quality mothers" are proof that there are different forms of active commitment to a novel, highly subjectified lifestyle marked by an almost complete blurring of work and life.

Young, well-connected, self-employed entrepreneurs tend to constitute another field that is not (or no longer) dominated by Fordist patterns of thinking and acting. Martina Schwingenstein, a Munich graduate, explored in her master's thesis the formation of a new field of discourse and practice dominated by "social entrepreneurs". They are members of the educational elite; in their self-image and activities, they attempt to reconcile conceptions of "sustainable business" and "sustainable production" with neo-liberal values such as "self-activation", "risk management" and "self rationalization". In other words, in their business models, personal attitudes and career aspirations, they mix values and practices usually ascribed to post-Fordism with "re-invented" Fordist traditions, for instance having a special feeling of obligation towards colleagues, customers and suppliers, who often come from under-developed countries. In certain milieus, "social entrepreneurs" are portrayed and promoted as role models for a new kind of entrepreneurship (Schwingenstein 2013).

In her Ph.D. project in progress, Barbara Lemberger also deals with a group of small and medium entrepreneurs who combine post-Fordist practices of self-economization with Fordist-like ideas of patronage, responsibility and leadership: In today's Germany, there are many extremely successful businesspeople of Turkish origin having climbed up to the middle class. In a historical and individual biographical situation requiring mobility, determination and the ability to cope with hardship, they profit from inter-generational experiences of migration and are able to "imprint" their experiences on the urban landscape of trade, business, and consumption. Undoubtedly, the developments in this milieu will feed into future debates on new bourgeois lifestyles influenced by the experience of migration (Lemberger 2011).

All in all, work research should pay more attention to synchronicities of the asynchronous and to the emergence of orientations in the world of work like these, which go beyond dichotomies such as Fordism/post-Fordism. Fordist and post-Fordist forms of production – and the corresponding modes of work and life – continue to co-exist in different contexts; as a result, alternative forms and *hybrid forms* integrating contradictory tendencies emerge (see Huber 2013). And yet, it is safe to say that industrial work has lost its "hegemonic position in terms of being a guiding principle" (Schönberger 2007: 69); and there surely is an advance of "service work", "knowledge work", and "affective work" (Lazzarato 1998) as well as lifestyles based on mobility and technology-guided forms of communication. In this situation, one thing is certain: a new type of worker is required, which is aptly called the "entrepreneurial self" by Ulrich Bröckling (2007). Workers of this type invest personal traits in the labor process by taking personal responsibility and involving their "ego", and they adapt their qualifications to rapidly changing job descriptions and locations of work. Their ability of coping with the "de-standardization" of the life-course (Kohli 1985) depends on the resources and expectations of the milieus they inhabit.

Instead of either subscribing to cultural pessimism or invoking an age of "new work", European ethnology can contribute to a more differentiated view by conducting explorative, empirical studies. A broad view on work biographies and the world of work is needed: They should not be analyzed from a perspective that sees the old welfare state as the norm, organized in national regimes, Fordist institutions and oriented towards traditional middle-class milieus. Rather, work cultures are characterized also by the perspective of migrants, both the work practices and lifestyles of new elites and of those less established coming from the margins of Europe, and ethnographic research should consider the transnational networks of mobile and immobile people – as Regina Römhild has suggested recently (Römhild 2010). We should transcend ethnocentric, traditional, middle-class perspectives and their regional and historical biases. In this process, the historical nature of discourses, individual practices, and individual attitudes will be uncovered.

Ethnographies of the New Work Life: A Short Postscript

Ethnographic case studies tend to adopt a holistic approach, which involves analyzing both micro- and macro-contexts and describing a range of insider perspectives. The examples drawn from the Munich research project demonstrated once again that qualitative research produces deep insights into the diversity of "(post-)Fordist" work settings; and that there are different ways in which workers take part in constructing these settings and attributing a meaning to their work. The micro-analytical approach adopted allowed the researchers to consider and judge how physical as well as immaterial forms of labor are embedded in existing pragmatic settings at work; and in certain broader social, moral and political frames that are often at odds with more traditional settings, beliefs and habitual orientations.

Ethnographic case studies enable us to explore the *vocabulary* used by interactive partners when they interpret work-related, interactive procedures. Moreover, they allow us to describe in how far the actors are attached or detached, committed or uncommitted; and whom they blame for their situation, or who they think is in charge. According to neo-liberal ideology, for example, they are to blame themselves and not an external instance like the market or the leaders of a company. Conversely, like in the picture frame factory, they often blame the "bosses" for hardly tolerable working conditions, but do not grasp the all-encompassing economic and political pressures faced by both employers and employees, which means that they struggle together – or, in times of precarity, as single individuals.

The work environments discussed are, in one way or another, deeply influenced by the processes of the subjectification, deregulation, and rationalization caused by the predominance of unrestricted market forces and by neo-liberal strategies of restructuring. The values of post-Fordism and the hegemonic practices of "reengineering" reflect a new "spirit of capitalism" centered on "employability" and commodification (Boltanski & Chiapello 2003). The new economic strategies and practices have not only transformed Fordist institutions, but they have also advanced into the organization of family life. In addition, they are also a serious challenge to the social aspects of work – for example the Fordist powers of collectivity and solidarity – as well as to the preservation of social peace. Currently, flexible capitalism is advanced by powerful new actors, such as the migrants who are constituting new, productive, bourgeois urban milieus and transnational economic networks. In some respects, the new forms of capitalism are marked by the blurring of the old social and spatial boundaries. In other respects, these boundaries are being reestablished, separating the winners and losers created by the new economic strategies. Thus, work ethnography should discover and reflect on the novel activities and creations of new social groups and move beyond terms with the fashionable prefix "post", such as "post-Fordism" and "post-modernity".[18]

Notes

1 Cf. Schmidt (2012) and Schmidt & Götz (2010). The aim of this interview-based study was to explore how new principles informing domestic work are developed in a changed work environment, and what kind of effects they have at the level of praxeology. The aim was to show the discrepancy between the traditional role of the mother and new demands placed on women in terms of self-management, flexibility, and the reconciliation of work and life.

2 See Götz, Huber & Kleiner (2010). This collection of case studies also contains the final report of the research project in question, which was led by the author of this article and conducted by 12 graduate students between 2008 and 2009. Some of the master theses originating in this context have also been published elsewhere. See Schweiger (2011), Braun (2013), Schmidt (2012). Further information can be found here: http://www.lernforschung.volkskunde.uni-muenchen.de/lernforschung/spaetmoderne_arbeit/index.html.

3 This strategy promises to boost the efficiency of staff; to increase the contentment of both staff and customers; and to make staff adapt to market conditions. It is centered on weekly meetings dedicated to quality assurance: The performances of the employees are monitored; mistakes are supposed to be corrected permanently, so that there is a *Continuous Improvement Process* (*Kaizen* in Japanese).

4 In this article, I will mainly concentrate on the German-language studies in question in order to introduce some of their approaches to the international research community.

5 Obviously, this concept was coined by Richard Sennett (1998: 9).

6 The term "Fordism" refers to an epoch in the history of capitalism named after Henry Ford, the pioneer of the mass production of cars. It is usually associated with clear-cut temporal, spatial and content-related boundaries between work and non-work, but also with specific social boundaries, hierarchies and positions. Both blue and white collar workers and their trade unions negotiated with the employers over "class compromises" (relating, for example, to reductions in work hours and improved working conditions) (see Schönberger 2007: 73ff.). Fordism also refers to the fact that optimized labor processes in the factories led to increases in productivity and declining costs of production. The factory regime was based on detailed, fixed plans concerning the labor process and labor units, which were calculated and evaluated on the grounds of the Taylorist principle of "scientific management" (Taylor 1917). It was part of the Fordist class compromise that workers benefited from increases in productivity through rising wages. This created a productivist circle, where additional demand and rising levels of consumption secured economic growth.

7 In their book about the "normal chaos of love", Ulrich Beck and Elisabeth Beck-Gernsheim (1990) discuss the "structural hostility towards the family" characterizing the late modern world of work.

8 Another case study from our project (Schweiger 2010, 2011) looked at the styles of work of eldercare workers. Through participant observation, the researcher established that the compulsion to rationalize eldercare work due to reforms of healthcare in Germany meant that the immaterial aspects of the work were neglected. The workers had to execute a number of predetermined, timed steps when they did their care work: lifting the old people out of their beds; washing them; "filling them up" with bread rolls; "mobilizing" them to walk.

9 Reznikova's categories were based on Wittel's (1998) distinction between a "worker habitus" and a "bourgeois habitus". Wittel examined the introduction of team work. He showed that the post-Fordist paradigm of work is an update and an expansion of the historically rooted, bourgeois habitus and its ideal of personal responsibility.

10 As Reznikova points out in the case study above, the suffering and the fear, the expectations and the strategies of coping of many workers, in particular older ones, are still more or less based on Fordist ideas. Following the tradition of Pierre Bourdieu's "weight of the world" (Bourdieu et al. 1997), Franz Schultheis and

Kristina Schulz have produced reports on contemporary social life (2005) and have also detected a Fordist habitus. In the Western post-war societies, Fordist wage labor was *the* mechanism producing collective identities and communities (under different preconditions characterized by economic planning, this is also true of the socialist countries; see Friedreich 2008). It had including effects; once it was absent, processes of exclusion started (cf. Moser 1993).

11 For instance, recent texts by Chavdarova (2010) and Petrova (2010) suggest that the Fordist forms of wage labor did not act as a guiding principle shaping the thoughts and actions of the people everywhere in Europe. In Bulgaria, illicit employment and precarious forms of securing one's livelihood have for some time enjoyed a high degree of legitimacy and are widely accepted. Bulgaria is a country where there is a high degree of mistrust in the State and in state institutions. As a result, the shadow economy has a long tradition as a legitimate institution.

12 In the article in question, Bausinger (1978) conducted a "re-study" of the "Fischerkommünen" (fishing collectives) on the Baltic islands of Rügen and Hiddensee originally studied by ethnographer Reinhard Peesch (1961). He observes that these pre-industrial fishing collectives sharing boats were only working on a temporary basis; for several months a year, the fishermen worked in other areas. This suggests that even back then, "patchworks" of work activities existed that are usually seen as a recent phenomenon. On this type of combined economy, see also Warneken (2006) and Hauser (2009).

13 It is a characteristic trait of modernity that wage labor determined people's self-image, status, lifestyle and social environment – at least to the same degree as family origin, denomination and local, socio-cultural hierarchies and networks. Qualifications endorsed by the State became tickets to higher positions in the social hierarchy; they undermined the old, feudal class boundaries (even if there were of course limits to upward social mobility through education). A certain division of labor – blue vs. white-collar work – was seen, not just by Marxist-materialist social theories, as an important mechanism in the constitution of classes and identities.

14 On this blind spot of social research, see Schulte Beerbühl & D. Dahlmann (2011) and Lucassen (1993).

15 Lehnert (2012) also stresses that itinerant traders were of importance for the emergence of capitalist consumer markets. Other contributions that are exceptional in their attention to short-distance mobilities can be found in particular in Austrian migration research. A good example is Oberpenning & Steidl (eds. 2001). Obviously, there are extensive accounts of working life in the nineteenth century; see Kocka (1983, 2012) and Kocka & Offe (2000). And yet, there is a lack of historical work research focusing on mobile people, especially those operating locally. Much of the current work in German language in this area examines the multifaceted forms of spatial, social and intellectual mobility, which are presented as by-products of post-modern globalization (see, e.g., the contributions to Götz et al. 2010). But it often operates without a historical comparative perspective looking at pre-industrial societies.

16 Michael Vester (2009), a political scientist, provides analyses of the social structure for the German case based on representative opinion polls. These provide evidence for growing social polarization: firmly established middle-class milieus are increasingly threatened by precarity and downward social mobility. In the French case, Castel (2009) has worked extensively on the "return of social insecurity" in the last thirty years.

17 For a summary of the debate in the social sciences on the multiple reasons for the transition from Fordism to post-Fordism, see Schönberger (2007) and the contributions to Castel & Dörre (2009) and Boltanski & Chiapello (2003).

18 I would like to thank Barbara Lemberger, Katrin Lehnert and Petra Schweiger for their many helpful comments regarding this article, and Alexander Gallas for his professional help in translating and editing the first German text version deriving from a lecture that bears the title "Arbeit in neuen Zeiten. Ethnografien zu Ein- und Aufbrüchen", see, e.g., the online-video of the LMU Ringvorlesung "Arbeit im Wandel" (November 29, 2011), see http://videoonline.edu.lmu.de/node/3281.

References

Barth, M. 2009: Wir nennen es Kreativität: Inszenierung von „alter" und „neuer" Arbeit in Werbebildern der Informations- und Kommunikationstechnologie. In: I. Götz & B. Lemberger 2009 (eds.), *Prekär arbeiten, prekär leben: Kulturwissenschaftliche Perspektiven auf ein gesellschaftliches Phänomen.* Frankfurt/M. & New York: Campus, pp. 183–204.

Bauman, Z. 1997: *Postmodernity and its Discontents.* New York: New York University Press.

Bausinger, H. 1978: Identität. In: H. Bausinger et al. (eds.), *Grundzüge der Volkskunde.* Darmstadt: Wissenschaftliche Buchgesellschaft, pp. 204–263.

Beck, U. 1986: *Risikogesellschaft:* Auf dem Weg in eine andere Moderne. Frankfurt/M.: Suhrkamp [*Risk Society: Towards a New Modernity.* London: Sage].

Beck, U. & E. Beck-Gernsheim 1990: *Das ganz normale Chaos der Liebe.* Frankfurt/M.: Suhrkamp.

Beck, U. & W. Bonß 2001: *Die Modernisierung der Moderne.* Frankfurt/M.: Suhrkamp.

Beck-Gernsheim, E. 1976: *Der geschlechtsspezifische Arbeits-*

markt. Frankfurt/M.: Campus.
Berger, P.L. & Th. Luckmann 1966: *The Social Construction of Reality: A Treatise in the Sociology of Knowledge.* Garden City: Doubleday.
Boltanski, L. & E. Chiapello 2003: *Der neue Geist des Kapitalismus.* Konstanz: UVK [*Le nouvel esprit du capitalism.* Paris: Gallimard] [*The New Spirit of Capitalism.* London & New York: Verso].
Bourdieu, P. et al. (eds.) 1997: *Das Elend der Welt: Zeugnisse und Diagnosen alltäglichen Leidens an der Gesellschaft.* Konstanz: UVK, Universitätsverlag [*La misère du monde.* Paris: Seuil] [*Weight of the World: Social Suffering in Contemporary Society.* Cambridge: Polity].
Braun, S. 2013: Hairdressers as Managers of Well-being: A Multi-Dimensional Perspective of Emotional Labor in Service Industry. In: G. Koch & S. Everke Buchanan (eds.), *Pathways to Empathy: New Studies on Commodification, Emotional Labor and Time Binds.* Frankfurt/M.: Campus, pp. 141–158.
Bröckling, U. 2000: Totale Mobilmachung: Menschenführung im Qualitäts- und Selbstmanagement. In: U. Bröckling, S. Krasmann & Th. Lemke (eds.), *Gouvernementalität der Gegenwart: Studien zur Ökonomisierung des Sozialen.* Frankfurt/M.: Suhrkamp, pp. 131–168.
Bröckling, U. 2007: *Das unternehmerische Selbst: Soziologie einer Subjektivierungsform.* Frankfurt/M.: Suhrkamp.
Bröckling, U., S. Krasmann & Th. Lemke (eds.) 2004: *Glossar der Gegenwart.* Frankfurt/M.: Suhrkamp.
Castel, R. 2009: Die Wiederkehr der sozialen Unsicherheit. In: R. Castel & K. Dörre (eds.), *Prekarität, Abstieg, Ausgrenzung: Die soziale Frage am Beginn des 21. Jahrhunderts.* Frankfurt/M. & New York: Campus, pp. 21–34.
Castel, R. & K. Dörre (eds.) 2009: *Prekarität, Abstieg, Ausgrenzung: Die soziale Frage am Beginn des 21. Jahrhunderts.* Frankfurt/M. & New York: Campus.
Chavdarova, T. 2010: Mobilisierungsstrategien in bulgarischen Privatbetrieben nach der Wende: Kontinuitäten und Wandel im Umgang mit formalen und informellen Beziehungen im Arbeitsleben. In: I. Götz et al. (eds.), *Mobilität und Mobilisierung: Arbeit im sozioökonomischen, politischen und kulturellen Wandel.* Frankfurt/M. & New York: Campus, pp. 315–332.
Dörre, K. 2006: Prekäre Arbeit und soziale Desintegration. *Aus Politik und Zeitgeschichte* 40/41, 7–14.
Friebe, H. & S. Lobo 2006: *Wir nennen es Arbeit: Die digitale Bohème oder das Ende der Festanstellung.* München: Heyne.
Friedreich, S. 2008: *Autos bauen im Sozialismus: Arbeit und Organisationskultur in der Zwickauer Automobilindustrie nach 1945.* Leipzig: Leipziger Universitätsverlag.
Gottschall, K. & G.G. Voß (eds.) 2005: *Entgrenzung von Arbeit und Leben: Zum Wandel der Beziehung von Erwerbstätigkeit und Privatsphäre im Alltag.* München: Rainer Hampp Verlag.
Götz, I. 1997: *Unternehmenskultur: Die Arbeitswelt einer Großbäckerei aus kulturwissenschaftlicher Sicht.* Münster & München: Waxmann.
Götz, I. 2011: *Deutsche Identitäten: Die Wiederentdeckung des Nationalen nach 1989.* Köln & Wien: Böhlau.
Götz, I. 2013: Encountering Arlie Hochschild's Concept of "Emotional Labor" in Gendered Work Cultures: Ethnographic Approaches in the Sociology of Emotions and in European Ethnology. In: G. Koch & S. Everke Buchanan (eds.), *Pathways to Empathy: New Studies on Commodification, Emotional Labor and Time Binds.* Frankfurt/M.: Campus, pp. 183–200.
Götz I. & B. Lemberger 2009 (eds.): *Prekär arbeiten, prekär leben: Kulturwissenschaftliche Perspektiven auf ein gesellschaftliches Phänomen.* Frankfurt/M. & New York: Campus.
Götz, I. et al. (eds.) 2010: *Mobilität und Mobilisierung: Arbeit im sozioökonomischen, politischen und kulturellen Wandel.* Frankfurt/M. & New York: Campus.
Götz, I., B. Huber & P. Kleiner (eds.) 2010: *Arbeit in „neuen Zeiten": Ethnografien und Reportagen zu Ein- und Aufbrüchen.* München: Utz Verlag.
Hauser, A. 2009: Prekäre Subsistenz: Eine historische Rückschau auf dörfliche Bewältigungsstrategien im Umbruch zur Industrialisierung. In: I. Götz & B. Lemberger (eds.), *Prekär arbeiten, prekär leben: Kulturwissenschaftliche Perspektiven auf ein gesellschaftliches Phänomen.* Frankfurt/M. & New York: Campus, pp. 263–285.
Heid, Th. J. 2010: Der Anlagekapitalismus lebt: Wie selbständige Finanzberater die Wirtschaftskrise überstehen. In: I. Götz, B. Huber & P. Kleiner (eds.), *Arbeit in „neuen Zeiten": Ethnografien und Reportagen zu Ein- und Aufbrüchen.* München: Utz Verlag, pp. 99–118.
Herlyn, G., J. Müske, K. Schönberger & O. Sutter (eds.) 2009: *Arbeit und Nicht-Arbeit: Entgrenzungen und Begrenzungen von Lebensbereichen und Praxen.* München & Mering: Rainer Hampp Verlag.
Hochschild, A.R. 1983: *The Managed Heart: Commercialization of Human Feeling.* Berkley, Los Angeles & London: University of California Press.
Hochschild, A.R. 2003: *The Commercialization of Intimate Life: Notes from Home and Work.* San Francisco & Los Angeles: University of California Press.
Huber, B. 2013: *Arbeiten in der Kreativindustrie: Eine multilokale Ethnografie der Entgrenzung von Arbeits- und Lebenswelt.* Frankfurt/M. & New York: Campus.
Illouz, E. 2006: *Gefühle in Zeiten des Kapitalismus: Adorno-Vorlesungen 2004, Institut für Sozialforschung an der Johann-Wolfgang-Goethe-Universität.* Frankfurt/M.: Suhrkamp.
Illouz, E. 2009: *Die Errettung der modernen Seele: Therapien, Gefühle und die Kultur der Selbsthilfe.* Frankfurt/M.: Suhrkamp.
Keupp, H. et al. (eds.) 2010: *Erschöpfende Arbeit: Gesundheit und Prävention in der flexiblen Arbeitswelt.* Bielefeld: Transcript Verlag.

Kleemann, F., I. Matuschek & G.G. Voß. 2003: Subjektivierung von Arbeit – Ein Überblick zum Stand der Diskussion. In: M. Moldaschl & G.G.Voß (eds.), *Subjektivierung von Arbeit*. München: Rainer Hampp, pp. 53–100.

Kocka, J. 1983: *Lohnarbeit und Klassenbildung: Arbeiter und Arbeiterbewegung in Deutschland 1800–1875*. Berlin & Bonn: Dietz.

Kocka, J. 2012: *Work in a Modern Society: The German Historical Experience in Comparative Perspective*. New York: Berghahn Books.

Kocka, J. & C. Offe (eds.) 2000: *Geschichte und Zukunft der Arbeit*. Frankfurt/M. & New York: Campus.

Kohli, M. 1985: Die Institutionalisierung des Lebenslaufs. *Kölner Zeitschrift für Soziologie und Sozialpsychologie* 73, 1–29.

Konvalinka, N.A. 2013: *Gender, Work and Property: An Ethnographic Study of Value in a Spanish Village*. Frankfurt/M. & New York: Campus.

Krohn, J. 2008: *Wir verkaufen Mode: Subjektivierung von Arbeit im Filialverkauf eines Textilkonzerns*. München & Mering: Rainer Hampp Verlag.

Lauterbach, B. 1998: *Angestellten-Kultur: „Beamten"-Vereine in deutschen Industrieunternehmen vor 1933*. Münster & München: Waxmann.

Lazzarato, M. 1998: Immaterielle Arbeit: Gesellschaftliche Tätigkeit unter den Bedingungen des Postfordismus. In: T. Negri, M. Lazzarato & P. Virno (eds.), *Umherschweifende Produzenten: Immaterielle Arbeit und Subversion*. Berlin: ID-Verlag, pp. 39–52.

Lehnert, K. 2009: *„Arbeit, nein danke"!? Das Bild des Sozialschmarotzers im aktivierenden Sozialstaat*. München: Utz Verlag.

Lehnert, K. 2012: „Der Streit um den Hausierer ist ein Kampf der durch seine Thätigkeit berührten Interessen" – Wanderhandel im Zeichen ländlicher Modernisierungsprozesse. *Volkskunde in Sachsen* 24, pp. 141–163.

Lemberger, B. 2007: *„Alles für's Geschäft!": Ethnologische Einblicke in die Unternehmeskultur eines kleinen Familienunternehmens*. Münster: LIT.

Lemberger, B. 2011: Mobilität als Kapital: Zur Entstehung einer migrantisch-türkischen Mittelschicht in Deutschland (Berlin). In: R. Johler, M. Matter & S. Zinn-Thomas (eds.), *Mobilitäten: Europa in Bewegung als Herausforderung kulturanalytischer Forschung*. Münster, New York, München & Berlin: Waxmann, pp. 98–104.

Lessenich, S. 2008: Die Neuerfindung des Sozialen: Der Sozialstaat im flexiblen Kapitalismus. Bielefeld: Transcript.

Löfgren, O. 1995: Leben im Transit? Identitäten und Territorialitäten in historischer Perspektive. Historische Anthropologie 3:3, 349–363.

Löfgren, O. 2003: Cult of Creativity. In: Institut für Europäische Ethnologie der Universität Wien (ed.), *Volkskultur und Moderne: Europäische Ethnologie zur Jahrtausendwende. Festschrift für Konrad Köstlin zum 60. Geburtstag am 8.Mai 2000*. Wien: Veröffentlichungen des Instituts für Volkskunde der Universität Wien, pp. 157–167.

Lucassen, L. 1993: A Blind Spot: Migratory and Travelling Groups in Western European Historiography. *International Review of Social History* 38, 209–235.

Matuschek, I., F. Kleemann & G.G. Voß 2008: Subjektivierte Taylorisierung als Beherrschung der Arbeitsperson. *Prokla: Zeitschrift für kritische Sozialwissenschaft* 38:150, 49–64.

Moser, J. 1993: *Jeder der will kann arbeiten: Die kulturelle Bedeutung von Arbeit und Arbeitslosigkeit*. Wien & Zürich: Europaverlag.

Müske, J. 2010: *Arbeitsalltag und technischer Wandel: Arbeiterinnen in einem Hamburger Versandhandelsunternehmen und ihre Arbeitswelt (1969–2005)*. Berlin: LIT Verlag.

Oberpenning, H. & A. Steidl (eds.) 2001: *Kleinräumige Wanderungen in historischer Perspektive*. IMIS-Beiträge H. 18. Osnabrück: Universität Osnabrück.

Peesch, R. 1961: *Die Fischerkommünen auf Rügen und Hiddensee*. Veröffentlichungen der Institut für Deutsche Volkskunde 28. Berlin: Akad.-Verlag.

Petrova, I. 2010: Mobilisierungsstrategien in bulgarischen Privatbetrieben nach der Wende: Kontinuitäten und Wandel im Umgang mit formalen und informellen Beziehungen im Arbeitsleben. In: I. Götz et al. 2010 (eds.), *Mobilität und Mobilisierung: Arbeit im sozioökonomischen, politischen und kulturellen Wandel*. Frankfurt/M. & New York: Campus, pp. 333–350.

Pongratz, H.J. & G.G. Voß (eds.) 2004: *Typisch Arbeitskraftunternehmer?* Berlin: Edition sigma.

Reznikova, O. 2010: „Die Arbeit war nicht so wie jetzt" – Auswirkungen der ökonomischen Umstrukturierung in einer kleinen Münchner Rahmenfabrik auf die Lebenswelt und den Habitus der Beschäftigten. In: I. Götz, B. Huber & P. Kleiner (eds.), *Arbeit in „neuen Zeiten": Ethnografien und Reportagen zu Ein- und Aufbrüchen*. München: Utz Verlag, pp. 39–52.

Römhild, R. 2010: Prekarität und Kreativität in Europa: Die soziale Erosion des Nationalstaats und die Mobilisierung sozialer Praxis in der Perspektive einer politischen Anthropologie. *Zeitschrift für Volkskunde* 106:1, 23–44.

Rosenbaum, H. 1982: *Formen der Familie: Untersuchungen zum Zusammenhang von Familienverhältnissen, Sozialstruktur und sozialem Wandel in der deutschen Gesellschaft des 19. Jahrhunderts*. Frankfurt/M.: Suhrkamp.

Schmidt, P. 2012: Mit Leib und Wissen Mutter: Zur zunehmenden Professionalisierung von Mutterschaft innerhalb der erwerbsfreien Sphäre. In: G. Koch & B.J. Warneken (eds.), *Wissensarbeit und Arbeitswissen: Zur Ethnografie des kognitiven Kapitalismus*. Frankfurt/M. & New York: Campus, pp. 153–166.

Schmidt, P. & I. Götz 2010: Supermami – Rabenmutter: Antagonistische Leitbilder und Subjektivierungsansprüche im Bereich Familienarbeit. In: I. Götz, B. Huber & P. Kleiner (eds.), *Arbeit in „neuen Zeiten": Ethnografien und Reportagen zu Ein- und Aufbrüchen*. München: Utz Verlag, pp. 165–180.

Schönberger, K. 2007: Widerständigkeit der Biografie: Zu den Grenzen der Entgrenzung neuer Konzepte alltäglicher Lebensführung im Übergang vom fordistischen zum postfordistischen Arbeitsparadigma. In: M. Seifert, I. Götz & B. Huber (eds.), *Flexible Biografien? Horizonte und Brüche im Arbeitsleben der Gegenwart*. Frankfurt/M. & New York: Campus, pp. 63–94.

Schulte Beerbühl, M. & D. Dahlmann (eds.) 2011: *Perspektiven in der Fremde? Arbeitsmarkt und Migration von der Frühen Neuzeit bis zur Gegenwart*. Essen: Klartext.

Schultheis, F. 2007: Der Lohn der Angst: Zur Normalisierung von Prekarität im grenzenlosen Kapitalismus. In: P. Gazareth, A. Juhasz & Ch. Magnin (eds.), *Neue soziale Ungleichheit in der Arbeitswelt*. Konstanz: UVK, pp. 59–73.

Schultheis, F & K. Schulz (eds.) 2005: *Gesellschaft mit beschränkter Haftung: Zumutungen und Leiden im deutschen Alltag*. Konstanz: UVK.

Schweiger, P. 2010: „Bevor man sie angeleitet hat, hat man's schon selber gemacht" – Arbeitsstile in der stationären Altenpflege zwischen Ökonomisierungszwang und „guter Pflege". In: I. Götz, B. Huber & P. Kleiner (eds.), *Arbeit in neuen Zeiten: Ethnografien zu Ein- und Aufbrüchen*. München: Utz Verlag, pp. 89–101.

Schweiger, P. 2011: *„Wir haben zwar Geduld, aber keine Zeit": Eine Ethnografie subjektivierter Arbeitsstile in der ökonomisierten Altenpflege*. München: Utz Verlag.

Schwingenstein, M. 2013: *„Der Sozialunternehmer": Kulturwissenschaftliche Analyse einer Leitfigur postmaterieller Ökonomie*. München: Utz Verlag.

Seifert, M. 2010 (ed.): *Zwischen Emotion und Kalkül: Heimat als Argument im Prozess der Moderne*. Leipzig: Leipziger Universitätsverlag.

Sennett, R. 1998: *The Corrosion of Character: The Personal Consequences of Work in the New Capitalism*. New York & London: W.W. Norton & Company.

Taylor, W. 1917: *Die Grundsätze wissenschaftlicher Betriebsführung*. München: Oldenbourg.

Vester, M. 2009: Klassengesellschaft in der Krise: Von der integrierten Mitte zu neuen sozialen und politischen Spaltungen. In: I. Götz & B. Lemberger (eds.), *Prekär arbeiten, prekär leben: Kulturwissenschaftliche Perspektiven auf ein gesellschaftliches Phänomen*. Frankfurt/M. & New York: Campus, pp. 55–106.

Voß, G.G. 2009: Subjektivierung und Mobilisierung. Und: Was könnte Odyssesus zum Thema „Mobilität" beitragen? In: I. Götz et al. (eds.), *Mobilität und Mobilisierung: Arbeit im sozioökonomischen, politischen und kulturellen Wandel*. Frankfurt/M. & New York: Campus, pp. 95–136.

Voß, G.G. & K. Rieder 2005: *Der arbeitende Kunde, wenn Konsumenten zu unbezahlten Mitarbeitern werden*. Frankfurt/M.: Campus.

Warneken, B.J. 2006: *Die Ethnographie popularer Kulturen: Eine Einführung*. Wien, Köln & Weimar: Böhlau.

Witte, A. 2007: Ich-AGs zwischen selbstbestimmtem Arbeiten und Prekarität: Zu Aspekten arbeitsmarktpolitischer Gründungsförderung und der Erwerbsform Alleinselbständigkeit. In: M. Seifert, I. Götz & B. Huber (eds.), *Flexible Biografien? Horizonte und Brüche im Arbeitsleben der Gegenwart*. Frankfurt/M. & New York: Campus, pp. 125–149.

Wittel, A. 1998: Gruppenarbeit und Arbeitshabitus. *Zeitschrift für Soziologie* 27:3, 178–192.

Irene Götz is a professor in the Department of European Ethnology at Ludwig-Maximilians-Universität München. Her main research fields are work ethnography and new nationalism in Europe after 1989. A recent publication is *Deutsche Identitäten: Die Wiederkehr des Nationalen nach 1989* (Cologne and Vienna: Böhlau, 2011).
(i.goetz@vkde.fak12.uni-muenchen.de)

HEX AND THE CITY
Neo-Pagan Witchcraft and the Urban Imaginary in Berlin

Victoria Hegner

The paper focuses on neo-pagan witches in Berlin and the role of the urban context in forming their identity and a new religion. The interplay between the city and a specific spiritual practice and thinking becomes particularly obvious in moments of public representations and space making. Following this idea, the article's ethnographic focus lies on the Pope's visit to Berlin in 2011 and the public protest neo-pagan witches organized in the heart of Berlin-Kreuzberg. The analysis reveals how religious imaginations and experiences were recast and how the urban imaginary of Berlin came into play and was thus reproduced.

Keywords: neo-pagan witchcraft, new religiosity, urban imaginary, Berlin, urban ethnography

This article is about neo-pagan witches in Berlin and the role of the urban context in forming their identity and establishing a new religion.[1] New religions have been flourishing since the end of World War II. Men and women in Western societies increasingly search for religious meaning and practices beyond the dominant belief systems. They take up and blend together different forms and traditions of practice and thought which stem from sources that are considered archaic, mystic, Eastern, and occult. The individual transcendent experience is most important. Dogmas and the idea of a single truth are wholeheartedly thrown overboard. The self is seen as the one and only authority and is thus sacralized (Luckmann 1967; Bochinger 1994; Hanegraaff 1996; Melton 2004; Heelas & Woodhead 2005; Knoblauch 2005, 2009; Beck 2008; Mohrmann 2010).[2]

Topographical headquarter for those new forms of religion appears to be the (post-)modern city. As the cultural anthropologist Werner Schiffauer and the theologist Leo Penta recently put it: "The city renders religious innovations, much more so than the countryside." This should not imply a rigid opposition between "the city and the rest". Still, the city holds particular social and cultural qualities. As Schiffauer und Penta go on to explain:

> The everyday encounter and confrontation with different social groups and cultural and religious practices within confined space grinds down tradition and gives way for alternatives. Social developments and ... grievances manifest themselves more immediately; cities offer the necessary space, network as well as mobility for innovation (...). (Quoted by metroZones 2011: 20)

Although this has widely been acknowledged (e.g., Cox 1984; Luhrmann 1989; Höhn 1994; Beaumont 2008; Andersson et al. 2011), studies on the interdependency between new religions and urban context, space and place (making) are still difficult to find. The few researches that do consider the importance of the *urban* within religious developments almost exclusively concentrate on dominant belief systems such as Christianity, Judaism and Islam as well as on so-called immigrant religions, that is, Voodoo in the US. Robert A. Orsi's edited volume *Gods of the City* (1999) as well as Lowell Livezey's book *Public Religion and Urban Transformation* (2000) are groundbreaking within this context. Concerning the interplay between religion, religious practitioners and the urban setting, Orsi pointedly wrote:

> ... specific features of the urban (...) landscape (...) are not simply the setting for religious experience and expression but become the very materials for such expression and experience. City folk do not live in their environments; they live *through* them. (...) Religion is always, among other things, a matter of necessary places, sites, where the humans and their deities, ancestors, or spirits may most intimately communicate ... (Orsi 1999: 44, emphasis in the text)

Programmatically he followed: "We examine how religious practice in the cities recasts the meaning of the urban environment as the city re-creates religious imagination and experience" (ibid.). For the following analysis on the interplay between neo-paganism and the urban context, I will take up Orsi's inspiring perspective and theoretically refine the lens by bringing in the concept of the *urban imaginary. Urban imaginary* refers the idea that

> a city is not a neutral container, which can be arbitrarily filled, but a historically saturated culturally coded space already stuffed with meanings and mental images. It is these meanings and mental images which determine what is "thinkable" and "unthinkable", "appropriate" and "inappropriate", "possible" and "impossible". (Lindner 2006: 210)

Hence, concerning the study the central question is what images of the politics and culture of Berlin are at work when practicing neo-pagan witchcraft there. What kind of witchcraft is possible and gets represented? Based on data of a yearlong fieldwork among a loosely knitted group of women witches with its leading figure Xenia, I will sharpen the focus of analysis and draw attention to ritual performance. I will specifically ask what kind of rituals neo-pagan witches create. Where do the rituals or specific performative acts take place? The question is also how these neo-pagan witches create urban space as a sacred *public* space – a space of inclusion beyond social and cultural boundaries, where people outside of neo-pagan witchcraft are encouraged to take part in or, at least, take notice of the witches' peculiar spiritual practice as well as their political activism.[3]

These moments of "publicity" show that Luckmann's often quoted perspective on the new social form of religion as *invisible* and thus privatized remains only partially applicable nowadays. As the Swiss scholars of religious studies Dorothea Lüddeckens and Rafael Walthert as well as the German sociologist Hubert Knoblauch recently postulated, new religions and religious practices become more and more *visible* and *fluid*. Knoblauch talks about forms of spirituality that have become *popular*. It means they have diffused into broader social contexts and thus started to move away from the social (and thus as well academic) margin (Lüddeckens & Walthert 2010; Knoblauch 2010). The paradigmatic locale for this development, again, appears to be the city (metroZones 2011). The city's imagined and practiced cultural openness, the diversity of highly individualized and intellectualized people as well as the accessibility to a wide range of different economical niche existences give way to this process. However, the interplay between new religions and the city remains ambivalent, as cultural anthropologists Ina Maria Greverus and Gisela Welz have already pointed out in 1990. Hence, new religious practitioners including neo-pagan witches might praise the modern city for its cultural liberalism but they also perceive it "as the root of all evil": as the place of anonymity and of the destruction of nature, as the place of self-alienation and fragmentation of living worlds. Thus, the city contradicts the new religious ideal of a holistically led life. The practice of new religiosity is seen as an attempt to master the resulting "stressfulness" of urban existence (Welz 1990: 9).

The present article concentrates on the idea of a growing *fluidity* of new religions, since I see fluidity as a central expression of new religions' urbanity. Hence, I will track the way in which neo-pagan witchcraft has become *visible* and thus public or publically represented in Berlin. The analysis focuses on how the urban imaginary of Berlin comes into play in those moments.

In doing so, I will divide the article into two parts. In the first part, I will provide some data concerning the neo-pagan witches in Berlin and their historical and religious distinctiveness. I will show how the emerging scene in the 1980s has to be understood in the context of a divided city and the special island situation of West Berlin. This part of the article also gives insight into Xenia's and her group's specific interpretation of witchcraft.

In the second part, I turn to the ethnographic description and analysis of the Pope's visit to Berlin in September 2011 and the protest that Xenia's group organized in the heart of Berlin-Kreuzberg. I will show how this particular ritual performance could be read as both an expression and a production of a specific image of Berlin, with the "myth of Kreuzberg" acting as catalyst.

Overall, the article emphasizes the need for more ethnography and the latter's strength in studying new religions in relation to the urban; it is time to bring the anthropology of the city and the anthropology of religion closer together.

Hex in Berlin

Since the beginning of the 1980s, Berlin has developed into one of the centers of neo-pagan witchcraft practice within Germany. There are hardly any statistics available for Berlin or for the whole of Germany.[4] Still, the number of neo-pagan witches in the German capital seems to be so high, that the journal *Body, Spirit, Soul* (German: Körper, Geist, Seele) – a major esoteric magazine in Berlin – lately claimed, that the German capital has the "highest concentration of witches in all of central Europe" (Schäfer 2010: 32). The term "witch" refers to a wide range of very different manifestations of neo-pagan religiosity/spirituality. It comprises followers of neo-Germanic groups such as Asatru as well as practitioners of a rather feminist spirituality – Goddess spirituality – with a pantheon that is not necessarily bound to a specific locale. The "lowest common denominator" is the worship of nature as immanently sacred. Some witches are followers of Gardnerian Wicca – a specific interpretation of neo-pagan witchcraft created by the British occultist Gerald B. Gardner (1884–1964) during the 1950s (von Schnurbein 1993; Bötsch 2005; Rensing 2006). The basic organizational principle is the *coven* – a circle of witches – in which one has to be ritually initiated (Gardner 1959). Wicca first arrived in Berlin during the 1980s, at that time still a divided city. Hence, it is important to note that it was West Berlin where Wicca was first introduced. Vivianne Crowley, a well known witch from the UK, visited the city and started to initiate people into this specific way of practicing and thinking of witchcraft. Estimates on how many covens exist in Berlin nowadays range from four to ten covens.

Xenia and "her" group could be best described as followers of Goddess spirituality. Like the majority of neo-pagans, they too claim that their spiritual practice is much older than Christianity and has been aggressively disrupted by it. In restoring "the old path" or "the old wisdom", they turn to multiple ancient pantheons and take up folkways they consider to stem from European pre-Christian peasants or "indigenous" peoples. Their witchcraft practice has one primary goal: to empower women's spirituality and to foster female liberation from patriarchy. In the center of worship they put the Great Goddess, which they see as immanently present in every human being. Their vision of spiritual witchcraft comes close to what has been developed by the so-called *Reclaiming Network* (Salomonsen 2001). *Reclaiming* originated in San Francisco, USA, in 1979/1980 and traveled quickly – via publication and individual people – to Europe, arriving in Berlin during the 1980s, like Wicca. Back then, Starhawk, the network's prominent representative and probably "the most famous witch in the world" (Hutton

1999: 345), visited the divided city, and, as in the case of Vivianne Crowley, only West Berlin. Like Vivianne Crowley, she clearly had an impact on the local witch scene. As one of the veterans from the 1980s and a Gardnerian Wicca, Natol claims: "It was Starhawk, it was her and Vivianne. It all started off with them, when they had come to Berlin in 1986 and 1988" (Conversation with Natol, February 24, 2011).

Within this context, it is important to note that the decade before the wall came down as well as the last years of the 1970s had in general been culturally as well as politically highly dynamic in West Berlin. Out of West Berlin's unique situation to be a political and economical island in the heart of the Eastern Bloc – a "frontier city" – the city had developed into a kind of "laboratory of social fantasies". This did not only concern niche existences and subcultures – like the vivid punk, art and squatter scene – but main stream social and cultural structures as well. For example: Berlin was the first West German city besides Bremen, where the ecologically oriented Green Party (*Alternative Liste* at that time) made it into parliament in the beginning of the 1980s. Berlin was also one of the first within the West German context, where anti-authoritarian kindergardens – *Kinderläden* – received substantial communal funding. Again, Berlin was the very first among West German cities where a local left-wing independent newspaper was founded and was successful (the *tageszeitung*, referred to as "taz"). In addition, Berlin was the only West German city with a paid rock-commissioner during the decade, who took care of the many newly founded music bands in the city and helped them to get successfully started (*Geo Special Berlin*, No. 6, 1986; Lindner 1993).[5]

City guide books – which always catalyze and fashion the cultural uniqueness of a city and thus help to turn it into a touristic resource – described Berlin at that time as *the* place to be – as "fancy", "strange" and "hot" (Schweinfurth 1986: 39, in *Geo Special Berlin*, No. 6, 1986), as a place, that "was ahead of all the smug West German cities when it comes to the feeling of restlessness" (Rosh 1986: 37, in *Geo Special Berlin*, No. 6, 1986). "This is mirrored in the city's music, art, writing, theater, fashion, off-scene, punks", as one author explained and went on: "Every detail taken by itself might be found somewhere else as well (…). Still, nowhere else all those things come together" (ibid.).

The emerging scene of neo-pagan witches, one can say, was an outcome and part of the city's cultural dynamics during that decade. It depicted an additional, a "spiritual", expression of Berlin's "restlessness" and its ascribed "walled-in" hotness and strangeness.

Xenia herself came to the conviction of being a witch during the 1980s after reading Starhawk. Working as an actress for one of West Berlin's small, alternative theaters at that time, she had to prepare for a comedy play and took the research very seriously. As she unfolds her story of how she found out about neo-pagan witchcraft, she states:

> It was a comedy. Its central character was a witch. I took the research very seriously and read everything I could get on witches. I also read Starhawk. Right away I was caught by her ideas. I knew: That's it. I had done some tarot before. But, Starhawk described what I really wanted to be: a witch. (Fieldnotes, October 22, 2010)

Since then, Xenia has explored and practiced neo-pagan witchcraft intensively. In 2000, she decided to open up a Center for Old Wisdom in Berlin. There she offers her spiritual healing abilities to interested women – to a lesser extent also to men. Most importantly, she organizes the eight neo-pagan festivals of the "earth year" and exclusively invites women to celebrate the moon as a symbol as well as the actual embodiment of the Great Goddess. Among other witches in Berlin, the group is known as the Moon-Women. Most of them come from a middle-class background, two are artists (photographer and painter), one is a professional astrologer, again one works in the pharmaceutical industry, three are nurses or teachers and one has her own business and works as a hairdresser, some are retired. The cast of the group, however, changes time after time. There is a number of core attendees, but even they do not come regularly. The social dynamic is deliberately set. For Xenia, it corresponds deeply with Berlin's city life which is, as she says, also ever changing, never static. Never have I witnessed a sabbat or esbat,[6] where *all* of the Moon-Women were there. Yet when they plan a public event such as a performance, where they want to be seen and acknowledged as neo-pagan witches with a specific understanding of the world by people outside of witchcraft and by the media, they make sure that everybody shows up. They even activate the loose network among the different groups of neo-pagans, Wiccans and individual – "solitary" – witches in Berlin. The network is rarely used, due to the fact "that everybody is always so busy in Berlin and only finds the time to mind her own business and group" (Interview with Xenia, September 30, 2010). Only in those rare public moments does the network get to work. One of those few events, where "everybody comes", had been the protest against the visit of Pope Benedict XVI. The demonstration had to be officially registered with the police beforehand, which presented the very first moment of creating and thus claiming "publicity" by the witches – a moment of getting "fluid".

The following thick description is an analytical experiment. I try to show how the urban imaginary of Berlin is reproduced though the ritual protest performance of the witches and simultaneously I aim to lay open the way in which Xenia's group generated a public space as a future *lieux de mémoire* (Nora 1990) of their religion.

The Pope, the Witches and the Myth of Kreuzberg

On September 22, 2011, Pope Benedict XVI visited Berlin. Xenia had the idea of organizing a "public witch event" on this day. Xenia thought of the event as a joyful protest against the Catholic Church and against its patriarchal dogmatism. During the process of planning the protest she wrote an e-mail to me:

> The idea is: Berlin witches sing a lullaby for the Pope. I know where the Pope will stay overnight. It is at Lilienstraße, at the Apostolic Nuntiatur. The lullaby should say that the Pope overslept modernity. The Catholic Church still closes its eyes to the fact that at its order 9 million witches (…) had been murdered.[7] (…) Somehow it must be a funny campaign as well; a campaign that catches the attention of the media. I imagine a horde of brave women who gather in Middle Age clothing or in witch-robes of our times. (…) They climb the cemetery wall. (I have already checked out how to break through the barricades on this day.) At midnight we have to be as close as possible to the Nuntiatur in order to sing the lullaby. (E-mail, May 7, 2011)

About 40 women and men gathered for the witch event in an area not far from the Pope's apartment, in front of the subway station Südstern and right in the heart of Kreuzberg – one of the "alternative", yet symbolically always gentrifying quarters of Berlin (Lang 1995, 1998). According to a recent, sociological survey of Berlin inhabitants' life situation and sense of living, Kreuzberg can be classified as a *creative quarter*, where

> a lot of artists, creative minds …, students and migrants … live, with an innovative and risk-taking mentality … The financial situation and status remain … below average [within the city, V.H.]. This is, however, compensated by the high degree of urbanity [in this quarter, V.H.] and the feeling of social cohesion. (Hertie-Berlin-Studie 2009)

Certainly, the geographical place for the gathering was determined by the Pope's address. Still, the location Kreuzberg and its ascribed status as being "creative" or "alternative" seemed to suite the gathering group and its social and cultural characteristics very well. To a certain extent, the demonstration with its concrete site could tentatively be interpreted as a play on and reproduction of the overall urban imaginary of Berlin. Surely, Berlin's imaginary is shaped by a diverse set of images or motives (e.g. being "provincial", "unrefined", "proletarian", a representative of Germany yet an exceptional case – hence "not German"). The reputation of being "creative"/"alternative" (and bankrupt, but nobody seems to worry – summarized in the narcissist city slogan *poor but sexy*) appears to be one of the most important images of the city. As part of Berlin's imaginary, it belongs to the city's "symbolic economy" that fashions Berlin's cultural singularity and turns into an economic resource.[8] In short: to be "poor" but "alternative" and "creative" sells very well. Kreuzberg still appears as a cultural and topographical manifestation of this image. As the German urban anthropologist Rolf Lindner points out:

> Since the 1960s, since the building of the Berlin wall turned Kreuzberg ... into an enclave, the quarter has appeared to be something like a Land's End, a territory, where the last indigenes – the so-called "Icke"-Berliners [Icke: colloquial for "I", proper German word: ich, V.H.] – met with the first wave of Turkish migrant workers and with the frugal yet hard-drinking cynics, who all had chosen this redevelopment area with low rents as their exile. During those years Kreuzberg became "a refuge of the not adapted or not yet adapted people, where the colorful and the dreary chaos as well as the artistic proliferation prospered." (...) For almost 30 years Kreuzberg was something like a "Mecca for dropouts". During this time Kreuzberg became a myth (...). (Lindner 1998: 9f.)

In this mythical area witches started to gather at sunset (for the following description: fieldnotes, September 22, 2011). Some of them I saw for the first time. Several people had put on their self-made Wicca garment and some were dressed in linen robes which were indeed supposed to invoke associations with the late medieval/early modern period and

Ill. 1: A woman dressed up as the Element Fire at the witch-demonstration against the Catholic Church and the Pope, September 22, 2011 in Berlin-Kreuzberg. (Photo: Victoria Hegner)

the Renaissance – the epoch often remembered as the "burning times" among witches. Others came in their casual clothes. A few had dressed up as the elements: air, fire, water and earth. Some had put on their ponchos. With their choice of clothes they demonstrated that part of their spirituality drew on [Indian] shamanism as it is practiced in Latin America. There were two women who wore a T-shirt with Lakshmi on it, the Hindu Goddess of wealth and prosperity. Finally, some brought along brooms. In their fancy outfits they looked like the fairytale witch from the *Grimms*. This mixture of dress semantics already made clear the joy and wide range of self positioning as witches.

Furthermore, it was a remarkable material manifestation of the eclectic nature of the witches' spiritual practice. One of the Moon-Women started to draw a huge spiral using flour. Aside from the initial gathering, it was one of the first steps to claim and construct concrete public ground for the witches and their performance. The spiral represents the eternal circle of death and rebirth. It symbolizes the female principle of life for neo-pagan witches since, in their cosmology, it is the Goddess and not the God who creates life, gives birth and who – as the Crone (the old wise woman) – signifies death and dies and is reborn. The symbolism, however, is hardly known by outsiders of neo-paganism. Yet, particularly for the Moon-Women, it works, so they call it a "super-sign" within the urban context. Drawing the spiral, according to the Moon-Women, seems to unfold a form of energy, through which city dwellers attain an awareness of the "interconnectedness" of every living organism and their own connectedness to the earth – an awareness that is supposedly lost in the city. As Xenia once explained to me:

Ill. 2: Xenia gave a passionate speech at the witch-demonstration against the Church and the Pope, September 22, 2011 in Berlin-Kreuzberg. (Photo: Manuela Schneider)

> These are so-called super signs [spirals together with ritual performance, V.H.], which we create, in order to evoke (...) within the archaic consciousness of people the feeling of reconnection with the earth. It should evoke a form of attentiveness (...). We do this for the other people (...) basically for the consciousness of the city dwellers. (Interview, September 30, 2010)

Once the woman had finished drawing the spiral, an impressive spectacle of neo-pagan witchcraft unfolded. Women and men gathered in a circle, they sang songs from the Reclaiming repertoire. They also sang spiritual songs and rounds they created right on the spot, and which were afterwards forgotten. They started to dance. After some time, Xenia gave a passionate speech invoking the Church's guilt and responsibility for the "burning times" and proclaiming female emancipation and free sexuality. Overwhelmed by the enthusiastic reactions of the group as well as of Kreuzberg bystanders and some curious policemen and women, she exclaimed: "Our female bodies belong to us. Let's have multiple orgasms." More and more nosy bystanders joined the assembly; newspaper- and TV-journalists showed up and began interviewing the *Hexen*.

Some well-known urban characters came along, such as the "Comet", who usually hangs around the Mauerpark, a touristic public park in Berlin's Prenzlauer Berg. Everybody seemed to know him. The "Comet" joined dancing, while artfully blowing huge soap bubbles. It was a great happening which came to an end when the two women who wore the Lakshmi-T-shirts stroke up the mantra in honor of the Hindu Goddess and the policemen started to shake hands with the *Hexen* – thanking each other for "good and inspiring cooperation".

Reflecting back on this event, the Moon-Women saw it as one of the rare, yet ideal public realizations not only of the eclectic character of witchcraft, but of the anarchic nature of witchcraft, in so far as nothing was planned beforehand besides the date and the location. No strict hierarchy seemed to rule the event, even the policemen seemed to have had partly joined the event, and still it was a great public success. The event left such a deep impression that Xenia suggested declaring the Südstern as one of their central ritual places. For Xenia as well as the other women, the square in front of the subway station with its densely populated apartment blocks, its different corner bars and the constant busy flow of people, provided an urban space to effectively go public and create a diverse audience for the witches' spiritual practice and messages. The mythical image of the area, the witches' (spiritual and political) goals and the concrete architecturally formed appearance of the place intensely interacted and coincided. Hence, at the following *Totensonntag*, an Evangelical holiday to remember the deceased, the Moon-Women planned the next public performance in commemoration of "the wise and free spirited women, men and children" that had been burned at the stake by the Church. This demonstrated an additional form of eclecticism: to incorporate a tradition of the "enemy" – as Xenia likes to call the Church – and ascribe one's own meaning to it. Thereby the women created a place of remembrance – *a lieu de mémoire* – and started to put neo-pagan witchcraft on the symbolic as well as concrete map of Berlin. Kreuzberg is certainly not a spatial coincidence. Considering its mythical image, it is one of the Berlin areas where there is the possibility to go public as witches, as eccentric as this self-ascribed identification might sound, because to call yourself a witch suits the myth and place of Kreuzberg well.

Conclusion

For a long time, new religious developments have been a marginal field of research within cultural anthropology/European ethnology. In view of the lively and highly differentiated discourse on the growing significance of religion/religiosity in post-modernity, it is time to throw one's hat and expertise of ethnography in the ring. Although new religions are a global phenomenon, locality matters decisively, and it is precisely long-term, qualitative research which has the capacity to bring the latter's significance to the surface. In times where we find that national cultural identifications, images and boundaries not only become more fundamental but seem to simultaneously crumble rapidly, it appears to be the (post-)modern city with its (staged) cultural singularity that shapes practices of new religions deeply. New religiosities in themselves become an expression of the urban. They mirror and enforce urban transformation. Thus, to understand the on-going cultural religious processes in post-modernity, studies on new religious practices and cosmologies have to be more closely linked to an anthropology *of* the city.

As I tried to show in the case of neo-pagan witchcraft – one of the fastest growing new religious branches worldwide – the interplay between the city and the specific spiritual practice and thinking becomes particularly obvious in moments of public representations and space making. Hence, when the Pope came to Berlin and neo-pagan witches organized a public protest, forms of expression where clearly shaped by the cosmology of a Goddess spirituality: drawing a spiral, dressing up as the nature elements, singing and dancing to Reclaiming chants and claiming free sexuality and female emancipation. Being situated at a loud and exhaust-laden cross road, in front of a subway station and across many corner bars, the representation got a decisive *urban* twist. Even the spiritual meaning of the spiral was urbanized by being interpreted as a "super sign" within the city, which should evoke a feeling of "reconnection" to nature. As religious imagination and experience were thus re-cast, the image of Berlin as "alternative" and "creative" was staged and reproduced. The "myth of Kreuzberg" was once more publically manifest.

Notes

1 The women from the Moon-Women-Group and the Reclaiming Group welcomed me into their homes and rituals. To all of them I owe a special dept. I am particularly grateful to Xenia Fitzner, Melany Matzky and Faye as well as the anonymous peer-reviewers for their pointed comments on the first draft of the paper. Thanks also to Matthew Finnemore for proofreading the text and sensibly correcting my English. All translations from the German language are by the author.

2 Within the academic discourse, we find different approaches towards the definition of new religions. Some scholars emphasize the undogmatic character of new religions. Others, again, don't see the rejection of dogmatism as a criterion for classifying new religions at all. Within their studies, they focus particularly on contemporary split-offs of dominant belief systems such as Pentecostal churches. See, e.g., metroZones (eds.) (2011). Some researchers substitute the word "new" with "alternative" religion. They take into account, that the latter is not a historically *new* phenomenon. Again, some scholars suggest the term "new spirituality" and avoid the word "religion", since for them, the term implies a certain theological coherence, which they do not see in new/alternative forms of religion/religiosity. I will use the term "religion/religiosity/spirituality" throughout the article. In doing so, I avoid the dualistic schema, which the differentiation between religion/spirituality implies (coherent vs. incoherent). I will use the terms new/alternative religion/religiosity/spirituality synonymously.

3 This concept of *public space* is shaped by the *ideal of inclusion* as it is put forward by city planners. See the study by Beate Binder (2009).

4 The only statistics I could find was in an article by Reena Perschke. According to her, 300 to 400 Wiccans and solitary witches live in Berlin. She extrapolated the number from interviewing ca. 10 Wiccans and solitary witches who told her that they are organized in groups of 10–20 people. Perschke then estimated that she had interviewed representatives of approximately half of the existing groups (Perschke 2003).

5 See other Berlin city guide books, e.g., *Richtig Reisen Berlin* from 1982. The latter has a chapter on Berlin's "alternative scene and subculture". It begins: "Nowhere else in Germany does such a multifarious alternative movement exist which is at the same time firmly anchored in projects, collective companies of any kind, in women's centers, *Kinderläden*, bars (...) and law firms" (1982: 92).

6 Sabbats: the eight festivals of the earth year; esbats: rituals at full moon.

7 Today's researchers on the witch hunt estimate that the number of burnt witches did not go beyond 50,000. Concerning the creation and reproduction of the idea of the "nine million witches burnt", see the article by Wolfgang Behringer (1998).

8 In her study The Cultures of Cities, Sharon Zukin employs the term "symbolic economy" of cities to describe urban culture – urbanity – as a new economical resource of global metropolises.

References

Andersson, Johan, Robert M. Vanderbeck, Gill Valentine, Kevin Ward & Joanna Sadgrove 2011: New York Encounters: Religion, Sexuality and the City. *Environment and Planning* A 43:3, 618–633.

Beaumont, Justin 2008: Faith-Based Organizations and Urban Social Isssues. *Urban Studies* 45:10, 2011–2017.

Beck, Ulrich 2008: *Der eigene Gott: Von der Friedensfähigkeit und dem Gewaltpotential.* Frankfurt am Main: Verlag der Weltreligionen.

Behringer, Wolfgang 1998: Neun Millionen Hexen: Entstehung, Tradition und Kritik eines populären Mythos. *Historicum.net:* URL: http://www.historicum.net/no_cache/persistent/artikel/826/. Accessed January 10, 2013.

Binder, Beate 2009: *Streitfall Stadtmitte: Der Berliner Schlossplatz.* Wien: Böhlau Verlag.

Bochinger, Christoph 1994: *"New Age" und moderne Religion: Religionswissenschaftliche Analysen.* Gütersloh: Kaiser.

Bötsch, Barbara 2005: *Leben mit der großen Göttin: Biografien, Glaubensweisen, Hintergründe zur Göttinreligion in Deutschland.* Regensburg: Lipa.

Cox, Harvey G. 1984: *Religion in the Secular City: Toward a Postmodern Theology.* New York: Simon and Schuster.

Gardner, Gerald 1959: *The Meaning of Witchcraft.* London: Aquarian Press.

Geo Special Berlin 1986: No. 6. Hamburg: Gruner + Jahr.

Hanegraaff, Wouter J. 1996: *New Age Religion and Western Culture: Esotericism in the Mirror of Secular Thought.* Leiden & New York: E.J. Brill.

Heelas, Paul & Linda Woodhead 2005: *The Spiritual Revolution: Why Religion Is Giving Way to Spirituality.* Malden, Mass.: Blackwell Pub.

Hertie-Berlin-Studie 2009: Sieben Berliner Lebenswelten: Kurzbeschreibungen: http://www.hertieberlinstudie.de/presse/pressematerial/texte/Lebenswelten_Ueberblick.pdf. Accessed January 10, 2013.

Höhn, Hans-Joachim 1994: *Gegen-Mythen: Religionsproduktive Tendenzen der Gegenwart*. Freiburg im Breisgau: Herder.

Hutton, Ronald 1999: *The Triumph of the Moon: A History of Modern Pagan Witchcraft*. Oxford & New York: Oxford University Press.

Knoblauch, Hubert 2005: Einleitung: Soziologie der Spiritualität. *Zeitschrift für Religionswissenschaft* 13, 123–131.

Knoblauch, Hubert 2009: *Populäre Religion: Auf dem Weg in eine spirituelle Gesellschaft*. Frankfurt am Main: Campus.

Knoblauch, Hubert 2010: Vom New Age zur populären Spiritualität. In: D. Lüddeckens & R. Walthert (eds.), *Fluide Religion: Neue religiöse Bewegungen im Wandel. Theoretische und empirische Systematisierungen*. Bielefeld: transcript, pp. 149–174.

Lang, Barbara 1995: Berlin-Kreuzberg: Bilder einer Vorstellung. *Zeitschrift für Volkskunde* 91:2, 223–247.

Lang, Barbara 1998: *Mythos Kreuzberg: Ethnographie eines Stadtteils (1996–1995)*. Frankfurt am Main: Campus.

Lindner, Rolf 1993: Berlin – Zone in Transition. *Anthropological Journal on European Cultures* 2:2, 99–111.

Lindner, Rolf 1998: Vorwort. Von "Freakland" zu "Slumland": Zur Mythologie Berlin Kreuzbergs. In: B. Lang (ed.), *Mythos Kreuzberg: Ethnographie eines Stadtteils (1961–1995)*. Frankfurt am Main & New York: Campus, pp. 9–15.

Lindner, Rolf 2006: The Imaginary of the City. In: G.H. Lenz, F. Ulfers & A. Dallmann (eds.), *Toward a New Metropolitanism: Reconstituting Public Culture, Urban Citizenship, and the Multicultural Imaginary in New York and Berlin*. Heidelberg: Winter, pp. 209–216.

Livezey, Lowell W. 2000: *Public Religion and Urban Transformation: Faith in the City*. New York: New York University Press.

Luckmann, Thomas 1967: *The Invisible Religion: The Problem of Religion in Modern Society*. New York: Macmillan.

Lüddeckens, Dorothea & Rafael Walthert 2010: Fluide Religion: Eine Einleitung. In: D. Lüddeckens & R. Walthert (eds.), *Fluide Religion: Neue religiöse Bewegungen im Wandel. Theoretische und empirische Systematisierungen*. Bielefeld: transcript, pp. 9–17.

Luhrmann, Tanya 1989: *Persuasions of the Witch's Craft: Ritual Magic in Contemporary England*. Cambridge, Mass.: Harvard University Press.

Melton, Gordon 2004: Toward a Definition of "New Religion". *Nova Religio* 8:1, 73–87.

metroZones 2011: Einleitung. In: metroZones (eds.), *Urban Prayers: Neue religiöse Bewegungen in der globalen Stadt*. Berlin & Hamburg: Assoziation A, pp. 7–24.

Mohrmann, Ruth E. (ed.) 2010: *Alternative Spiritualität heute*. Münster, New York, München & Berlin: Waxmann.

Nora, Pierre 1990: *Zwischen Geschichte und Gedächtnis*. Berlin: Klaus Wagenbach.

Orsi, Robert 1999: Introduction: Crossing the City Line. In: R.A. Orsi (ed.), *Gods of the City: Religion and the American Urban Landscape*. Bloomington, IN: Indiana University Press, pp. 1–78.

Perschke, Reena 2003: Neuheidnisches Hexentum. Wicca. Pagan. Freifliegende. In: N. Grübel & S. Rademacher (eds.), *Religion in Berlin: Ein Handbuch*. Berlin: Weißensee Verlag, pp. 525–529.

Rensing, Britta 2006: Der Glaube an die Göttin und den Gott: Theologische, rituelle und ethische Merkmale der Wicca-Religion, unter besonderer Berücksichtigung der Lyrik englischsprachiger Wicca-Anhänger. Ph.D. thesis, unpublished manuscript, Friedrich-Schiller-University, Jena.

Richtig Reisen Berlin 1982: Köln: DuMont, pp. 1–78.

Rosh, Lea 1986: Der wunde deutsche Punkt. *Geo Special Berlin* 6, 36–37.

Salomonsen, Jone 2001: *Enchanted Feminism: Rituals, Gender and Divinity among the Reclaiming Witches of San Francisco*. London & New York: Routledge.

Schäfer, Heidrun 2010: Kreativ oder reaktiv? *Körper, Geist, Seele* 2, 31–33.

Schnurbein, Stefanie von 1993: Walküren des Neuen Zeitalters: Zum Frauenbild neugermanisch heidnischer Gruppen der Gegenwart. In: D. Pahnke (ed.), *Blickwechsel: Frauen in Religion und Wissenschaft*. Marburg: Diagonal-Verlag, pp. 143–174.

Schweinfurth, Reiner 1986: Schön schräg und schrill und scharf. *Geo Special Berlin* 6, 39–44.

Starhawk 1979: *The Spiral Dance: A Rebirth of the Ancient Religion of the Goddess*. San Francisco: Harper & Row.

Welz, Gisela 1990: Urbanität und Spiritualität: New Age als städtische Subkultur. In: I.-M. Greverus & G. Welz (eds.), *Spirituelle Wege und Orte: Untersuchungen zum New Age im urbanen Raum*. Frankfurt am Main: Institut für Kulturanthropologie und Europäische Ethnologie, pp. 9–29.

Zukin, Sharon 1995: *The Culture of Cities*. Cambridge, MA: Blackwell.

Victoria Hegner, Ph.D., is a postdoctoral researcher at the Institute for Cultural Anthropology/ European Ethnology at the University of Göttingen. Using ethnographic methods, she is particularly interested in the interplay between new religious practices and the urban context and culture. A recent publication is Urban Witchcraft and the Issue of Authority, in: A. Fedele & K. Knibbe (eds.), *Gender and Power in Contemporary Spirituality: Ethnographic Approaches* (New York: Routledge, 2012).
(Victoria.Hegner@phil.uni-goettingen.de)

THE STUDY OF CULTURE AT THE INTERSECTION OF ACTOR-NETWORK THEORY AND ETHNOLOGY

Carina Ren and Morten Krogh Petersen

"To describe the real is always an ethically charged act." (Law 2009: 155)

A number of ethnologists have taken up the material-semiotic approaches of Actor-Network Theory (ANT) to study and describe a broad variety of phenomena. Drawing upon our own analytical engagements with ANT, we critically address the opportunities and challenges, which ANT provides within the field of ethnology. We see ANT as a new way of describing and "interfering" with cultural differences, an endeavor deeply rooted in ethnological studies, while at the same time challenging the ethnological study of culture. Through our discussion we hope to address the position of culture in the wake of its material-semiotic exploration and discuss the types of knowledge created when ethnology interferes with ANT, hence inquiring into contemporary ethnological knowledge production.

Keywords: the concept of culture, difference, actor-network theory, multiplicity, ontological politics

Recently, European ethnologists have been greatly inspired by studies conducted within the field of Actor-Network Theory (ANT). Ethnologists have taken up material-semiotic approaches to study and describe a broad variety of phenomena. In Denmark for instance, a good number of ethnology scholars have produced what we may call ANT-inspired dissertations (Jespersen 2008; Sandberg 2009; Ren 2009; Munk 2010; Petersen 2011; Boll 2011). Also, an anthology has been published (Damsholt et al. 2009) and as examiner and teacher respectively at the University of Copenhagen, we see that various courses and course literature at the Section of Ethnology draw inspiration from ANT.

ANT-inspired ethnological research has dealt with very different empirical fields such as the medical consultation, national borders, the tourist destination, flood risks, government organizations and tax compliance. It utilizes a wide range of notions developed within and around the empirically, analytically and theoretically diverse field of ANT and connects to other disciplines and fields of research in different ways. Yet in spite of – or maybe because of – this diversity in empirical fields, analytical resources and disciplinary positioning, we find it relevant to ask and discuss: *what makes the material-semiotic approach of ANT so compelling to ethnologists?* In the following, we wish to direct our attention to this production of what we broadly term ANT-inspired ethnology as well as its consequences. We will do so by turning primarily to our own analytical engagements with ANT.

Our aim with this article is not to lump together ANT-inspired ethnological studies in their entirety and argue for a new material-semiotic trend in Danish ethnology through sheer quantity. Rather, taking our own drawing on and wrestling with material-semiotic approaches and our ongoing discussions with colleagues as a point of departure, we wish to address the arguments, knowledges, and realities that the material-semiotic approach of ANT enable us to (attempt to) produce – or not to produce. Through such a hopefully transparent display, we wish to foster a discussion of the relationship between the discipline of ethnology and ANT.

At a first glance, the material-semiotic methods, sensibilities and analytical resources of ANT resonate well with many "classic" virtues of the discipline of ethnology. Through close empirical scrutiny of socio-material practices, ANT studies show a great interest in describing various kinds of differences and their interactions. However, ANT – especially in its recent, multiplicity-oriented versions (Vikkelsø 2007) – can also be described with regard to its specific interventionist ambitions, which – as we argue – differ from "traditional" ethnological engagements in and with the world.

John Law, sociologist and one of the key contributors to the field of ANT, has outlined a number of modes of mattering, which he delineates from the wider field of Science and Technology Studies (STS). A mode of mattering can be described as a specific way for researchers (and others) to attempt to come to matter in a given empirical field of scrutiny. Drawing upon his own work and work by empirical philosopher Annemarie Mol (Mol 2002), he delineates a specific and ANTish mode of mattering and entitles it "interference". Within this mode of mattering "contributing turns into the form of ontological interference" (Law 2004: 5). To the question of what this means, Law replies threefold:

> One, it says that realities are being done. Not just knowledges, but realities too. Everywhere. This is enactment. We know about this already. Two, it says that they are complex, non-coherent, uncertain, and in interference with one another. This is difference. And three, it says that if we recognize this and work it right, we can interfere and make a difference. This is the ontological politics. (Law 2004, emphasis in original)

As stressed above, ANT comes in different versions. ANT's insistence on relationality applies to ANT itself and ANT can thus be seen as continually "becoming with" (Haraway 2008: 4) its explorations and engagements with various empirical fields. In the above quote, Law draws on well-known ANT studies of how one network gains strength and, hence, does a reality. He does however take this insight in a new direction, namely that of multiplicity. In our own work, we have found this notion of multiplicity analytically fruitful and in this paper we suggest that our liking of the notion of multiplicity has to do with the longstanding interest of ethnology in studying cultural differences and to make such differences matter. We suggest, in other words, that a central aspect of ethnology's mode of mattering is partially connected (Strathern 2004) with interference's mode of mattering as Law describes it. This turns the quote into a well-suited point of departure for our ambition to pursue the question of what kinds of arguments, knowledges, and realities are worked up in the intersection of ethnology and ANT.

The relevancy of such an enquiry is further substantiated in a situation where ethnology is coming to grips with a growing operationalization with fields such as innovation and consumer research (O'Dell & Willim 2011; Damsholt et al. 2011; see also Cefkin 2009) and, subsequently, with the realization that ethnological research creates new and different sorts of effects and interventions (Jespersen et al. 2012). In relation to this, the question remains: how can we grasp and come to terms with the interventional capacity that arises in the intersection of ethnology and ANT? In the following sections we will discuss our own use of the material-semiotic methods, sensibilities and analytical resources of ANT by way of Law's description of interference as a mode of mattering. We aim to make transparent the "modus operandi" of our work and discuss its results through the notions of enactment, difference and ontological politics. Lastly, we will offer some concluding remarks on the implications and challenges that arise in the intersection of ANT and ethnology. First however, we offer a brief introduction to ANT.

ANT and Culture

Phenomena such as a national border, a tourist destination or a government organization might at first seem like rather closed-off boxes; they seem to have clear boundaries and they work in the way we expect them to. However, taking a second look, one might notice how a jumble of entities, actors and relations, all of which are very hard to define and delineate, makes up such phenomena. How can one describe phenomena that at one point appear as closed and efficient boxes and at another as a jumble of entities, actors and relations? This is the basic question of ANT. ANT is about thinking not in boxes but in nodes, connections and relations and to describe how through such nodes, connections and relations, at certain moments, boxes may appear (Elgaard Jensen 2005: 185–186; see also Callon & Law 1997). John Law elaborates upon this as he introduces ANT in the following way:

> Actor-network theory is a disparate family of material-semiotic tools, sensibilities and methods of analysis that treat everything in the social and natural worlds as a continuously generated effect of the webs of relations within which they are located. It assumes that nothing has reality or form outside the enactment of those relations. Its studies explore and characterise the webs and the practices that carry them. Like other material-semiotic approaches, the actor-network approach thus describes the enactment of materially and discursively heterogeneous relations that produce and reshuffle all kinds of actors including objects, subjects, human beings, machines, animals, "nature", ideas, organisations, inequalities, scale and sizes, and geographical arrangements. (Law 2009: 141)

One of the central and hitherto closed-off boxes that ANT has sought to open is Western science and technology. How can one explain its impressive success? One exemplary study is Bruno Latour and Steve Woolgar's *Laboratory Life* (1986). In this study Latour and Woolgar explore how a biological laboratory constructs scientific facts. Their study shows how the construction of scientific facts happens in a chain of materially and discursively heterogeneous events, from the handling of rats, chemicals, and other materials of the laboratory to the publishing of a scientific article. In this chain of events, the heterogeneous materials and discourses of the laboratory are *translated* into a scientific fact (see also Latour 1990, 1999).

The idea of studying the laborious and continual translation of a myriad of heterogeneous *things* into (scientific) *facts* stemmed from the mid-1970s, when Latour investigated why it was so difficult for black executives in the Ivory Coast to adapt to modern industrial life. Going through literature on African philosophy and in comparative anthropology, Latour noticed how this literature sought explanations in "the African 'mind'" (Latour & Woolgar 1986: 273), as opposed to simpler social factors as, for instance, very limited contact with the machines of modern industrial life (see also Verran 2001). This lead to the following question:

> What would happen to the Great Divide between scientific and prescientific reasoning if the same [ethnographic] field methods used to study Ivory Coast farmers were applied to first-rate scientists? (Latour & Woolgar 1986: 274)

What happens is that the Great Divide between scientific and prescientific reasoning can no longer be explained with reference to cognitive or cultural differences such as "Western rationality" as opposed to "the mystery of the East" (Elgaard Jensen 2005). Rather, "[i]f there is a difference between the West and the Rest it is, Latour tells us, not because the Rest is radically Other, but because the West has accumulated a series of small and practical techniques that generate cumulative advantage" (Law 2009: 150).

These early studies show an interest in deconstructing the idea that the success of the West is due to some particular Western rationality. In this approach, culture and cultural differences cannot be used to explain anything. Rather, what needs to be explained is how culture and cultural differences *come into being* as effects of the on-going connecting and disconnecting of a wide range of materially and discursively heterogeneous entities and actors. This interest is pursued through empirical studies of scientific practices, of practices of colonization and long-distance control (Law 1986, 1987), and of practices of technological-scientific engineering projects (Callon 1986). This view on culture commonly denominates the ethnological research that draws upon analytical resources from the field of ANT.

What loosely characterizes these earlier ANT studies is a focus on the strategies by which certain entities or facts come into being and gain strength. According to STS researcher Signe Vikkelsø, such strategy-oriented analyses focus on "the strategic movements of actors (...) in order to describe the successive relations that are established or cut off and the simultaneous translation of programs and actors" (Vikkelsø 2007: 301). To Vikkelsø, these endeavors are contrasted by later, multiplicity-oriented approaches (see for instance Law 1994; Mol 2002; Moser 2000, 2011), which attempt to describe how things hold together through their heterogeneous assemblages. Multiplicity-oriented approaches explore "the multiplicity of a phenomenon, that is, of the ways in which coexisting and partly connected versions of reality are enacted" (Vikkelsø 2007: 301).

Vikkelsø's categorization is illuminating in understanding parts of the theoretical and analytical diversity of the field of ANT studies. In this paper, however, our aim is not to put the labels of "strategy-oriented" or "multiplicity-oriented" on the body of ANT-inspired ethnological research discussed. Rather, our point is that Law's description of interference as a mode of mattering draws upon insights from both types of ANT studies and that it emphasizes the study of differences that matter, making it especially suitable for discussing the nature of the arguments, knowledges and realities produced in the intersection of ANT and ethnology. How we do this is further explained in the following section.

Methodology

The above described ANT studies invite us as ethnologists to explore not what or how culture "is", but rather how culture is continuously and recursively made up or "done" as relations between heterogeneous entities and actors are established or cut off. Reflexively applying this insight to the discipline of ethnology, we can say that our aim here is not to define current Danish ethnology, but to explore how ethnological work is recognized as such as relations between heterogeneous entities and actors are established or cut off. Our designation of the entities and actors that are connected to the discipline of ethnology and the effects of such connections does not take place from a neutral position outside of the discipline itself. We both have a background in ethnology and draw upon resources from the field of ANT in our research. This means that we are in all possible ways a part of the field, which we seek to explore in this article.

We understand this position with aid from Donna Haraway, a key contributor to what may be termed feminist material semiotics, and her call to situate ourselves in relation to, or in this case, right in the middle of, the phenomena we explore (Haraway 1991). To Haraway, there is no position outside, and thus it is impossible to step out of the phenomenon of study by, for instance, employing a neutral language. Our concern here, then, is not to question or explain away our messy attachments (Jensen 2007) to the phenomenon we explore, the intersection of ethnology and ANT. Instead, it is first to see this situatedness as a unique "empirical opportunity" (Elgaard Jensen 2012: 16) and second to make transparent how we have operated within this situatedness in our drawing upon and wrestling with the intersection of ethnology and ANT.

Accordingly, we have decided to put our own

ANT-inspired doctoral work "in the middle" in going about the task pursued in this article. We look for analyses, which can enable us to illustrate the implications that ANT has for the study of culture. Our wish is to show how our own and others' work is reproducing culture and cultural differences as central, ethnological objects of study while simultaneously radically reshaping the content of these notions of culture and cultural differences. As mentioned above, this endeavor is structured following Law's three implications of the "interfering" mode of mattering, namely enactment, difference and ontological politics.

Reality as Enacted

> One, it says that realities are being done. Not just knowledges, but realities too. Everywhere. This is enactment. (Law 2004: 5, emphasis in original)

What does it entail to see realities as being done? Paraphrasing Latour (2005) and his point that what needs exploration is how the social comes into being as opposed to assuming that social phenomena already exist out there and form a specific subset of reality, it entails not providing a cultural explanation of anything, but rather to explain culture in and through the things, facts and artifacts of which it is continuously made up. In the following we provide a number of examples of such attempts to describe cultural assemblages. We show that since an ANT approach does not start with an idea of culture as a specific part of reality (different from, say, "economy" or "nature"), what is described is how laborious assemblages make them up. In the following, we will first look at and exemplify how reality is seen as made up of various entities, proceeding to discuss the consequences of describing culture not as a distinct and delineable part of reality, but as made and done in relations between heterogeneous or messy entities and actors.

Culture and Tourism: Enacting the Tourist Destination

The way of studying and describing culture as something performed in a web of relations is exemplified in the dissertation *Constructing the Tourist Destination: A Socio-Material Description* (2009) by Carina Ren. In her dissertation, Ren shows how local highland Górale culture is used as a way to sanction a number of tourism offers in Zakopane, a Polish tourist destination. Taking as a starting point a painting from 1845 picturing a Górale guiding bourgeois ladies into the wilderness of the Tatras, Ren challenges the common separation of (authentic) culture and tourism, which is usually drawn within the field of tourism studies. Instead of taking the dichotomy as a point of departure for analysis, Ren shows how local and tourism culture intertwine while at the same time reinforcing each other. In the painting:

> a relational exploration of culture at the destination of Zakopane suggests that tourism and culture have locally been identified, defined and practiced in a process of material and embodied reciprocity for over a century, if not longer. This suggests an alternative to what McFall (2004) terms "the invocation of an idealized past in which economy and culture existed in a more bounded sealed-off world" (ibid.: 30). The narrative of the painting supports an alternative understanding in which the internal Górale heritage consumption is based on, created and articulated in connection to and partly by non-Górale to which it is therefore inextricably linked. The painting itself, its exposition at (and building of) the Tatra Museum in Zakopane, the scene of the painting and countless other motifs in music and literature, both national and Górale, are all part of the creation of what Górale is, what it means and how it is perceived and presented. As argued by McFall, (...) the analytical distinction between culture and economy is "surprisingly difficult to apply in instances of material practice" (ibid.: 29). Instead, "the economy and the cultural can be understood as performed in material practices under particular arrangements and utilizing particular socio-technical devices" (ibid.). This is how Górale culture and tourism may be approached as they have, previously and today, mutually engaged and developed over time at the destination through guiding, architecture,

> the appreciation of nature, food stuffs, cultural productions and other tourism related practices and artifacts. This connection has not turned culture and tourism into "a whole", but has made them incomprehensible as separate and disassociated absolutes. (Ren 2009: 165)

By pursuing what locals identify as authentic culture in relation to tourism and by looking at how culture is legitimated and "activated" through its connection to tourism, Ren shows how distinctive and separated characteristics of culture and tourism are continuously blurred. Also, the possibility of referring and aligning with (or rejecting) specific notions of Górale is described as a strategy through which hierarchy, class, unity and inclusion can be established.

This initial investigation of what Górale *is*, is followed by a scrutiny of how Górale is performed at the tourist destination. This is motivated in the following way:

> The notion of Górale is one, which is frequently referred to when asking to the specificity of the destination of Zakopane. A striking observation in Zakopane is the omnipresent references to "Górale" in print and visual representations, through historical references, in the soundscape of the town centre, in symbols and iconography, in statues and art work, foodstuff and other sales items, in costumes worn by waiters and coach men or in tourism offers such as bonfires, sledge rides and dance and music performances. To the cultural analyst it is also a striking notion because of its elasticity and apparent broadness, which makes it connect to a broad range of services and products (...). Because Górale is not a solid character, the unproductive questioning (...) of *what* the notion is, is better replaced with an interrogation of what it looks like, what forms a part of it and where its boundaries are identified. (Ren 2009: 170)

An example of exploring the question of "how Górale?" is provided through the case of the Górale restaurant, which in many interviews with local cultural "authorities" (for instance musicians, artists and ethnologists) was identified as "a place of culture". The restaurant was seen as a place, where one might be lucky not only to taste traditional Górale food, but also to encounter really skillful musicians. In several cases, the awareness of Górale culture was identified through the musical performance of restaurant musicians. Most often, the true Górale restaurant was appraised for the music played, as is exemplified with the very popular and according to many Górale informants very authentic restaurant of Karczma Sopa described here by Małgorzata Wnuk, a restaurant owner herself:

> There is one restaurant in this street where you can always listen to good music. This is the Sopa. It is also a restaurant in traditional style. The owner, a friend of mine, is also a Highlander and musician, and that is why he sometimes plays there. He always has good musicians, good music. I envy him. (Ren 2009: 175)

Asked whether this good music is based on the owner's skills to hire good musicians, the interviewee – herself a successful Górale restaurant owner – repudiates: "No, he is a musician, and they are his friends also. And he has very good ears. So he wouldn't allow [others] playing badly" (ibid.). The authentic performance of "Góralness" in the terms of music making cannot be referred to as a strictly "cultural" or "work related" sphere. Rather, the music comes together through friendship, "good ears", being the owner as well as a Highlander and musician, through both *having* good music and *making* good music. As sides of culture and identity are joined together with musical and business-related skills in this informant's statement, it is unclear whether she envies him his skills as a musician, his ability to attract other good and authentic musicians or the reputation and economic success of his restaurant.

The Górale restaurant music is deployed as a marker of authentic Górale culture and of real Górale restaurants and shows a clear connection between identity, tourism, culture and business and between the production and consumption of music as both a cultural practice and a product. Hereby, overlapping, mutually defining and entwining relations are displayed. The analysis of the Górale restaurant describes it as a place simultaneously questioning and reaffirming a "correct" cultural practice of Góralness, but also challenges cultural practices as "purely" cultural, showing how economy, work, identity and practice are not separate but interfering. It is through its many shifting combinations, that Górale is enacted and made possible, that it is made strong and durable. By claiming both authenticity and "good business" Górale is not only constructed and legitimized as an identity, but also performs as a political actor at the tourist destination.

By looking at the ongoing enactment of Górale culture, attention is directed towards the consequences of the often strategic enterprise of relating and ordering heterogeneity into seemingly coherent wholes. This work defies the idea that something is *purely* authentic or commercial. To explore reality as enacted in places (or networks) such as the tourist destination entails a number of consequences, which is not only displayed but also reiterated in our descriptions. This brings us to our next discussion, namely what kinds of differences are created in the enactment of realities.

Enacting Difference

> Two, it says that they are complex, non-coherent, uncertain, and in interference with one another. This is <u>difference.</u> (Law 2004: 5, emphasis in original)

In the above, it has been shown how the heterogeneous and enacted character of reality is purported in ethnological studies that have drawn upon analytical resources from the field of ANT studies. In the present section, we move on to the second part of the answer to the question of how recent multiplicity-oriented studies within the field of ANT attempt to matter. They attempt to matter by showing how different socio-material practices enact different realities and that these different realities interfere with one another. The notion of difference, thus, describes differences between various enactments or performances.

Different Socio-Material Practices – Different Realities

In order to clarify the notion of difference put forward by recent analyses from the field of ANT it is fruitful to discuss how this specific notion of difference deviates from other notions of difference. Mol notes that "[t]alking about reality as *multiple* depends on another set of metaphors. Not those of perspective and construction, but rather those of intervention and performance. These suggest a reality that is *done* and *enacted* rather than observed" (Mol 1999: 77, emphasis in original). Multiplicity is a step away from thinking about differences with the metaphors of perspective and construction, but what does this mean?

To see difference as a matter of multiplicity is a step away from difference as exclusively a matter of differences in *perspectives*. It is a step away from epistemological differences and what might be termed ontological passiveness. This, to be clear, is not to deny the existence of different perspectives, different ways of knowing. It is to say that such perspectives are not perspectives on a passive reality that lies around "waiting to be glanced at" (Gad & Jensen 2010: 71). Rather, perspectives are – on par with all other actors and entities – seen as taking part in describing *and* enacting certain realities as opposed to others (Gad & Jensen 2010: 73).

To conceptualize differences in terms of multiplicity is also a step away from the metaphor of *construction*, both in its social and socio-material variants. Social constructionism tells us how different social groups with different perspectives support one specific version of truth or reality as opposed to another (see for instance Pinch & Bijker 1989), while constructionist stories emphasize how a specific version of truth or reality needs the support not only of social groups, but a wide range of heterogeneous materials (see for instance Latour & Woolgar 1986). According to Mol, the metaphor of construction enables stories about the "might-have-beens" (Mol 1999: 76). The metaphor, in other words, enables stories that can question the "taken-for-grantedness" of the present.

The alternative offered by the metaphors of intervention and performance is that reality – or, rather, realities – are manipulated and enacted differently in different socio-material practices and that these realities are in interference with one another. Research becomes a matter of exploring how realities are enacted, rather than choosing between perspectives on a rather passive reality. An example follows.

Public Administration and Management as a Case of Multiplicity

Morten Krogh Petersen's dissertation, *"Good" Outcomes: Handling Multiplicity in Government Communication* (2011), explores government communication as a case of contemporary public administration and management. The doctoral research was conducted within a so-called Industrial Ph.D. project, which was hosted by a communications agency and Copenhagen Business School. Further, the project involved five government organizations that acted both as clients of the communications agency and as the empirical field of the doctoral research. The overall aim of the Industrial Ph.D. project was to develop new and better ways of producing and, especially, assessing the outcomes of the government organizations' communication initiatives. One of the main aims of the doctoral research was to provide "thick descriptions" (Geertz 1973) of the present working practices of the government communicators that could inform the innovation of new so-called communication measurements.

The ethnographic investigations of the working practices of communicators from each of the five government organizations involved suggested that there was something ambivalent about the government organizations. As the study focused on how the production and assessment of communicative solutions and the implied formulation of applicable success criteria unfurled, this ambivalence primarily came out empirically in discussions of what constitutes a "good" outcome of a given communicative endeavor. To give an example: Petersen was able to ethnographically follow a rather large communication project entitled *The Group Communication Project* concerning internal communication in one of the government organizations involved. In an interview, Petersen discusses the project's specific way of measuring the success of the project with the project manager. Here are her reflections:

> Bad measurements are when they just note what has been done! (…) In those instances you formulate success criteria saying: "This is what we are going to do." (…) You don't formulate success criteria that focus on the outcome [of a given activity]. [If you focus on what you are going to do] then, when the year is coming to an end, you can simply and lyrically note: "Well, we've reached our goal because we've done what we said we'd do a year ago" (…). In the ministerial department we've been working like that [and we've been focusing on what's been done] for a number of years. However, I know that our Financial Office – that's where the work on our performance contracts happens – is focusing on this to a still rising degree. They ask: "Well, but what do you want to achieve by this? It's not enough to say that you will do it." It's a change in mentality, really (…). Especially in *The Group Communication Project* we've had a focus on making sure that what we put into this world has an outcome. Otherwise it's just a waste of everybody's time. That is why our success criteria are formulated in a way that ensures that we'll measure the project's outcomes. (Petersen 2011: 163)

An exclusive focus on outcomes, as highlighted by the project manager in the interview, is one of the core characteristics of New Public Management (Hood 1991). Further, the project manager suggests that the government organization where she works is in a state of change: it is on its way to become a "pure" New Public Management organization. However, in other instances there seemed to be limits as to how pure the government organization in question could actually become. One such instance came to fore through a fieldwork activity, during which a communicator who was working in the same government organization on the same communication project briefly noted, contrary to the project manager, that success criteria must be formulated rather loosely. During an interview with this communicator Petersen notes that it must be rather difficult to work around two such very different ways of formulating success criteria. She responds:

> Yes, but I'm still of the opinion that in connection to where we are now [with *The Group Communication Project*]... I mean, actually that's a problem we have in connection to the group communication policy right now. The policy formulates quite rigidly what we're to do, right? And that's a little... Now we... Well, actually, we don't think that that's suitable. However, we have a team of group managers who've finalized this policy and fundamentally that means that we have to do it. Unless we go all the way up the system again... And that's [not really an option]... You have to be really careful not to commit yourself to something that you cannot carry out subsequently, right? (Petersen 2011: 170)

Empirical examples such as this one left Petersen somewhat confused: in accordance with the core principles of New Public Management, the communicators would stress the need to manage and organize their work in connection with rather rigid and finalized formulations of its desired outcomes only to suggest an instance later that this was actually a bad idea: to manage and organize work around rigidly formulated outcomes did not fit the organizations' more bureaucratic traits where, for instance, policies and decisions that have traveled "all the way up the system" are practically impossible to change.

Instead of effacing this ambivalence by, for instance, viewing it as a methodological failure – a lack of ability to generate a clear empirical material or a lack of ability to choose a univocal perspective on the work of the communicators (Law & Singleton 2005) – Petersen decided to turn this ambivalence into his object of study. Maybe the government organizations were both one thing, and another and maybe a third thing as well? Maybe the government organizations were both New Public Management organizations and Weberian, administrative organizations?

In turning the ambivalence into his object of study, Petersen took inspiration from the notion of *modes of ordering*, first introduced by Law in his study of a British research laboratory in the era of Thatcherism. The notion of modes of ordering is developed as an analytical tool for describing what Law describes as the materially and discursively heterogeneous networks of the social, in his case the networks of the laboratory. Law states that modes of ordering catch much of the same, as a notion of Foucauldian mini-discourses would do. The idea is that different modes of ordering describe the performance of different, often implicit, strategies. A mode of ordering describes a strategy, "which runs through, shaping, and being carried in the materially heterogeneous processes which make up the organisation" (Law 2001: 1f.). With that, the analytical challenge for Petersen became one of developing specific modes of ordering that could be used in an attempt to analytically order and not dismiss the ambivalence that seemed to characterize the government organizations in question. A second related challenge became one of describing how the different performances of the same organization coexist.

Petersen argues that many attempts are made at turning the government organizations under scrutiny into pure or singular New Public Management organizations. He develops the notion of *singularizing* to describe this specific way of handling multiplicity. However, such attempts at singularizing never fully succeeded. A second way of handling multiplicity, which also finds support in the project's empirical material, is therefore described. This second way is a *sequencing* of the different performances, and the dissertation suggests that it is through such sequencing that the government organizations involved handle their situation of ambivalence.

Difference: A Question of Diversity or Multiplicity?

As seen in our exemplifications of how ANT understands realities as enacted and in interference with one another, cultural differences as an object of study take on a certain flavor in the studies that draw upon resources from the field of ANT. In Ren's case, an interest in culture is kept up, but the question is less about diversity amongst people and groups. Ren shows how culture, in her case the Górale culture, is continuously enacted as a wide range of heterogeneous actors and entities connect and disconnect. She thereby broadens what an analysis of culture should take into account. In Petersen's case, culture and cultural differences are strangely absent seen from an ethnological perspective. The study is not concerned with organizational culture in the sense of beliefs, values, meanings, ideologies and practices within the organization (see for instance Ashkanasy et al. 2011). Rather, it describes how such elements of culture and a wide range of other elements connect and disconnect in different ways and perform the organization differently through such connections and disconnections. Thus, it is a study not of the diversity, but the multiplicity of the organizations involved.

The ANT-inspired conceptualization of culture shifts from seeing cultural differences as a matter of cultural diversity amongst people or groups to conceptualizing differences through the notion of multiplicity. Firstly, this implies seeing practices not only as human, but socio-material. Secondly, the enacted character of reality creates a whole new understanding of the performative role of culture *as well as* other elements that are made to matter in a specific practice. This is investigated through the concept of ontological politics. As we show in the following, the notion of multiplicity implies a shift in how to think about and deal with the interventionist and political nature of inquiring into cultural differences (see also Mol & Mesman 1996).

Ontological Politics, Intervention and Multiplicity

> And three, it says that if we recognize this and work it right, we can interfere and make a difference. This is the ontological politics. (Law 2004: 5, emphasis in original)

Newer ANT studies question whether the focus on a single actor-network and its translation into a strong center still carries the same potency – analytically and politically – as it did thirty years ago. Instead, these newer and multiplicity-oriented studies explore "the multiplicity of a phenomenon, that is, of the ways in which coexisting and partly connected versions of reality are enacted" (Vikkelsø 2007: 301). As we have shown, ANT does not provide any a priori theoretical models of explanation to filter or to categorize our empirical material. For instance, the choices of which actors to follow (see for instance Latour 2005: 68), how and where to "cut the network" (Strathern 1996) and how to communicate heterogeneity, mess, non-coherence and fluidity creates new challenges for the researcher. In this section, we point to how two interventionist strategies can be identified from ANT-inspired ethnological work. The first concerns multiplicity as an interventionist strategy, while the second focuses on small stories, based on Law's credo of a modest sociology (or ethnology, in this case), meaning a version of knowledge production that "acknowledges the partiality of its own ordering attempts and makes transparent wherein this partiality lies" (Petersen 2011: 84; see also Law 1994).

Multiplicity as Intervention

Recent ANT studies have engaged in ontological politics, for instance by addressing what "good" care is (Mol 1999, 2008). According to Law, Mol "defended 'care' against individualist models for practicing diabetes control" (Law 2009: 155). Rather than diversity politics, Mol's approach invites us to engage in ontological politics. It is no longer about attempting to matter by making room for, giving voice to or showing politicians and bureaucrats cultural diversity amongst peoples and groups and how to handle this cultural diversity. It is about attempting to matter by taking part in the enactment of specific realities – and acknowledging the researcher's role herein. Having shown how ethnographic descriptions of multiplicity and its unfurling becomes an analytical "result" because of ANT's insistence on reality as enacted and on material-discursive heterogeneity, we could now ask whether and how multiplicity is seen as a relevant interventionist strategy to engage in ontological politics. How do ethnographic descriptions of multiplicity intervene?

In Petersen's case it is relevant to ask the question: was the multiplicity of the government organizations involved an ontological starting point or rather to be understood as an outcome of the study's interventions? As we have seen, multiplicity-oriented ANT studies take as their point of departure that reality is enacted differently in different socio-material practices. For instance, Law states that "[p]ractice is larger, more complex, more messy, than can be grasped within any particular logic" (Law 2002: 34). However, and this is the crucial point, to attend to and appreciate this complexity and messiness by not reducing practice to be graspable with one particular logic only is "an *act*. It is something that may be done – or left undone. It is an intervention. It intervenes in the various available styles for describing practices" (Mol 2002: 6, emphasis in original).

Based on experiences with being part of the Industrial Ph.D. project gained through fieldwork, research by peers, discussions with supervisors and colleagues and working at the communications agency, Petersen chose to highlight the multiplicity of the government organizations involved. Through ethnographic descriptions, Petersen shows that multiplicity is what enables practices of public administration management to work well, meaning to address and handle the many, diverging and incommensurable criteria of success for government organizations. Thus, Petersen's work is about offering an empirically, theoretically, politically and personally thoroughly grounded and transparent alternative to the idea that full-blown New Public Management is the only cure for all the perceived ills of contemporary public administration and management.

Modest Stories as Intervention

Ren's aim of providing small stories is drawn from Law's idea of a "modest sociology" (Law 1994: 9), a sociology which, as mentioned, acknowledges partiality as an inevitable condition for knowledge production and which, accordingly, seeks to bring this partiality to the fore and refrains from making grand scale claims from nowhere. Following this idea, Ren reflects in the following way on the ethnographic descriptions of her thesis and their claims, arguing that they do not

> (...) reflect very strong network effects or tell representative or very hegemonic versions of the destination. Rather, they are versions which have *worked*, although sometimes modestly, and which have somehow created an outcome, whether contingently or strategically. (Ren 2009: 14f., emphasis in original)

As Ren later explains, the intention behind these descriptions of modest workings and the leaning toward contingency in describing the tourist destination, "is to render specific ordering efforts visible, but also simultaneously to point to both ordering and heterogeneity as ways to generate a new understanding of the destination" (Ren 2009: 36). Such endeavors to unearth small stories of lack of contingency and the laborious work to (at least for a while) order and stabilize heterogeneity, shows how ANT through its empirical sensitivity challenges strong stories or theories by avoiding to utilize these as either a starting point for analysis or a desirable result. As shown by this example, the studying of mundane practices and routines combined with an interest in performing (ontological) politics by means of *modest accounts of multiplicity* are some of the things which have made ANT fit so well into the field of ethnology.

Concluding Remarks: Culture, Cultural Differences and Intervention

In this paper we have focused on what happens at the intersection of ethnology and the field of ANT studies. ANT studies conceptualize reality as enacted, multiple and political in an ontological sense. Relating these ontological commitments to ethnology, this has, at least, three important implications. First, culture loses any a priori, essential or primary explanatory status or power, because it is not understood as a distinct part of reality, but as continuously performed in materially and discursively heterogeneous practices. Second, the main object of study shifts from being a question of diversity amongst peoples and groups to being one of differences between partially connected versions of reality. Finally, the researcher is understood as engaged in the enactment of such partially connected versions of reality. She is engaged in ontological politics rather than in what may be termed diversity politics.

As the approach is increasingly gaining momentum within ethnology, we as researchers must critically re-address and evaluate its significance and impact in order to avoid a "naturalized", non-reflexive application. As noted by STS-researchers Christopher Gad and Casper Bruun Jensen, "[ANT] cannot equip the researcher with a failsafe method for doing ANT. Indeed, it just might be a mistake to follow the actor in some cases. Thus, we read ANT texts neither as sociological theories or methodological guides but as additions to and transformations of the study of various networks" (Gad & Jensen 2010: 73f.). Through concrete examples of analytical work, we have shown how ANT has managed to add to and transform the study of culture and cultural differences, but – and just as important – also to question the role and use of theories and methodology. In accordance with the point of ANT not being a theory or a failsafe method, we have emphasized how ANT has led us to re-think how we produce empirical material, utilize notions for analysis and attempt to make the outcomes of our research matter. This also means, that we do not intend to claim that a "turn to ANT" transforming the discipline beyond recognition has taken place within ethnology. Our point is that ANT urges us to reconsider the application of the broad arsenal of concepts and methods at our disposal. Perhaps notions from our ethnological baggage may be dug out and reinvested in order to study and attempt to bring into being cultural differences that matter within the empirical fields of investigation.

References

Ashkanasy, N.M., C.P.M. Wilderom & M.F. Peterson 2011: *The Handbook of Organizational Culture and Climate.* Thousand Oaks, California & London, United Kingdom: Sage.

Boll, K. 2011: *Taxing Assemblages: Laborious and Meticulous Achievements of Tax Compliance.* Ph.D. thesis, IT University of Copenhagen.

Callon, M. 1986: Some Elements of a Sociology of Translation: Domestication of the Scallops and the Fishermen of Saint Brieuc Bay. In: J. Law (eds.), *Power, Action and Belief: A New Sociology of Knowledge? Sociological Review Monograph.* London: Routledge and Kegan Paul, pp. 196–233.

Callon, M. & J. Law 1997: After the Individual in Society: Lessons on Collectivity from Science, Technology and Society. *Canadian Journal of Sociology* 22:2, 165–182.

Cefkin, M. Book 2009: *Ethnography and the Corporate Encounter.* New York & Oxford: Berghahn Books.

Damsholt, T., C. Mordhorst & D.G. Simonsen 2009: *Materializations: New Perspectives on Materiality and Cultural Analysis (Materialiseringer: Nye perspektiver på materialitet og kulturanalyse).* Aarhus: Aarhus Universitetsforlag.

Damsholt, T., K. Salomonsson, A. Wiszmeg & L.S. Hvalsum 2011: *Culture-driven Innovation: New Methods, New Possibilities (Kulturdreven innovation: Nye metoder, nye muligheder).* Copenhagen & Lund: University of Copenhagen and Lund University.

Elgaard Jensen, T. 2005: Actor-Network Theory: The Material Semiotic of Latour, Callon, and Law (Aktørnetværksteori: Latours, Callons og Laws materielle semiotik). In: A. Esmark, C.B. Laustsen & N.Å. Andersen (eds.), *Socialkonstruktivistiske analysestrategier (Analytical Strategies of Social Constructionism).* Frederiksberg: Roskilde Universitetsforlag/Samfundslitteratur, pp. 185–210.

Elgaard Jensen, T. 2012: Intervention by Invitation: New Concerns and New Versions of the User in STS. *Science Studies* 25:1, 13–36.

Gad, C. & C.B. Jensen 2010: On the Consequences of Post-ANT. *Science Technology Human Values* 35:1, 55–80.

Geertz, C. 1973: Thick Description: Towards an Interpretive Theory of Culture. In: C. Geertz, *The Interpretation of Cultures: Selected Essays.* New York: Basic Books, pp. 3–30.

Haraway, D.J. 1991: Situated Knowledges: The Science Question in Feminism and the Privilege of Partial Perspective. In: D.J. Haraway, *Simians, Cyborgs, and Women: The Reinvention of Nature.* New York: Routledge, pp. 183–201.

Haraway, D.J. 2008: *When Species Meet.* Minneapolis: University of Minnesota Press.

Hood, C. 1991: A Public Management for All Seasons? *Public Administration* 69:1, 3–19.

Jensen, C.B. 2007: Sorting Attachments: Usefulness of STS in Healthcare Practice and Policy. *Science as Culture* 16:3, 237–251.

Jespersen, A.P. 2008: *Commitment at Work? Danish General Practitioners' Consultation Processes*. Ph.D. thesis, University of Copenhagen.

Jespersen, A.P., M.K. Petersen, C. Ren & M. Sandberg 2012: Guest Editorial: Cultural Analysis as Intervention. *Science Studies* 25:1, 3–12.

Latour, B. 1990: Visualisation and Cognition: Drawing Things Together. In: M. Lynch & S. Woolgar (eds.), *Representation in Scientific Practice.* Cambridge, Mass.: MIT Press, pp. 19–68.

Latour, B. 1999: Circulating Reference: Sampling the Soil in the Amazon Forest. In: B. Latour, *Pandora's Hope: Essays on the Reality of Science Studies.* Cambridge, MA & London, UK: Harvard University Press, pp. 24–79.

Latour, B. 2005: *Reassembling the Social: An Introduction to Actor-Network-Theory*. Oxford: Oxford University Press.

Latour, B. & S. Woolgar 1986: *Laboratory Life: The Construction of Scientific Facts.* Princeton, New Jersey: Princeton University Press.

Law, J. 1986: On the Methods of Long Distance Control: Vessels, Navigation and the Portuguese Route to India. In: J. Law (eds.), *Power, Action and Belief: A New Sociology of Knowledge?* London: Routledge, pp. 234–393.

Law, J. 1987: Technology and Heterogeneous Engineering: The Case of Portuguese Expansion. In: W.E. Bijker, T.P. Hughes & T. Pinch (eds.), *The Social Construction of Technological Systems: New Directions in the Sociology and History of Technology*. Cambridge, MA: MIT Press, pp. 111–134.

Law, J. 1994: *Organizing Modernity*. Oxford: Blackwell.

Law, J. 2001: Ordering and Obduracy. Accessed April 12, 2010, from http://www.comp.lancs.ac.uk/sociology/papers/Law-Ordering-and-Obduracy.pdf.

Law, J. 2002: Economics as Interference. In: P. Du Gay & M. Pryke (eds.), *Cultural Economy: Cultural Analysis and Commercial Life*. London: SAGE Publications Ltd, pp. 21–38.

Law, J. 2004: Matter-ing: Or How Might STS Contribute? Accessed April 15, 2011, from http://www.lancs.ac.uk/fass/sociology/papers/law-matter-ing.pdf.

Law, J. 2009: Actor Network Theory and Material Semiotics. In: B.S. Turner (eds.), *The New Blackwell Companion to Social Theory.* Oxford: Blackwell Publishing Ltd, pp. 141–158.

Law, J. & V. Singleton 2005: Object Lessons. *Organization* 12:3, 331–355.

McFall, L. 2004: The Culturalization of Work in the "New" Economy: An Historical View. In: T.E. Jensen & A. Westenholz (eds.), *Identity in the Age of the New Economy: Life in Temporary and Scattered Work Practices.* Cheltenham: Edward Elgar Publishing, pp. 9–33.

Mol, A. 1999: Ontological Politics: A Word and Some Questions. In: J. Law & J. Hassard (eds.), *Actor Network Theory and After.* Oxford: Blackwell Publishers, pp. 74–89.

Mol, A. 2002: *The Body Multiple: Ontology in Medical Practice.* Durham & London: Duke University Press.

Mol, A. 2008: *The Logic of Care.* Oxon: Routledge.

Mol, A. & J. Mesman 1996: Neonatal Food and the Politics of Theory: Some Questions of Method. *Social Studies of Science* 26:2, 419–444.

Moser, I. 2000: Against Normalisation: Subverting Norms of Ability and Disability. *Science as Culture* 9:2, 201–240.

Moser, I. 2011: Dementia and the Limits to Life: Anthropological Sensibilities, STS Interferences, and Possibilities for Action in Care. *Science, Technology & Human Values* 36:5, 704–722.

Munk, A.K. 2010: *Risking the Flood: Cartographies of Things to Come.* Ph.D. thesis, University of Oxford.

O'Dell, T. & R. Willim 2011: Irregular Ethnographies: An Introduction. *Ethnologia Europaea: Journal of European Ethnology* 41:1, 5–13.

Petersen, M.K. 2011: *"Good" Outcomes: Handling Multiplicity in Government Communication.* Ph.D. thesis, Copenhagen Business School.

Pinch, T.J. & W.E. Bijker 1989: The Social Construction of Facts and Artifacts: Or how the Sociology of Science and the Sociology of Technology might Benefit each Other. In: W.E. Bijker, T.P. Hughes & T.J. Pinch (eds.), *The Social Construction of Technological Systems: New Directions in the Sociology and History of Technology.* Cambridge, Massachusetts: The MIT Press, pp. 17–50.

Ren, C. 2009: *Constructing the Tourist Destination: A Socio-Material Description.* Ph.D. thesis, University of Southern Denmark.

Sandberg, M. 2009: *The Present/Absent Border: Europeanization Processes in a Twin Town on the Polish-German Border.* Ph.D. thesis, University of Copenhagen.

Strathern, M. 1996: Cutting the Network. *Journal of Royal Anthropological Institute* 3:2, 514–535.

Strathern, M. 2004: *Partial Connections.* Updated edition. Walnut Creek, CA: AltaMira Press.

Verran, H. 2001: *Science and an African Logic.* Chicago: University of Chicago Press.

Vikkelsø, S. 2007: Description as Intervention: Engagement and Resistance in Actor-Network Analyses. *Science as Culture* 16:3, 297–309.

Carina Ren is Assistant Professor at the Department of Culture and Global Studies, Aalborg University Copenhagen. She is affiliated with the Tourism Research Unit, where she researches cultural tourism and place branding from a socio-material and relational perspective. Recently, she has co-edited the book *Actor-Network Theory and Tourism: Ordering, Materiality and Multiplicity* (2012).
(ren@cgs.aau.dk)

Morten Krogh Petersen is Assistant Professor at the Department of Learning and Philosophy, Aalborg University Copenhagen. In his current research he focuses on how contemporary design and innovation projects explore, utilize knowledge of and create intricate links to everyday life, drawing upon material-semiotic methods of analysis. He has recently co-edited a special issue of *Science Studies* on cultural analysis as intervention (2012).
(mkp@learning.aau.dk)